# NO OTHER NAME

# No Other Name

*An Investigation into the Destiny
of the Unevangelized*

John Sanders

WILLIAM B. EERDMANS PUBLISHING COMPANY
GRAND RAPIDS, MICHIGAN

Copyright © 1992 by Wm. B. Eerdmans Publishing Co.
255 Jefferson Ave. S.E., Grand Rapids, Mich. 49503
All rights reserved

Printed in the United States of America

**Library of Congress Cataloging-in-Publication Data**

Sanders, John, 1956–
    No other name : an investigation into the destiny of the
unevangelized / John Sanders.
        p.        cm.
    Includes bibliographical references and index.
    ISBN  0-8028-0615-5 (pbk.)
    1. Salvation outside the church.   2. Salvation after death.
3. Evangelistic work — Philosophy.   I. Title.
BT759.S29      1991
234 — dc20                                          91-41816
                                                        CIP

*To*
*Jody, Lexi, Rajesh,*
*Amanda, Caleb, and Alaethea*

# Contents

# Foreword

John Sanders addresses an unresolved problem in evangelical theology, a problem having to do with the credibility of God's plan to save humanity. Evangelicals say rhetorically that God desires all men and women to be saved, but their position logically denies all those outside the church any meaningful access to salvation. The bottom line of their reasoning is that the vast majority of people who have lived on the earth have no possibility of salvation because they have not heard the good news through no fault of their own and therefore cannot respond to it. If these are the only redemptive arrangements set in place, it is hard to believe God is serious about loving the world, despite what we say.

Many are asking today whether it is conceivable that the God who reconciled the world in Jesus Christ would allow the majority of humankind to perish without having been told of his love for them or having an opportunity to receive or reject salvation. I am not the only evangelical who does not believe this makes good sense of God's gracious way with humanity and who wants a better explanation.

What John Sanders proposes by way of inclusivism is surely a better explanation and should help to close the credibility gap in current evangelical theology. It has come none too soon, in that liberal theologians are jumping all over us for not making better sense of God's universal salvific will and are capitalizing on our vulnerability to mount outrageous proposals of their own which deny the Incarnation and promote what they call theological pluralism but which is really only religious relativism. Our position on the accessibility of salvation to the unevangelized gives liberals a window of opportunity to float really heretical notions. By sticking stubbornly to what Sanders calls *restrictivism,* evangelicals have made it ridiculously easy for liberals to attack classical theology (in particular, its christology). Scholars such as John Hick have been making mincemeat out of us, arguing all too convincingly that evangelicals have nothing to contribute to the discussion of religious pluralism.

It has seemed for some time now, not only to liberals but to many evangelicals as well, that traditional theology is stuck in deep mud, having no new ideas to put forward and no defense to the serious criticisms made of it. Even the minority of evangelicals who are not restrictivists have not been able to construct a decent full-scale defense of the inclusivist paradigm, only bits and pieces of which have been available in print. Well, they can breathe a sigh of relief now, for help has arrived. Sanders's book is a full-length defense of the wider hope and offers the church a satisfying answer to the problem of the final destiny of the unevangelized.

The book distinguishes itself on at least three counts. First, no other book offers its readers so much primary information. Drawing on extensive research, Sanders has conducted a thorough, biblical, historical, and theological investigation of the issues. He tells us where theologians have stood over the years on this important question, what the exegetical and theological issues are, and what is at stake in making one's decision. The book leaves people free to choose what they should believe, but whatever one's position, no reader will fail to come away from reading it wiser and better informed.

Second, the book is brilliantly crafted and a model of systematic, constructive theology. The reader will notice the orderliness, the depth of analysis, the insight and expertise, the spectrum of opinion neatly laid out by way of five paradigms. Clear, subtle reasoning makes the book a fine example of theological understanding and evaluation. Again, whatever the opinion of the readers, they will be impressed by the fairness of critical interaction and the abundance of the sort of data they need in order to make up their minds, one way or another.

Third, Sanders provides an exposition of the wider hope that is superior to anything we presently possess. Widely held by evangelicals already, inclusivism receives a fine explanation and defense which it has not received before. As such, the book will also pose a serious challenge to the theology of restrictivism, which dominates the current evangelical leadership, if not the people in the pew. It is bound to spark a tremendous discussion.

The book will be indispensable for the study of the final destiny of the unevangelized. Serious students will be required to consult it, regardless of the position they hold on the topic, and it is likely to frame the discussion for years to come. The judgments of God will contain surprises, of course, and we are in no position to give the final word on the final destiny of any group of people. We will all stand before God, and it will be God's prerogative to judge sinners. What this book does is to open up a possible understanding of Scripture in which the divine judgment, whatever the surprises, can be contemplated as a judgment that is fair and full of mercy.

Clark H. Pinnock

# *Preface*

The question of the destiny of the unevangelized has long intrigued Christians and non-Christians alike. During my first year in college, a non-Christian asked me about the fate of the millions of people who have never heard of Christ. Could they receive the salvation Jesus offered, or were they all automatically damned to hell? I didn't have any easy answers, but I was convinced of the significance of the question. It not only tugged at my heart to think of the destiny of untold billions but it also raised serious questions about God's love for the world and his stated desire that all people come to share in his gift of eternal life. And beyond this the issue of salvation or damnation of the unevangelized raises questions about God's justice and the problem of evil. How can we believe that God is just and loving if he fails to provide billions of people (including infants who die) with any opportunity to participate in salvation through Jesus Christ? Why did God create so many people if he knew that the vast majority of them would have no chance of ultimate salvation? On the other hand, if the unevangelized do have an opportunity for salvation, how is it made available to them?

I have been reading and reflecting on the issue of the destiny of the unevangelized ever since that encounter during my first year in college. In 1984 I wrote a short paper discussing three views on the topic. Clark Pinnock read it and encouraged me to seek publication. Later he surprised me by suggesting that I expand it into a book. Appearances to the contrary, I promptly acted on his suggestion. The reason it took so many years to complete the project is that I do research the same way I fish. Just as there is always one more cast to make when fishing, so there is always one more index to search through. After spending six years canvassing the subject of the unevangelizéd, I feel confident that I have located all the major views and identified many of the key figures throughout church history who have held them. This is not to say I think I've caught every fish in the lake, however. Indeed, my intent has been to offer a survey of positions that will serve as a guide for those after me desiring to wet a line in this topic.

Several people deserve special thanks for having assisted me in the production of this book. Clark Pinnock has been particularly helpful along the way. My colleague Ron Spreng read the manuscript and gave many useful suggestions. Donald Bloesch was kind enough to read the manuscript and give his encouragement for the project even though critical of aspects of my theology. Donald McKim also read the manuscript and was helpful in discussing my interpretation of John Calvin. Stephen Davis made some insightful comments on Chapter 3. My colleagues at Oak Hills Bible College have been supportive and stimulating even when disagreeing with me. Ralph Quere and Keith Bridston provided beneficial dialogue on Lutheran positions. Fr. Keough Patnode assisted me in the translation of several Latin texts. Tim Straayer, my editor at Eerdmans, did a good job improving the writing. I would also like to give special thanks to several librarians who helped me procure so many books and articles: J. T. Salley, Kathy Vann Eeckhout, and the librarians of Wartburg Theological Seminary. Finally, commendation must go to my wife, Jody, who performed a work of supererogation in listening to my ideas even when she was not very interested, and to my five children, who encouraged me even when they thought I should have been writing a children's story book.

# Introduction

Anne, away at college, eagerly opened the letter from Mrs. Lynde. It was full of news about her hometown of Avonlea. Part of the letter was concerned with affairs at church. Mrs. Lynde was upset with the ministers being sent to fill the Avonlea pulpit.

> I don't believe any but fools enter the ministry nowadays, she wrote bitterly. Such candidates as they have sent us, and such stuff as they preach! Half of it ain't true, and, what's worse, it ain't sound doctrine. The one we have now is the worst of the lot. . . . He says he doesn't believe all the heathen will be eternally lost. The idea! If they won't all the money we've been giving to Foreign Missions will be clean wasted, that's what! Last Sunday night he announced that next Sunday he'd preach on the axehead that swam. I think he'd better confine himself to the Bible and leave sensational subjects alone. Things have come to a pretty pass if a minister can't find enough in Holy Writ to preach about, that's what.[1]

Mrs. Lynde's humorous letter wonderfully captures the reaction many conservative Christians have when someone sug-

1. L. M. Montgomery, *Anne of the Island* (New York: Bantam Books, 1980), pp. 39-40.

1

gests that there might be hope for the salvation of the "heathen": if there is any hope, then evangelistic missions are a waste of time. This reflects an unfortunately limited understanding of the motivation for mission. Furthermore, Mrs. Lynde's letter expresses the common notion that the salvation of the unevangelized is not in the Bible at all. Although the topic is not explicitly addressed, there certainly are passages that suggest a direction toward an understanding.

The issue of the "salvation of the heathen" is a favorite among Christians. I have been asked about it many times in church and on college campuses. At no time, however, did the issue become more poignant than when my ten-year-old daughter Lexi, whom we adopted from India, asked my wife whether her birth mother, who had died, would be in heaven. My wife suggested she ask me since I was writing a book about her question. Lexi explained to me that she did not think her birth mother had ever heard about Jesus. Was there any hope for her mother's salvation? We had a long talk during which we discussed the importance of two truths — that Jesus is the only savior and that Jesus desires to save everyone. I told her that God wants us to experience the fullness of redemption that Jesus provides but that he also "desires all people to be saved." Keeping these two truths together, I was not able to say with any assurance whether or not her birth mother was now in the presence of Jesus. I am sure Lexi will ask me about this subject again. And when her brothers, also from India, grow up, they too will no doubt ask me about the salvation of their respective birth parents. In this book I attempt to give a more complete answer to my daughter's question. I had much more to say to her than she was able to understand at age ten. It is my hope that my children will find this study helpful in their future inquiries.

It is also my hope that the book will prove useful to other Christians as they seek to address the subject. Although the topic is much discussed, there have been no detailed studies of the sort I am attempting here for over ninety years. This lack of theological attention strikes me as irresponsible. Just as Christians through the ages have addressed the issues they encountered, so we must seek an answer to one of the central questions of our day — the destiny of the unevangelized. The Western church has become increasingly aware of the magnitude of the problem of the unevangelized since the discovery of new lands and peoples in the sixteenth century.

Today we face "plural shock" in the encounter with other religions. This shock has caused what Gabriel Fackre calls "christological heart failure" in some Christians.[2] These thinkers assert that we must surrender the uniqueness of Jesus in order to accommodate today's global sensitivities. Radical pluralists such as Paul Knitter and John Hick argue that conservative Christians cannot produce anything but fruitless speculations regarding the unevangelized or assertions that their destiny is simply unknowable.[3] Such avant-garde pluralists will think this study antiquarian, belonging to a "Ptolemaic" universe. They call for us to "cross the Rubicon" or take part in a "Copernican shift" in theology by abandoning the finality and particularity of Jesus Christ. Evangelicals are not prone to this type of christological heart failure. For us, such siren calls go unheeded since we have two nonnegotiable truths: the finality of Jesus Christ and God's universal salvific will. But evangelicals are not without health problems — notably, hardening of the arteries. Many have concluded that these two essential truths imply that the majority of the human race is automatically a *massa damnata*. I will be arguing that there are other more biblically and theologically satisfying alternatives.

Using Scripture as the source of ultimate authority and tradition as a guide, we can address the issues of our day afresh

2. Fackre, *The Christian Story: A Narrative Interpretation of Basic Christian Doctrine*, rev. ed. (Grand Rapids: William B. Eerdmans, 1984), p. 219.
3. See Knitter, *No Other Name? A Critical Survey of Christian Attitudes toward the World Religions* (Maryknoll, N.Y.: Orbis Books, 1985); and Hick, *God Has Many Names* (Philadelphia: Westminster Press, 1982), pp. 49ff.

and formulate a theological understanding of the destiny of the unevangelized — an endeavor that faithful Christians in every age have undertaken. I hope to uncover a viable third alternative to the two extremes commonly thought to be the only options on the theological market — the claim that there is absolutely no hope for the unevangelized on the one hand and assertion of universalism or even relativistic pluralism on the other. Perhaps the tide will turn from the modern flow toward pluralism if a theologically sound alternative can be provided.

Some comments on the structure of the book may help direct readers to those sections most significant to them. The book falls into three parts. Part 1 sets the issue in the context of church history and particularly of contemporary evangelical thought. It also introduces the key scriptural texts and theological ideas used in the study. Part 2 reviews the two extreme positions concerning hope for the unevangelized. In Chapter 2 I explore and evaluate what some consider to be *the* evangelical view — a view that I refer to as *restrictivism* (viz., the belief that all the unevangelized are automatically damned to hell). The key idea in restrictivism is that access to salvation is not universal but limited to those who hear the preaching of the gospel from human agents. In Chapter 3 I outline the other extreme, classical universalism, the belief that all human beings will finally come to salvation in Jesus Christ. This chapter also includes an excursus on the radical pluralists who reject the particularity and finality of Christ. It is my contention that neither of these positions adequately holds together the two essential evangelical truths. In Part 3, I review three theological constructions affirming that salvation through Jesus Christ is universally accessible to every human being. In Chapter 4 I introduce the crucial ideas for this section. In Chapter 5 I present a variety of ways in which all people (or at least those seeking God) are presented with the gospel before they die or are judged on the basis of how they would have responded had they heard the gospel. In Chapter 6 I examine an idea developed in the early church and currently being revived in popularity:

the assertion that all unevangelized will be given an opportunity after death to receive Christ. In Chapter 7 I examine inclusivism, the contention that salvation is presently universally accessible even if people are never evangelized, that if they make a faith commitment to God they will be saved by the atonement of Jesus even though they never heard about that grace. In Chapter 8 I offer my conclusions regarding the various points of view that have been presented. Finally, I have included an appendix on the question of salvation for young children and mentally incompetent people.

I have attempted to structure the material in this book to make it easily accessible to the reader. Most chapters contain five sections: (1) the biblical texts used to support the position being defended, (2) the theological beliefs used to give the view cogency, (3) an exposition of some of the leading defenders of the view, (4) an evaluation of the position, and (5) a historical bibliography detailing the people who have held the view throughout the history of the church.

Something should be said regarding the type of argumentation and the nature of the conclusions in this book. The character of theological construction and argumentation used in this book is that of a "cumulative case" or "good reasons" approach.[4] Say you awake one morning to find that your car will not start. You suspect that the problem is a frozen fuel line even though you don't have any specific proof that this is the case. Building a cumulative case for your suspicion would involve adducing plausible evidence, such as the fact that it is thirty degrees below zero outside, you kept your battery in the house all night, and you recently had your car tuned up. Of course the real problem could be that you forgot to put a proper weight of oil in the crankcase last fall, but you would have to weigh the signifi-

---

4. For a discussion of this form of argument, see Basil Mitchell, *The Justification of Religious Belief* (Oxford: Oxford University Press, 1981); and Trudy Glover, *A Practical Study of Argument* (Belmont Cal.: Wadsworth, 1985), pp. 259-61.

cance of that fact against the other facts of the case to determine
whether it warranted overturning your initial suspicion. The
good-reasons approach involves a consideration of whether there
is enough contrary evidence (both quantitatively and qualita-
tively) to overthrow the conclusion. For instance, if you found out
that your mechanic had added gas line antifreeze the day before,
it might well lead you to reject the thesis that the gas line is frozen.
As should be evident, cumulative-case arguments are not able to
provide absolute certainty regarding the conclusion. All that can
be attained is a certain degree of plausibility.

Finally, a word about why this book was written. I had
five reasons for writing it. First, the God I see presented in the
Bible has great love for all humanity. Yet restrictivism, which
claims that all the unevangelized are damned to hell, seriously
puts this conception of God in jeopardy. Personally, I am deeply
saddened by the picture of God given by some of my conservative brethren when discussing the unevangelized. They seem
to believe that God does little in the way of seeking the redemption of the great majority of human beings. The recognition of God's concern for all people has been re-emerging in
Western theology for many years, and it should be applied to
this important issue. I wish to defend the notion that it is God's
will to save everyone and that he works tirelessly to that end.
But on the other end of the spectrum lies universalism, claiming
that absolutely everyone will be saved. Again, I believe this view
reflects a distortion of the biblical God. I want to argue that a
reasonable alternative to both restrictivism and universalism can
be developed that affirms salvation as universally accessible.

Second, I am concerned that restrictivism gives far too
much ammunition to the critics of Christianity. If it is true that
God automatically damns all the unevangelized to hell, then
perhaps the arguments against the goodness and justice of God
have some merit. In other words, the problem of evil rears its
ugly head. But if it can be shown that salvation is universally
accessible, then a step toward a theodicy will have been provided
for this aspect of the problem of evil.

Third, I want to challenge those involved in missions to develop sound motivations for the commitment to world evangelization in light of the universal accessibility of salvation. There are good reasons to pursue missionary activity even if salvation is not out of the reach of the unevangelized, but these need more attention than they have been given by conservative Christians. Roman Catholic writers are far ahead of us on this issue, having already worked through a missions strategy in light of their view of the wider hope (inclusivism).

Fourth, I trust this book will give those who now meekly believe in the wider hope the theological muscle they need to defend their convictions more adequately. Many Christians reject the idea that all the unevangelized are indiscriminately damned, but they do not know how to support that conviction with sound biblical and theological arguments. Moreover, they are usually unaware that belief in the wider hope has a long and venerable tradition in church history. I hope this book will supply them with the information they need.

Finally, I felt the need for a comprehensive typology and survey of the literature on this important topic.[5] I offer this work in the hope that it will provoke further study and responsible discussion of the important question concerning the possibility of salvation for the unevangelized — particularly among those in the evangelical Protestant community.

---

5. I am not aware of any comparable English-language works written in this century. Two significant works from the nineteenth-century are Edward Grinfield's *Nature and Extent of the Christian Dispensation with Reference to the Salvability of the Heathen* (London: Rivington, 1827) and E. H. Plumptre's *Spirits in Prison* (London: Isbister, 1898). In French, see L. Capéran's *Problème du Salut des Infidèles,* 2 vols. (Paris, 1934).

# PART ONE

## *Formulating the Issue*

# CHAPTER ONE

# *The Issue in Context*

## The Question

If Christ declares Himself to be the Way of salvation, the Grace
and the Truth, and affirms that in Him alone, and only to souls
believing in Him, is the way of return to God, what has become
of men who lived in the many centuries before Christ came?
. . . What, then, has become of such an innumerable multitude
of souls, who were in no wise blameworthy, seeing that He in
whom alone saving faith can be exercised had not yet favoured
men with His advent?[1]

The words are those of Porphyry, a third-century philosopher
and critic of Christianity. His questions are just as pertinent
today as when he first uttered them, for at issue is not merely
the salvation of those who lived before the incarnation of Christ
but also of those who have lived after the incarnation and yet
have not heard the gospel. In other words, what about the
salvation of those who live A.D. but who are still informationally

---

1. Porphyry, quoted by Augustine in a letter to Deogratias, in *Nicene
and Post-Nicene Fathers*, series 1, vol. 1, ed. Philip Schaff (1886; reprint, Grand
Rapids: William B. Eerdmans, 1974), p. 416.

B.C.? Are they without any hope? The destiny of the unevangelized is a common concern among Christians today. The following dialogue between two short-term missionaries in India captures the essence of a typical discussion of the topic. The missionaries have just left a village where an elderly man earnestly asked them about all his ancestors who had never heard of Christ.

*     *     *

"Carl, I can't get the picture of that man's face out of my mind. The deep sadness in his eyes. It haunts me. I'm still deeply committed to world evangelization, but I am really questioning whether our witness is injured when we have no answer to such an important question."

"Look, Dale, we're not theologians. How can we be expected to know what to say about such a difficult issue?"

"It just seemed so simple when we were back in the states during our training period. That was only three weeks ago, and I remember when Bill asked Prof. Lindum about the fate of those who had never heard about Jesus. The professor replied that if we were asked that question we were to just say that God has no other plan to save each person except they give their hearts to Jesus. He then quoted Acts 4:12, 'there is no other name under heaven given among men by which they must be saved.' That seemed satisfactory then, but when I have to look into the eyes of these people — real people and not statistics — I just can't bring myself to tell them that all their ancestors are damned to hell."

"I don't feel good about it either, but the truth is the truth. Jesus told us that he is the way, the truth, and the life. Nobody can get to heaven except through him. That man's ancestors didn't know about Jesus, so they can't be in heaven. That is all the more reason why we should get on with our evangelism, so more people don't end up in hell."

"Do you really believe, Carl, that nine-tenths of the people who have ever lived on this planet are condemned to hell just because they never heard of Jesus? Do you want to say that maybe twenty billion will be in hell while only a few million will be in heaven?"

"The truth is not discovered by counting numbers, Dale. That is just a false American idea. Besides, they will be in hell because they rejected the revelation that God gave them, not because they never heard of Christ."

"What would happen if somebody who hadn't heard of Christ did want to repent of sin and turn to God? Would God save them?"

"At one time I thought so, but Dr. Lindum told us that a person has to hear about the gospel of Jesus Christ in order to be saved. He also said that Scripture denies any other way, like a future chance after death. He referred to the verse that says 'after death comes judgment.'"

"But Carl, if people are damned for rejecting the light they have and can be saved only if they hear about Jesus, that would mean that the unevangelized only have an opportunity to be damned but not an opportunity to be saved. That just doesn't sound fair to me."

"Nobody said God had to be fair or that life is fair. It isn't fair, and that is why we who have experienced the grace of God in Jesus need to reach these people for Christ."

"Well, if God isn't fair, then what about when Peter says 'God is not willing that any should perish but that all should come to repentance' and Paul's statement that God desires everyone to be saved? Does God really want everyone to be saved or not?"

"We have to distinguish between what God wants and what God gets. God does want everyone to be saved, but most Christians have not been willing to share their faith with others, so God's will has been thwarted because of our sinfulness. Those Christians who've been unwilling to evangelize will be judged severely for their neglect."

"So what? They'll still be in heaven while most of the

people who've ever lived will be in hell! Why should they get
to go to heaven when they've been so disobedient?"

"Because nobody goes to heaven by obedience but only
because of Jesus. Have you forgotten so basic a truth as grace?"

"Oh Carl, I know that's right. It's just that I'm so confused
at the moment. I just don't see how God can condemn all of
them for no fault of their own."

"But it's their own fault that they are condemned, since
they've rejected the light God has given them."

"But if Jesus is the light of the world and God desires all
people to see that light, it just seems to me that God would do
something more than rely on a bunch of people like those in
the church who have generally been unenthusiastic about evangelism. Why should the unevangelized not have an opportunity
to be saved because of our neglect?"

"That's a good question. But if they could be saved apart
from missionaries like us, then why bother to raise support like
we did? Why should Christians spend so much money on
missions? We know that Jesus commanded us to evangelize the
world, so we know missions is the right thing to do."

"Do you think that all the infants who die go to hell too?"

"Of course not! God would not condemn them, because
they haven't done anything wrong. I believe all children who
die before the age of accountability will be in heaven."

"I'm glad to hear you say that, Carl. But how can you be
so confident about the salvation of children and at the same
time rule out all hope for the unevangelized? Why are you so
generous toward one group and not the other?"

"For two reasons. First, adults have all sinned against God.
Second, Jesus said to 'permit the little children to come to me.'
Heaven must be filled with children."

"Well, if you can push Jesus' statement that hard to say
heaven is filled with children, then I don't see why you try to
restrict what Paul and Peter said about God desiring to save all
people. If God is willing to save all children who die, then it
seems he'd do something about providing an opportunity for

salvation to the vast majority of human beings who have ever lived. Look, we're almost to the next village. Let's talk about this more tonight. We'd better pray before we reach the village."

## Should an Answer Be Attempted?

The conversation between Carl and Dale highlights many of the issues, questions, and answers that typically come up in discussions of the destiny of unevangelized.[2] It is difficult to arrive at accurate statistics for the number of unevangelized presently living. It is even more difficult to ascertain the number of unevangelized who have lived since the time of Christ. It is virtually impossible to know how much of the entire human race has lived and died without receiving any message from human missionaries about God's grace in Israel or in the church. Some statistics may be helpful in formulating an idea of just how large a group the unevangelized have been. It is estimated that in A.D. 100 there were 181 million people, of which one million were Christians. It is also believed there were 60,000 unreached people groups at that time. By A.D. 1000 there were 270 million people, 50 million of whom were Christians, and 50,000 unreached people groups. In 1989 there were 5.2 billion people, of whom 1.7 billion called themselves Christian, and

---

2. I chose the term *unevangelized* in hopes of avoiding the pejorative connotations of such terms as *heathen* and *pagan*. I use it here to refer to those who have died without hearing about or understanding the redeeming work of Jesus Christ — among whom I would include those who are too young to understand the gospel and those who are mentally or psychologically incapable of understanding it. I would also include among the unevangelized those who have been driven away from Christ not by the gospel but by the poor testimony or lifestyle of professing Christians. Our bigotry and greed, for instance, may prevent others from genuinely perceiving God's grace. Finally, I would argue that not all those who have heard a recitation of "gospel facts" have thereby come to understand the gospel. There is more to evangelism than just transferring information.

there were 12,000 unreached people groups.[3] Although there is no way of knowing with certainty how many of these people were unevangelized, it seems safe to conclude that the vast majority of human beings who have ever lived never heard the good news of grace regarding the God of Israel and the Father of our Lord Jesus Christ. In terms of sheer numbers, then, an inquiry into the salvability of the unevangelized is of immense interest and importance. Do we have anything to say about the destiny of countless billions who have lived and died apart from any understanding of the divine reconciliation obtained by Jesus? Are such people automatically damned to hell? Does God genuinely desire the salvation of all people?

There are those who say we should not seek to answer such questions. In the nineteenth century, Bishop Horne said that "to the curiosity, which . . . is ever anxiously enquiring into the future destination of those who have never heard of him, the proper answer, surely is, 'What is that to thee? Follow thou me.'"[4] In the twentieth century, there are many who claim our position should be one of "reverent agnosticism." According to the evangelical theologian James Packer, "if we are wise, we shall not spend much time mulling over this notion. Our job, after all, is to spread the gospel, not to guess what might happen to those to whom it never comes. Dealing with them is God's business."[5] Those who adopt this line of thought are fond of asking, "Will not the Judge of all the earth do right?" (Gen. 18:25, NIV). It is then stressed that we can draw neither negative nor positive conclusions from this because God simply has not told us the answer.[6] This approach is popular in both Eastern

3. The figures are from the *World Christian Encyclopedia* as cited in *World Evangelization* 16 (1989): 40.

4. Horne, quoted by Edward Grinfield in *The Salvability of the Heathen* (London: C. & J. Rivington, 1827), p. 2.

5. Packer, *Christianity Today*, 17 January 1986, p. 25.

6. See J. A. Motyer, *After Death* (Philadelphia: Westminster Press, 1965), pp. 65-66; for a perspective from the Lutheran tradition, see Ralph Quere, *Evangelical Witness* (Minneapolis: Augsburg, 1975), p. 139.

Orthodoxy and Protestantism. Those who advocate it are often very humble and responsible theologians who are not convinced that there is enough information to decide the question.

But I am dissatisfied with this stance. I believe enough information does exist for the construction of a biblically satisfying and theologically sound answer. It is true that our primary task ought to be following Jesus and spreading the good news of his kingdom to all the world. But accomplishing that task involves the theological activity of answering new questions as they arise. If we did not speculate about subjects not directly revealed in the Bible, we would have very little theology; we would have no doctrine of the Trinity, no doctrine of Jesus having both a human and divine nature in hypostatic union. These articles of faith, hammered out over several centuries by the early church, are not explicitly explained in Holy Scripture. They are theological formulations drawn from scriptural information to answer crucial issues raised in the intellectual (Hellenistic) context of the church at that time. The crisis in the church was such that it was not enough for the leaders simply to state a vague idea. The issue needed plausible clarification. In the same way, the church of today needs to address the subject of the unevangelized in a responsible fashion.

I am not suggesting that the issue of the unevangelized is as paramount as that of the Trinity or the dual nature of Christ, but there is a certain similarity between the way in which the intellectual climate of the early church raised some very serious theological questions and the way our contemporary context does the same. There is a crisis brewing both inside and outside the church regarding the unevangelized, and some serious attempts have been made to resolve the matter. At present, no consensus of the sort achieved at Nicea has been reached in the church concerning an answer to the problem of the unevangelized. In this regard the debate over the destiny of the unevangelized is similar to the debate over Christian eschatology: a considerable variety of positions (including various forms of millennialism) have been derived from the

biblical materials, but there is no clear consensus. My point
here is that theologizing is a legitimate enterprise for Christians;
we must not adopt an agnostic stance before we have made a
thorough investigation.

Moreover, as theologian Hans Küng states, "if Christian
theologians have no answer to the question of the salvation of the
greater part of mankind, they cannot be surprised when people
react again as they have done in the past: Voltaire pouring out his
scorn for the Church's presumption in claiming to be the sole way
of salvation; Lessing . . . with his fable of the three rings, all
supposed to be genuine and yet perhaps none of them really
belonging to the father."[7] Finally, I would note that those who
advocate the agnostic solution seldom take the same stance toward
the problem of evil. They quite readily enter into theodicies. If sin,
damnation, and the love of God are all part of the problem of evil,
then the issue of the destiny of the unevangelized is also part of
that problem, and it ought to be addressed forthrightly.

If a "reverent agnosticism" is unsatisfactory, then why
hasn't the issue been settled by now? In early Judaism the issue
of the salvation of unevangelized Gentiles was disputed, but
there was no settled opinion.[8] The New Testament does not
address the topic in a direct or systematic manner. A single
statement by our Lord Jesus could have settled the controversy
before it began, but this is also true concerning the sacraments,
the doctrine of the Trinity, church-state relations, and eschatology. It is a matter of debate *because* it is addressed only
indirectly in Scripture.[9] Consensus on the subject has not
emerged at any point in the history of the church.

7. Küng, *On Being a Christian* (Garden City, N.Y.: Doubleday, 1976),
p. 99.
    8. See E. P. Sanders, *Paul and Palestinian Judaism* (Philadelphia:
Fortress Press, 1977), pp. 206-12. See also Barnabas Lindars, "The Old
Testament and Universalism in Paul," *Bulletin of the John Rylands University
Library* 69 (1987): 512.
    9. See Hans Küng, *Freedom Today* (New York: Sheed & Ward, 1966),
pp. 132-33.

The topic was addressed from time to time by theologians in the early and medieval church, and one might expect that the systematicians of the Middle Ages would have arrived at a solution if anyone would have, but two factors hindered them. First, they were simply unaware of how many unevangelized there actually were. Aquinas thought that there were only a handful of such people. The magnitude of the problem became evident only after the great explorations and discoveries of new lands in the fifteenth and sixteenth centuries. Second, when the question of salvation outside the church was brought up, it was typically directed to heretics and schismatics rather than the unevangelized. Even Protestant documents such as the Thirty-Nine Articles of the Church of England, the Second Helvetic Confession, and the Westminster Confession give no definitive decision on the topic. Reformed theologians discussed the subject but disagreed among themselves, so it is not surprising that the confessions do not settle the question.

In the eighteenth and nineteenth centuries the issue of the "wider hope," as it was called, picked up steam, and many views were discussed.[10] The discussion has continued into the twentieth century, but, surprisingly, Protestant theologians have been reluctant to join in.[11] Karl Barth and the dialectical theologians, fearful of speculation, tend toward reverent agnosticism, while Ernst Troeltsch and the relativistic theologians think themselves to have outgrown the question, and Paul Tillich was not interested in the question of "personal" salvation after death.[12] Mean-

10. For an extensive bibliography of the period on this and related topics, see William Alger, *The Destiny of the Soul* (Boston: Roberts Brothers, 1880).

11. See George Lindbeck, "Fides Ex Auditu and the Salvation of Non-Christians," in *The Gospel and the Ambiguity of the Church*, ed. Vilmos Vajta (Philadelphia: Fortress Press, 1974), pp. 103-9.

12. According to Nels Ferré, Tillich became more interested in individual survival of death after he made a trip to the Orient late in life. He discussed the issue in his Ingersoll Lectures on Immortality. See Ferré, *The Universal Word* (Philadelphia: Westminster Press, 1969), pp. 235-36.

while Roman Catholic theologians of this century, notably Karl
Rahner, have taken the lead in theological reflection concerning
the salvability of the unevangelized.[13] Among evangelicals the
situation is quite varied and so merits a closer examination.


### The Topic within Evangelicalism

Evangelical leaders have managed to keep a tight lid on this
volatile topic. Many of these leaders appear to be extremely
fearful of discussing it because of its implications for missions.[14]
The lack of open discussion has led some to assume that there
is in fact an evangelical consensus on the issue, and when that
assumption is questioned, it often brings about a heated debate.[15] The lack of serious academic attention to the topic
among evangelicals is surprising, considering the popularity of
the issue in Sunday schools and on college campuses. There
have been some short academic pieces in journals and books,
but on the whole evangelical theologians have produced only
brief popular treatments or have mentioned the topic only in
passing in their systematic theologies. And this lack of attention

---

13. Lindbeck suggests that this is because Roman Catholic theology
is closely tied to missions and the church, while Protestant theology is primarily tied to the university ("Fides ex Auditu and the Salvation of Non-
Christians," p. 108).

14. James Davison Hunter claims to have statistical support for the
fear that inclusivism reduces support for missions; see *Evangelicalism: The
Coming Generation* (Chicago: University of Chicago Press, 1987), pp. 47,
258n.44.

15. I found evidence of this in several letters I received after publishing
an article entitled "Is Belief in Christ Necessary for Salvation?" (*Evangelical
Quarterly* 60 [1988]: 241-59) and also in the emotional reactions of evangelical theologians and mission leaders at conferences where the topic was
presented. For example, the three formal responses to the paper Clark Pinnock
presented on this topic to the 1989 Evangelical Theological Society national
meeting were particularly acrimonious.

may well be helping to obscure the fact that just as there has been no consensus in the history of the church regarding the unevangelized, so there is no single "evangelical view" on this topic.[16]

Harold Lindsell, former editor of *Christianity Today,* has stated that "evangelicals have always insisted and continue to insist that in order for men to be converted they must hear of Jesus Christ and respond to his invitation in faith. If they die without the knowledge of Jesus Christ, they perish."[17] But this is patently false! According to James Davison Hunter, only about two-thirds of evangelical college and seminary students hold that all unevangelized will be damned to hell; fully one-third hold to some kind of hope for the possible salvation of the unevangelized.[18] Among college professors at evangelical liberal arts colleges, only 56 percent ruled out all hope for the unevangelized.[19] Hunter claims there has been a discernible trend within evangelicalism as far back as the 1940s to presume at least some softening of the torments in hell for those who die unevangelized. He notices a growing trend among evangelicals to allow more hope for the unevangelized even though these same evangelicals firmly maintain the necessity of Christ for salvation.[20] I will show that it is incorrect to consider this "trend" to be of recent origin.

Evangelicals in the nineteenth century discussed the issue much more openly and held the same broad spectrum of views

16. See Malcom McVeigh, "The Fate of Those Who've Never Heard? It Depends," *Evangelical Missions Quarterly,* October 1985, pp. 370-79.

17. Lindsell, "Missionary Imperatives: A Conservative Evangelical Exposition," in *Protestant Crosscurrents in Mission,* ed. Norman Horner (Nashville: Abingdon, 1968), p. 57.

18. See Hunter, *Evangelicalism,* pp. 34ff.

19. Hunter, *Evangelicalism,* p. 174.

20. George Marsden has documented that Fuller seminary students tend to be much more hopeful for the unevangelized than their counterparts at other evangelical seminaries (*Reforming Fundamentalism: Fuller Seminary and the New Evangelicalism* [Grand Rapids: William B. Eerdmans, 1988], pp. 303-4).

found in evangelicalism today. In fact, "wider hope" positions
were present within evangelicalism long before 1940, even at
the height of the Fundamentalist-Modernist controversy, although Hunter is correct in indicating that the issue has become
more public. Public disagreement within evangelicalism is even
evident among those most concerned with missions. Whereas
the Frankfurt Declaration (1970) explicitly said all unevangelized are damned, the Lausanne Covenant (1974) left the issue
undecided.[21] This split is most apparent in the distinction between "progressive" evangelicals, who tend to have hope for the
unevangelized, and "establishment" evangelicals, who tend to
rule out any hope for them.

There is a general feeling that the dominant view of
evangelicalism is that all those who die unevangelized will be
damned to hell. This is so, I think, because the proponents of
this position tend to have more power in the evangelical community. Establishment evangelicals have traditionally had a
greater degree of control over evangelical publishing and educational institutions than have progressive evangelicals. And
concerns about reactions to their views among both establishment colleagues and constituencies have kept many progressive leaders from speaking their mind on the issue. Some of
these individuals have reason to fear that discussing their beliefs
would be politically and financially disastrous for the institutions they are associated with.[22] Even though the belief that
no unevangelized person can be saved is not in the doctrinal

21. See John Stott and David Edwards, *Evangelical Essentials* (Downers
Grove, Ill.: InterVarsity Press, 1989), p. 320.
22. Mark Noll points out that the Roman Catholics may turn to the
magisterium and the liberals to technical study as an authority for settling
disputes, but evangelicals can only turn to the court of popular acceptance.
If evangelicals challenge or seek to modify long-cherished doctrines, they can
expect to be treated like greenhorn politicians tampering with the Social
Security system. See Noll, *Between Faith and Criticism* (New York: Harper
& Row, 1986), pp. 153-56, and "Evangelicals and the Study of the Bible,"
in *Evangelicalism and Modern America*, ed. George Marsden (Grand Rapids:
William B. Eerdmans, 1984).

statements of many evangelical institutions, it can be safely said that it is for many an unwritten article of faith, and those who disagree with it can expect the same response as if they denied the deity of Jesus Christ. Nevertheless, I have found that many laypeople have hopes for the unevangelized but do not know how to articulate and defend such hopes. Within evangelicalism, the wider hope is more popular in the pews than in the pulpits.

There are indications that some evangelical leaders are not only certain of the correctness of their position but that they do not wish to see any alternatives to that position being discussed. Robertson McQuilken, president of Columbia Bible College, has said that it is "certainly dangerous, if not immoral" to discuss the subject of hope for the salvation of the unevangelized.[23] One pastor responded to an article I had written on the topic by asking, "Why have you put a question mark where God has placed a period?" Some charge those who openly advocate hope for the unevangelized with selling out the truth in hopes of getting their nonevangelical colleagues to like them.[24] Sometimes those espousing the wider hope are viewed as "heretical" despite the fact that they hold to all the orthodox tenets of the faith.[25] Some who hold the damnation of the

23. McQuilken, *The Great Omission* (Grand Rapids: Baker Book House, 1984), p. 50.

24. Joseph Stowell, president of Moody Bible Institute, made this sort of accusation at the "Evangelical Affirmations" conference at Trinity Evangelical Divinity School May 1989. See *Evangelical Affirmations*, ed. Kenneth Kantzer and Carl Henry (Grand Rapids: Academie Press, 1990), pp. 390-91. Aside from the questionable nature of the accusation, the fact remains that the psychological origin of a belief is irrelevant to its truth or falsity.

25. The reason for this, as George Marsden astutely observes, is that evangelicals have no creeds or ecclesiastical courts to settle disputes, and so "theological minutiae" — the doctrine of the rapture, for example — are called upon to play that role (*Reforming Fundamentalism*, p. 152). In the process, it becomes increasingly difficult to distinguish the truly fundamental doctrines from the peripheral. The topic of the salvation of the unevangelized is certainly one area in evangelical theology where the peripherals are often confused with the truly fundamental.

unevangelized to be an essential tenet of the faith believe that any challenge to it can lead to a serious loss of unity in the evangelical community.[26]

Despite such obstacles, the latter half of the 1980s witnessed a substantial increase in the number of times the topic was discussed in print and at significant evangelical gatherings. One very important discussion took place in May of 1989 at the "Evangelical Affirmations" conference held at Trinity Evangelical Divinity School. The conference was organized and directed by theologians such as Carl Henry and Kenneth Kantzer, and invitations were sent out to all evangelical "leaders" who wished to participate.[27] The goal was the production of a list of affirmations that would identify evangelical positions on a wide array of topics. J. I. Packer was chosen to speak on the unevangelized. He warned against speculating about the salvation of the unevangelized, yet he was careful not to shut the door so firmly as to rule out all hope. As the participants voted on the statements being produced, Robertson McQuilken objected that the wording of the affirmations did not specifically rule out the possibility of salvation for the unevangelized. He proposed a stricter formulation to the effect that explicit knowledge of Jesus is necessary for salvation and without it no one can be saved. This was a tremendously important modification for, if accepted, it would establish in a somewhat official way *the* evangelical position. A brief debate ensued but came to an

26. One sad example of this sort of disunity was Bill Bright's public refusal to participate in a national youth convention if Tony Campolo was allowed to speak (see *Christianity Today*, 20 September 1985, pp. 36-38, and 13 December 1985, pp. 52-54). Bright was reacting to Campolo's *A Reasonable Faith* (Waco, Tex.: Word Books, 1983), in which he argues that Matthew 25 gives great hope for the salvation of the unevangelized and that we should refuse to say who will *not* be in heaven.

27. In the end, the conference had a far greater representation of "establishment" evangelicals than "progressive" evangelicals, especially when it came to selecting the plenary speakers, the council of theologians, and the writers of the affirmations. For a list of conference personnel, see *Evangelical Affirmations*, pp. 527-35.

abrupt halt when theologian Roger Nicole (himself not an advocate for the wider hope) pointed out that McQuilken's proposal would consign all infants who die to hell. The tide turned abruptly after that. Apparently evangelicals are simply not willing to consign all such infants to eternal damnation. The final draft affirmed that all are saved only through Christ and that God reaches out to save all who believe in him, but that was as close as the conference came to answering the key question.

## Two Essential Truths

There are two theological axioms from which the problem of the unevangelized arises. The first is God's universal salvific will suggested in passages such as 1 Timothy 2:3-4 ("God our Savior, who desires all men to be saved and to come to the knowledge of the truth"). The second is the particularity and finality of salvation only in Jesus evidenced in texts such as Acts 4:12 ("And there is salvation in no one else, for there is no other name under heaven that has been given among men, by which we must be saved"). The attempt to hold both axioms together creates the problem of how God can genuinely desire all human beings to partake of salvation and yet claim that salvation is exclusively offered only in the person of Jesus Christ, of whom most of the human race has been ignorant. However, before going further into the problem we should establish that these two axioms are, in fact, biblically founded.[28]

28. The following survey of biblical texts is meant to be illustrative only. For in-depth discussions, see the following: Russell Aldwinckle, *Jesus — A Savior or the Savior?* (Macon: Mercer University Press, 1982), chap. 4; Leon Morris, *The Apostolic Preaching of the Cross* (Grand Rapids: William B. Eerdmans, 1956); Bernard Ramm, *An Evangelical Christology* (Nashville: Thomas Nelson, 1985); and H. D. McDonald, *The Atonement of the Death of Christ* (Grand Rapids: Baker Book House, 1985).

The term "finality" refers to the unsurpassibility and normativity of both the work (e.g., atonement) and the revelation of Jesus. The term "particularity" refers to the fact that the salvation provided by God is available *only* through Jesus. Jesus, as the Son of God, is the highest, clearest, and absolutely normative expression of the character of God. Furthermore, Jesus is *the* savior. There are no others. The finality of Jesus is taught in passages such as Hebrews 1:3 ("He is the radiance of His glory and the exact representation of His nature, and upholds all things by His word of power"). Jesus himself made claims that were audacious to his hearers — "He who has seen Me has seen the Father" (John 14:9). The particularity of salvation as being only through Jesus is clearly taught throughout the New Testament.[29]

In the gospels Jesus makes some claims that had to sound utterly ridiculous coming from a rabbi. When he told the paralytic that his sins were forgiven (Mark 2:1ff.), the audience reacted by asking "Who can forgive sins but God alone?" When Jesus made such statements as "he who believes in *me* will never die" and "*I* am the way, the truth and the life," he was not speaking like a rabbi or sage. Sages tell us what to believe and inform us about the way, the truth, and the life; Jesus claimed to *be* the truth. Jesus made it very clear that our eternal destiny hinges upon our belief in *him*. Such claims sounded blasphemous to his listeners, and in today's relativistic world they sound ludicrous. The modern world would be more comfortable with Jesus having said "I will tell you about a way of life" instead of "*I* am *the* life."

In the epistles Jesus is depicted as providing redemption for the sins of the entire human race. "He has delivered us from the domain of darkness, and transferred us to the kingdom of His beloved Son, in whom we have redemption, the forgiveness of sins" (Col. 1:13-14). "When He made purification of sins,

29. For a defense of particularity and finality in Paul's thought, see Sanders, *Paul and Palestinian Judaism*, pp. 447-74.

He sat down at the right hand of the Majesty on high" (Heb. 1:3). "He Himself is the propitiation for our sins; and not for ours only, but for those of the whole world" (1 John 2:2). Through this *one* savior is seen the highest expression of God's universal salvific will.

Jesus showed great compassion on those whose lives were ruined and battered. He told of his willingness to bring wholeness to their lives when he declared, "Come to Me, all who are weary and heavy-laden, and I will give you rest" (Matt. 11:28). In John 12:32 we read, "and I, if I be lifted up from the earth, will draw all men to Myself." Peter boldly claimed that God is patient, "not wishing for any to perish but for all to come to repentance" (2 Pet. 3:9). In the writings of Paul we find some of the most extensive expositions of the universal grace of God. He declares that "as one man's trespass led to condemnation for all men, so one man's act of righteousness leads to acquittal and life for all men" (Rom. 5:18, rsv) and that "He died for all" (2 Cor. 5:15). He speaks of "God our Savior, who desires all men to be saved and to come to the knowledge of the truth" (1 Tim. 2:3-4) and of "the living God, who is the Savior of all men" (1 Tim. 4:10). "For the grace of God has appeared, bringing salvation to all men" (Tit. 2:11).[30]

Holding these two axioms together is not always easy, but the New Testament offers some help. John held both the particular and the universal together when he said, "For God so loved the world, that He gave his only begotten Son, that whoever believes in Him should not perish, but have eternal life. For God did not send the Son into the world to judge the world, but that the world should be saved through Him" (John 3:16-17). The terms "world" and "whoever" emphasize universality, while "in him" and "through him" emphasize particularity. Paul does the same when he speaks of "God our Savior,

---

30. For more biblical references and a solid defense of God's universal salvific will, see *The Grace of God, the Will of Man*, ed. Clark Pinnock (Grand Rapids: Zondervan, 1989), chaps. 1-4, especially pp. 36-64.

who desires all men to be saved and to come to the knowledge of the truth. For there is one God, and one mediator also between God and men, the man Christ Jesus, who gave Himself as a ransom for all" (1 Tim. 2:3-6).

If we expand the discussion of the particular and the universal, we discover a wide array of texts that may be called exclusive and inclusive. The exclusive texts seem to indicate that the path to salvation in Jesus is very narrow indeed. "He who has believed and has been baptized shall be saved; but he who has disbelieved shall be condemned" (Mark 16:16). "He who believes in Him is not judged; he who does not believe has been judged already, because he has not believed in the name of the only Son of God" (John 3:18). "No one comes to the Father, but through me" (John 14:6). The Gentiles are depicted in the darkest of colors, "having no hope and without God" (Eph. 2:12) and "children of wrath" (Eph. 2:3). On the other hand, we find many inclusive texts which seem to indicate that God is very accepting and the path he has provided back to him is wide. "God is not one to show partiality, but in every nation the man who fears Him and does what is right, is welcome to Him" (Acts 10:34-35). God has "overlooked the times of ignorance" (Acts 17:30; cf. Rom. 3:25). Jesus is the "true light which, coming into the world, enlightens every man" (John 1:9). According to Romans 2:6-16, the Gentiles are capable of fulfilling the law by faith even though they do not have the written law, and thus they will receive "glory and honor and immortality, eternal life." Faith that is pleasing to God comes from those who "believe that He is, and that He is a rewarder of those who seek Him" (Heb. 11:6).

Holding both sets of texts together without neglecting either set requires careful theological balance. The Alexandrian church under the guidance of Clement of Alexandria and Origen emphasized the universalistic and inclusivistic texts and concluded that all human beings would ultimately be saved. The Western church, following Augustine, has tended to emphasize the particularistic and exclusivistic texts and thus has assumed that salvation is limited to those who have heard about

Jesus through the church. These two poles of thought are still present in the church today. Modern pluralists so emphasize the universalistic texts and play down the particularistic texts that they end up with a God who saves everyone by any (religious) means available to the person. Most evangelicals do the opposite, subordinating the universal/inclusive texts to the particular/exclusive texts to the extent that they end up with a God who does not seem serious about trying to save all people.

We must hold to both sets of texts and seek to arrive at a theological formulation that does justice to both. On the one hand, "in its eagerness to preach divine impartiality and the universal offer of salvation, the church must not diminish the scandal of the incarnation which comes to awesome expression in the cross. God has chosen to save all through one man: Jesus the Messiah, a member of the people of Israel."[31] On the other hand, we must be equally eager to preach that God desires to save all people. We must never underestimate the lengths to which God is willing to go to reconcile human beings to himself. The same God who is willing to search for the one lost sheep is the God who desires all people to be saved.

Some conservative Christians would object to this formulation of the two essential truths. Those from the Reformed tradition who adhere to limited atonement do not perceive any tension between the truths of salvation only in Jesus and God's universal salvific will. They maintain that God does not actually desire that all human beings experience redemption in Christ Jesus; if he did, they contend, then all people would be saved. Since God gets whatever he desires, if he truly desired all to come to salvation, then universalism would be true. And since universalism is not true, they argue, it must be the case that God does not desire all to be saved. That God gets whatever he wants was a key point of belief for Augustine: "the will of the omnipotent is always undefeated."[32] Calvin followed Augustine's lead in this

31. Frank Matera, "Acts 10:34-43," *Interpretation* 41 (1987): 65.
32. Augustine, *Enchiridion* 26.102.

regard and proceeded to argue that the verses ostensibly supporting God's universal salvific will do not refer to *all* human beings but only to those whom God has chosen to save. Terms such as "world" and "all" simply refer to the elect and to the fact that God saves from every group or class of humans.[33]

Although this is not the place to debate this important difference, it should be pointed out that most contemporary evangelicals espouse unlimited atonement and do not follow Augustine or Calvin on this point. But I would have to grant that those who do not, those who do continue to affirm the doctrine of limited atonement, will not be able to accept many of the conclusions in this book. I interpret the above quoted passages to support God's universal desire for each and every human being who has ever lived to experience redemptive grace, and of course this interpretation significantly informs my evaluation of the various positions I survey.[34]

Returning to the topic of the two essential truths, we can perhaps clarify the issue by distinguishing between the ontological and epistemological necessity of Jesus Christ for the salvation of individuals. Orthodox Christianity uniformly affirms the ontological necessity of Jesus Christ for salvation: if it were not for his atonement, we would all be left in our sins without any hope of reconciliation. But the matter of epistemological necessity — the question of whether a person must know about Jesus in order to benefit from the salvation he provided — is something else altogether. If such knowledge is necessary, is it made available to all people? If so, when and how does this occur? All the views surveyed in this book affirm the ontological necessity of Jesus for salvation but sharply disagree regarding the nature and timing of the epistemological necessity.

33. See Calvin, *Institutes of the Christian Religion,* Library of Christian Classics, vols. 20-21, ed. John T. McNeill, trans. Ford Lewis Battles (Philadelphia: Westminster Press, 1960), 3.24.16.
34. For a superb defense of God's universal salvific will as I have defined it and a thorough critique of the Calvinist perspective, see *The Grace of God, the Will of Man.*

## Control Beliefs

Although the theological perspective one holds affects the answer one gives to the question of the destiny of the unevangelized, it is interesting to note that this issue cannot be settled by appeal to denominational loyalties. As we will see, Baptists, Lutherans, Presbyterians, and even Roman Catholics disagree among themselves on this subject. Even Calvinist and Arminian backgrounds support quite a variety of different views regarding the unevangelized. More significant is the particular stance one takes regarding christology, faith, the nature and means of grace, the value of general revelation, the ministry of the Holy Spirit, and epistemology. The question of the unevangelized intersects with such vital issues as the nature of God (his love and power), the problem of evil, and election and damnation. The views we take on such subjects are of immense importance because they serve as "control beliefs" that guide and control the way we investigate and interpret evidence on other topics.[35] They form the boundaries within which answers are possible.

Control beliefs can be extremely powerful in influencing what we "see" in a text or the way we interpret our experiences. Christopher Columbus, for example, was influenced by two main control beliefs as he sailed west to find the Indies: (1) his absolute trust of Ptolemy's geography and (2) his assumption that the world is six parts land and only one part water (see 2 Esdr. 6:42). When he reached the Americas and found that it did not exactly fit the maps he had of the Indies, he simply modified his previous views to say there was a second very long peninsula on the coast of Asia.[36] Had someone suggested to Columbus that he had reached a "new world," he would have denied it! This story

35. See Nicholas Wolterstorff, *Reason within the Bounds of Religion*, (Grand Rapids: William B. Eerdmans, 1976).
36. See Daniel Boorstin, *The Discoverers* (New York: Vintage House, 1985), pp. 229, 244.

illustrates how powerfully control beliefs can influence our interpretation of data. All of us have and should have control beliefs.
It would be impossible to live meaningfully without them. They
give us stability as we encounter new ideas and experiences. But
sometimes we need to examine and modify — or even reject —
certain of our control beliefs.

I want to acknowledge at the outset of this study the
control beliefs that form the parameters within which the destiny of the unevangelized is considered. The following list is in
agreement with traditional evangelical theology: Christ alone,
grace alone, faith alone, Scripture alone.[37] These affirmations
delineate that salvation is offered only through the work of
Christ, that it is a complete work of God's free grace, that it is
appropriated only by faith, and that the Bible is the final authority for faith and practice. My treatment of the materials in this
work is also influenced by my belief in the substitutionary
atonement of Jesus for the sins of every human being, my
understanding of sin as rebellion against God that affects every
area of our lives, my belief that God desires to redeem every
human being who has ever lived, and my belief that an "act of
faith" is necessary for appropriating salvation into our lives. One
final guiding belief is that although the Bible is the authoritative
norm for theology, it must nevertheless be interpreted.[38]

37. For criticisms of some of these evangelical control beliefs, see Paul
Knitter, *No Other Name?* (Maryknoll, N.Y.: Orbis Books, 1985), pp. 90-96.
I am sympathetic to many of Knitter's criticisms, but I disagree that these
beliefs must be jettisoned to arrive at a successful solution to the problem of
religious pluralism.

38. More specifically, I endorse the position known as "critical inter-
pretationism," on which see David Wolfe, *Epistemology* (Downers Grove, Ill.:
InterVarsity Press, 1982), and Arthur Holmes, *Contours of a World View*
(Grand Rapids: William B. Eerdmans, 1983). Furthermore, I would argue
that evangelicals need to become more cognizant of their own interpretive
"horizon" in their handling of the biblical text. On this, see Anthony Thisel-
ton, *The Two Horizons* (Grand Rapids: William B. Eerdmans, 1980); Mark
Noll, *Between Faith and Criticism;* and chaps. 7 and 9 of *Evangelicalism and
Modern America.*

I want to stress the point about the authority of Scripture for two reasons. First, it is often the case in discussions of the unevangelized that those who espouse the wider hope are said to place human reason above biblical truth, in contrast to those who reject the wider hope, who are said to subordinate human reason to Scripture. While it is certainly possible and perhaps even tempting for us to use our own ideas to circumvent difficult teachings of Scripture, it is also the case that we have no alternative to using human ideas and reasoning to understand the Bible. Nor is anyone exempt from this task. Since we cannot avoid bringing our human ideas to the interpretive task, the real issue is which interpretation is best — and that should be settled by debate, not by *ad hominem* arguments or accusations.

The second point I want to make in this regard is that a genuine appeal to the authority of Scripture does not consist in merely citing a list of verses and then concluding that one's position has been proved.[39] This may sound obvious, but in discussions on the unevangelized it is amazing how often it occurs.[40] It consistently turns up in the classroom. When I

39. For an example of this sort of approach, see James Borland, "A Theologian Looks at the Gospel and World Religions," *Journal of the Evangelical Theological Society* 33 (March 1990): 8-11. Borland quotes a series of restrictivist texts, ignores all the universalistic and inclusivistic passages, and then asks, "Are we more enlightened than our Master? Do we know something that Jesus failed to understand?" He shows no awareness of how his own control beliefs affect his selection of texts, and he fails to interpret the texts he does cite in light of their original contexts. For more on the influence of the epistemology of naive realism in evangelical thought, see George Marsden, *Fundamentalism and American Culture* (New York: Oxford University Press, 1980), pp. 14-16, 55-62; and chaps. 6-9 of *Evangelicalism and Modern America*.

40. There is a general tendency among evangelical thinkers to put more effort into the defense of accepted doctrines than into fresh interpretation of Scripture as such. Some evangelicals even go so far as to give the appearance of equating the authority of established doctrine with that of biblical teaching. In such a context, critical discussion is virtually impossible, because alternative interpretations are dismissed from the outset as threats. See Wolfhart Pannenberg, *Basic Questions in Theology: Collected Essays*, 2 vols., trans. George H. Kehm (Philadelphia: Westminster, 1970-71), 1: 9.

teach about Calvin's or Arminius's position on election, my students typically quote verses to settle the issue, as if to suggest that Calvin or Arminius must have been unaware of them. Of course they were not unaware of them; they simply interpreted them differently because of significant differences in their control beliefs.[41] The same is true when it comes to those who disagree on the topic of the unevangelized.

Within the framework of these primary control beliefs, however, there is significant room for discussion and interpretation of Scripture. In the course of this study, I will frequently be referring to the control beliefs that are helping to shape the various positions.

41. For more on this, see my essay "God as Personal" in *The Grace of God, the Will of Man*, pp. 165-80.

# PART TWO

## The Two Extremes:
## Restrictivism and Universalism

# CHAPTER TWO

## *Restrictivism:*
## *All the Unevangelized Are Damned*

Many evangelicals hold that the only legitimate answer to the question of the destiny of the unevangelized is that there is no hope whatsoever for salvation apart from their hearing the message about the person and work of Christ and exercising faith in Christ before they die. The key belief that distinguishes this view — which I will be referring to as *restrictivism* — is that not everyone has an opportunity to be saved; access to salvation is not universal. Some restrictivists believe that Jesus died for the sins of every human being (unlimited atonement), but even these maintain that the opportunity for salvation is restricted to those who have heard and understood the gospel. Apart from human preaching there is no salvation. Just as Noah's ark saved only those on board, so the ark of salvation saves only those who board through the work of human missionaries. If the ark never reaches certain peoples, then they drown. Since the ark has not reached the vast majority of human beings, say the restrictivists, it must be the case that most human beings die condemned to hell.

## Key Biblical Texts

A number of familiar scriptural texts are commonly cited in support of restrictivism. These texts can be organized into four categories.

First, there are texts that affirm the particularity and exclusiveness of salvation in Jesus Christ. After testifying before the Sanhedrin that Jesus had been raised from the dead, Peter proclaimed that "there is salvation in no one else; for there is no other name under heaven that has been given among men, by which we must be saved" (Acts 4:12). Restrictivists interpret this to mean that a person must have explicit knowledge of the person and work of Jesus in order to have an opportunity to be saved. Paul declared to the Corinthians that "no man can lay a foundation other than the one which is laid, which is Jesus Christ" (1 Cor. 3:11). The writings of John contain a similar emphasis. Jesus told Thomas, "I am the way, and the truth, and the life; no one comes to the Father, but through me" (John 14:6). "And this is eternal life, that they may know Thee, the only true God, and Jesus Christ whom Thou hast sent" (John 17:3). "And the witness is this, that God has given us eternal life, and this life is in His Son. He who has the Son has the life; he who does not have the Son of God does not have the life" (1 John 5:11-12). Having cited these passages, Roger Nicole asks, "Why was it necessary for Christ to come at all if salvation can be obtained apart from him? When we reflect on the immensity of his suffering and the paramount significance of the incarnation, it appears incongruous, to say the least, that these great deeds should represent only one of several ways of being reconciled to God."[1]

A second group of passages points to the sinfulness of humanity and the utter hopelessness of life without Jesus. In Romans, Paul argues that all Gentiles and all Jews are guilty of rejecting God. The Gentiles have turned away from the light

1. Nicole, "One Door and Only One?" *Wherever* 4 (1979): 3.

of general revelation (1:20) and conscience (2:15), he says, and the Jews have refused to follow the light of special revelation (2:23). Consequently, both Jews and Gentiles are "under sin" and guilty before God (3:9). Gentiles could use the revelation of God given them to repent and seek God, but none of them do so (3:11). Instead, they "suppress the truth in unrighteousness" (1:18). Jews could use the revelation of God given them to repent and seek God, but none of them do so (3:11). In Ephesians Paul speaks in the darkest terms about those who are not "in Christ." The Gentiles, he says, were "strangers to the covenants of promise, having no hope and without God in the world" (2:12). Those without Christ are "darkened in their understanding, excluded from the life of God, because of the ignorance that is in them, because of the hardness of their heart" (4:18). Restrictivists understand these texts as indicating that apart from the special revelation of the gospel there is only sin and no salvation.

A third group of passages speaks of the importance of hearing the gospel and repenting. "After John had been taken into custody, Jesus came into Galilee, preaching the gospel of God, and saying, 'The time is fulfilled, and the kingdom of God is at hand; repent and believe in the gospel'" (Mark 1:14-15). Jesus told the disciples to "go into all the world and preach the gospel to all creation. He who has believed and has been baptized will be saved; but he who has disbelieved shall be condemned" (Mark 16:15-16). "He who believes in the Son has eternal life; but he who does not obey the Son shall not see life, but the wrath of God abides on him" (John 3:36). "Whoever denies the Son does not have the Father; the one who confesses the Son has the Father also" (1 John 2:23). In Romans 10 Paul explains the necessity of faith in Christ for salvation. He writes, "if you confess with your mouth Jesus as Lord, and believe in your heart that God raised Him from the dead, you shall be saved" (v. 9). A person finds out about Jesus from human preachers: "How then shall they call upon Him in whom they have not believed? And how shall they believe in Him whom they have not heard? And how are they to hear without a preacher?" (v. 14). "So faith comes from hearing, and hearing by the word of Christ" (v. 17). These texts are then used to interpret two significant events in the book of Acts.

In Acts 10, Peter is summoned to the house of Cornelius, a "God fearer" — that is, a Gentile who worshiped the God of Israel but was not a full proselyte to Judaism. Restrictivists maintain that although Cornelius was a God-fearing person, he needed to hear about Christ in order to be saved. If Cornelius had died before Peter brought him the gospel of Christ, they believe, he would have been damned to hell. If that were not so, why would God have gone to such great pains to see that the gospel was brought to him?[2] Furthermore, the angel had already informed Cornelius that Peter would "speak words to you by which you will be saved, you and all your household" (11:14). Hence, the argument goes, Cornelius was not saved until he became a follower of Jesus. This same line of reasoning is used to interpret another key event in Acts — Paul's sermon to the Epicurean and Stoic philosophers in Athens. These philosophers spoke a great deal about "God" and even had an altar dedicated "to an unknown god" (17:23). But Paul told them that they were ignorant of the true God and that he had been sent to preach the gospel to them. He said that God had made human beings "that they should seek [Him], if perhaps they might grope for Him and find Him, though He is not far from each one of us" (17:27). The word *if* here denotes, according to Gordon Lewis, "a contingency apparently not very likely to happen. . . . It seems clear that he did not consider the Athenians, in spite of their highest achievements, to have found Him. . . . If there had been a revelation through nature which could give life, then righteousness would indeed have been by general revelation. But through nature men did not find the Lord of All. Hypothetically, the Athenian outsiders

2. See Dick Dowsett, *Is God Really Fair?* (Chicago: Moody Press, 1985), p. 48.

could have sought and found God; realistically, the best of them had not."[3] The Athenians worshiped and served the creature rather than the Creator (17:29). On the basis of these verses, restrictivists argue that no one can be saved unless they receive the special revelation about Jesus from human messengers.

A fourth category of texts speaks of the narrowness of the true path to God and the few people that find this path. Jesus said, "enter by the narrow gate; for the gate is wide, and the way is broad that leads to destruction, and many are those who enter by it. For the gate is small, and the way is narrow that leads to life, and few are those who find it" (Matt. 7:13-14). On this basis, restrictivists argue that the majority of the human race is going to hell because few enter the narrow gate by accepting the gospel.[4]

When all of these passages are taken together, they present a rather bleak picture of humanity out of the reach of the gospel. Only those who have heard about and converted to Christ are true worshipers of God.

3. Lewis, "The Gospel on Campus," *HIS* 27 (1966): 12-13.
4. The great Princeton theologian Benjamin Warfield strongly objected to this interpretation of these texts. Although he believed that knowledge of the gospel is necessary for salvation (he repudiated the wider-hope theories), he insisted, along with Charles Hodge, that the number of those in heaven will be far greater than the number of those in hell. When Jesus spoke of the "narrow way," said Hodge, he was instructing his listeners to make their calling and election sure, not hinting at the relative population figures for heaven and hell. He suggests that the parable of the tares and the wheat teaches that the number of the damned will be inconsiderable in comparison the saved. How could Warfield and Hodge believe there will be more saved than damned when the vast majority of the human race has never heard of Christ? By appealing to the postmillennial doctrine that a period in history is coming when virtually every human being on earth will become a Christian. Assuming that the future population of the earth will be far greater than the total population throughout history, they believed that more will be saved than lost. See B. B. Warfield, "Are They Few That Be Saved?" in *Biblical and Theological Studies* (Philadelphia: Presbyterian and Reformed, 1952), pp. 334-50; and Hodge, *Systematic Theology*, 3 vols. (Grand Rapids: William B. Eerdmans, 1940), 3: 879-80.

## Theological Considerations

Six theological arguments will be considered here. All the advocates of restrictivism accept the first four, while only some accept the last two.

### 1. The Particularity and Finality of the Revelation and Salvific Work of Jesus

The first and most important control belief for restrictivists is the principle that Jesus is the only savior and that there is no way to possess saving faith other than to know him. The definition of "saving faith" is crucial for understanding this view. Most evangelicals would agree that saving faith involves personal trust in God and that one must have some knowledge (specific content) in order to trust. Furthermore, it is readily acknowledged that one can be saved with incomplete knowledge: Abraham was saved even though he was ignorant of the resurrection of Jesus. This, says Walter Elwell, raises a question: "If commitment to God is essential to salvation, and if the precise nature of the facts one must believe to be saved varies, how much does a person need to know (believe) to be saved, and where does that knowledge come from?"[5] The unequivocal answer given by restrictivists is that saving faith involves knowledge of biblical propositions or special revelation.

Philipp Melanchthon, Luther's colleague in the German reformation, included the sacraments as necessary for salvation: "it is certainly true that outside the Church, where there is no gospel, no sacrament, and no true invocation of God, there is no forgiveness of sins, grace, or salvation, as among the Turks, Jews, and heathen."[6] Jonathan Edwards wrote that "divine revelation

---

5. Elwell, "Heaven's Entrance Exam: How Much Do We Need to Know to Get In?" *Wherever* 4 (1979): 4.

6. Melanchthon, *On Christian Doctrine*, trans. Clyde Manschreck (New York: Oxford University Press, 1965), p. 212.

. . . is the only remedy which God has provided for the miserable, brutish blindness of mankind. . . . It is the only means that the true God has made successful in his providence, to give the nations of the world the knowledge of himself; and to bring them off from the worship of false gods."[7] The Princeton Calvinist Charles Hodge agreed with Edwards; citing Romans 10:17, he concluded that "there is no faith, therefore, where the gospel is not heard; and where there is no faith, there is no salvation."[8]

But if special revelation is necessary for saving faith to occur, what exactly is the content of the special revelation? Here there is some disagreement. Since the time of Augustine, most writers on this subject have contended that in Old Testament times people had to have faith in the "savior to come," whereas in New Testament times people have to have faith in the "savior who has come" in order to be saved. The French medieval ecclesiastic Bernard of Clairvaux, in agreement with Augustine, asserted that the statement "Abraham rejoiced to see my day" (John 8:56) means that Abraham was saved "because he had believed on him who would suffer. So are we to think of all the saints of that time, that they were born, just as we are, under the power of darkness because of original sin, but they were rescued before they died and by nothing else but the blood of Christ."[9] Roger Nicole agrees: "Abraham saw Christ's day (John 8:56); Moses wrote about Christ (John 5:46), and the Old Testament prophets sensed they were speaking about the salvation to come through the work of Christ (1 Pet. 1:10-12). . . . Now that the Messiah has come, it is not appropriate or even permissible to center our attention on these emblems."[10] Most proponents of covenant theology would agree that people living prior to the incarnation of Christ were saved by faith in

7. *The Works of Jonathan Edwards*, 2 vols. (Carlisle, Pa.: Banner of Truth, 1984), 2: 253.
8. Hodge, *Systematic Theology*, 2: 648.
9. Bernard, quoted by Ralph Turner in *"Descendit Ad Inferos," Journal of the History of Ideas* 27 (1966): 183.
10. Nicole, "One Door and Only One?" p. 3.

the Messiah to come, while all those after the incarnation must have faith that the Messiah has come.

Others take exception to the idea that people who lived during Old Testament times had to know about a future savior in order to be saved. Modern dispensationalists argue that Old Testament believers could not have known very much about the person and work of Christ from the rather obscure utterances in the Old Testament. Charles Ryrie states that "the *basis* of salvation in every age is the death of Christ; the *requirement* for salvation in every age is faith; the *object* of faith in every age is God; the *content* of faith changes in the various dispensations."[11] Ryrie holds that the content of faith for people in the Old Testament varied according to the specific revelation God gave them. The content of Abraham's saving faith, for example, was his belief that God would give him a son. The important point, according to Ryrie, is that the object of faith (God) was the same for Abraham as it is for us.

Both dispensational and covenant-theology restrictivists agree on three points, however. First, special revelation of some sort is necessary for salvation. Second, whatever the nature of the content of faith for those before Christ, "*now* it is not the same. . . . There is not the remotest hint in the New Testament of any way that people might be saved without personally putting their trust in Jesus and Him alone."[12] "Since Calvary, the unchanging required content of one's faith is the gospel. Nothing else saves, while all else damns."[13] Third, the ancient assertion that "outside the church there is no salvation" is understood in its most restrictive sense. Although the modern Protestants who hold this view would prefer to formulate it as "outside the word there is no salvation," they agree with the essence of the statement

11. Ryrie, *Dispensationalism Today* (Chicago: Moody Press, 1965), p. 123.

12. Dowsett, *Is God Really Fair?* p. 51.

13. James Borland, "A Theologian Looks at the Gospel and World Religions," *Journal of the Evangelical Theological Society* 33 (March 1990): 9.

by Fulgentius, a pupil of Augustine, that "not only all pagans, but also all Jews, all heretics and all schismatics who die outside of the present Catholic Church, will go to eternal fire, which is prepared for the devil and his angels."[14]

## 2. *General Revelation Does Not Provide a Means to Salvation*

The second theological control belief for restrictivists is the converse of the first. Harold Lindsell sums it up well: "General revelation, to be a vehicle of salvation, must insist that God is revealed sufficiently so as to restore the broken relationship with man . . . but the essence of special revelation is the truth that God is not revealed unto salvation in general revelation. . . . This much is perfectly evident: general revelation is totally insufficient as a vehicle for salvation."[15] Philipp Melanchthon held that natural knowledge of God is equivalent to law and so cannot save, since only the gospel of forgiveness can do that. The great philosophers, he said, knew only law, otherwise, "no distinction would be possible between us and the heathen if God saved men without knowledge of Christ and without faith!"[16]

Charles Hodge delineated and rejected various proposals about how saving knowledge may come without special revelation, and he also clearly opposed the notion that salvation is universally accessible: "The revelation of the plan of salvation is not made by the works or by the providence of God; nor by the moral constitution of our nature, nor by the intuitions or deductions of reason; nor by direct revelation to all men everywhere and at all times; but only in the written Word of God."[17] This is not to deny general revelation any teaching function, but it is to suggest that it has no

14. Fulgentius, quoted by Hans H. Henrix in "Judaism — Outside the Church, So No Salvation?" *Christian Jewish Relations* 17 (1984): 3.

15. Lindsell, *A Christian Philosophy of Mission* (Wheaton Ill.: Van Kampen Press, 1949), p. 107.

16. Melanchthon, *On Christian Doctrine*, pp. 6, 167.

17. Hodge, *Systematic Theology*, 2: 646.

salvific role. Bruce Demarest argues this forcefully in his study on general revelation. "General revelation elicits the anxious interrogation, 'What shall I do to be saved?' It prompts the question and poses the difficulty, but it cannot provide the solution."[18] But this does not imply that general revelation says nothing true about God or the human situation at all. Demarest goes on to suggest that there are "spiritual truths" about God and humanity in other religions and that people have genuine contact with God through general revelation — but no saving contact — because all people pervert God's universal revelation and "the light they do possess is too fragmentary and distorted to illumine the path that leads to a saving knowledge of God."[19]

### 3. Commitment to Christ Must Occur during One's Lifetime

A third key control belief for this position is that the "act of faith" must occur before a person dies — that is to say, there is no entertainment of the possibility of evangelization after death. In support of this belief, restrictivists typically cite Hebrews 9:27 ("it is appointed for men to die once and after this comes judgment"). The idea is also present in 2 Esdras 9:10 and in other early Christian writings such as 2 Clement 8:3: "for after we have gone out of the world, no further power of confessing or repenting will there belong to us."[20] In Roman Catholic theology and in most Protestant thought, it is assumed that death ends our period of probation and seals our destinies.

18. Demarest, *General Revelation* (Grand Rapids: Zondervan, 1982), p. 70.
19. Demarest, *General Revelation*, p. 259.
20. This belief has been extremely dominant in the Western church. See Alan Fairhurst, "Death and Destiny," *The Churchman* 95 (1981): 313-14. Aquinas agreed in his *Summa Theologica*, Part 3, q.52, a.7; as did Jonathan Edwards, *The Works of Jonathan Edwards*, 2: 515-25. This point is also raised in several Reformed confessions: Scottish Confession of Faith (1560), chap. 17; Second Helvetic Confession (1566), chap. 26; Westminster Confession (1646), 32.1; Westminster Larger Catechism (1647), Q. 86.

## 4. *The Unevangelized Deserve Condemnation*

The fourth restrictivist control belief pertains to the reason why the unevangelized are condemned to hell. How can God justly condemn someone simply because they never heard of Christ? Theologian R. C. Sproul argues that "if a person in a remote area has never heard of Christ, he will not be punished for that. What he will be punished for is the rejection of the Father of whom he has heard and for the disobedience to the law that is written in his heart."[21] Carl Henry concurs: "no man who has never heard of Jesus Christ is condemned for rejecting Christ; all men are condemned for their revolt against the light that they have. . . . Christ has an existence which antedates and is broader than his historical incarnation. He is the truth, and the source of all good. . . . In a real sense, a man who has never heard the name of Christ rejects him nonetheless, everytime he sins against whatever light he has."[22] Henry contends that every unevangelized person rejects Jesus Christ implicitly when he or she sins against the truth.

It is perhaps worth noting that many restrictivists seek to soften the bite of this "awful doctrine" by asserting that the unevangelized will not be punished as severely as those who have been evangelized but rejected Christ. Loraine Boettner says, for example, that "this, of course, does not mean that all of the lost shall suffer the same degree of punishment . . . (Lk 10:12-14, 12:47-8). . . . While the heathens are lost, they shall suffer relatively less than those who have heard and rejected the gospel."[23]

21. Sproul, *Reason to Believe* (Grand Rapids: Zondervan, 1982), p. 56. It is no longer commonly argued in evangelical circles that the unevangelized are worthy of condemnation solely on the grounds of original sin. Modern evangelicals tend to say they are sent to hell because of their own actual sin.

22. Henry, *Giving a Reason for Our Hope* (Boston: W. A. Wilde, 1949), pp. 40, 42.

23. Boettner, *The Reformed Doctrine of Predestination* (Grand Rapids: William B. Eerdmans, 1954), p. 120. For another statement along these lines, see Harry Buis, *The Doctrine of Eternal Punishment* (Philadelphia: Presbyterian and Reformed, 1957), p. 163. The similarity of this "softening" to the Roman Catholic idea of limbo for infants who die unbaptized should not go unnoticed.

## 5. The Implications of the Restrictivist Position for Missions

Some restrictivists — though not all — endorse the belief that
all the unevangelized are lost as a motivation for missionary
endeavors.[24] This argument came into use beginning in the
eighteenth century. Due to its widespread use by mission societies, it has come to be very familiar to evangelical audiences.
"In fact," says Boettner, "the belief that the heathen without
the Gospel are lost has been one of the strongest arguments in
favor of foreign missions. If we believed that their own religions
contain enough light and truth to save them, the importance
of preaching the Gospel to them is greatly lessened."[25] Some
nineteenth-century New England ministers said that this was
a terrible argument to use for missionary motivation, but Enoch
Pond, a pastor and theologian, disagreed:

> what a dreadful conclusion is this! . . . Not less than six hundred
> millions of the present inhabitants of our globe are hea-
> thens. . . . A mighty stream is ever pouring them over the
> boundaries of time; and when once they have passed these
> boundaries, where do they fall? Alas! . . . They fall to rise no
> more. . . . Now these are not fictions, but *facts* — facts fully
> established by the Scriptures. . . . Here is a broad current rush-
> ing downward from the heathen world into that lake which
> burneth with unquenchable fire, on which hundreds of millions
> of immortal beings are descending, and by which thousands
> upon thousands are every day destroyed.[26]

A little less florid but just as sweeping is Dick Dowsett's assertion that, "according to the Bible, the majority of people are

24. An example of restrictivists who do not subscribe to this argument
would be those in the Reformed tradition, who have traditionally not evidenced much interest in missions despite their belief that the unevangelized
are damned to hell.

25. Boettner, *The Reformed Doctrine of Predestination*, p. 119.

26. Pond, "The Future State of the Heathen," *Christian Review* 22
(Jan. 1857): 41.

'on the road to destruction' — terminally ill with the most desperate disease. . . . 98 percent of the people in Asia are a write-off. And they make up half the world's population."[27]

More tactful expressions of the same point can be found in two significant statements on missions by modern evangelicals. The Wheaton Declaration of 1966 says, "His saving grace is effective only in those who believe on Christ (John 1:12). . . . The mission of the Church inescapably commits us to proclaim the gospel which offers men the forgiveness of sins only through faith in Jesus Christ . . . [and] obliges evangelicals to preach the gospel to all men before they die in their sins."[28] The "Frankfurt Declaration," produced by the Tübingen evangelical theologian Peter Beyerhaus and approved by a convention of evangelicals in Germany in 1970, reads,

> we therefore oppose the false teaching . . . that Christ himself is anonymously so evident in world religions, historical changes, and revolutions that man can encounter him and find salvation in him without the direct news of the Gospel. . . . The adherents to the nonchristian religions and world views can receive this salvation only through participation in faith. They must let themselves be freed from their former ties and false hopes in order to be admitted by belief and baptism into the body of Christ.[29]

Statements such as these provide the impetus for powerful and emotional analogies. "The case may well be compared to that of a doctor who discovers a completely effective cure for all forms of cancer. He would not say, 'There may be some

27. Dowsett, *Is God Really Fair?* p. 16. For an objection to the glibness with which some evangelicals speak about those damned to hell, see David Edwards and John R. W. Stott, *Evangelical Essentials* (Downers Grove, Ill.: InterVarsity Press, 1988), p. 312.

28. *The Church's Worldwide Mission,* ed. Harold Lindsell (Waco, Tex.: Word Books, 1966), pp. 224-25. Although this passage does not explicitly rule out all universal accessibility views, commentary on the material provided by Arthur Climenhaga does (see pp. 105-6).

29. *Christianity Today,* 19 June 1970, pp. 5-6.

other treatments that succeed in isolated instances.' Instead he
would labor to the utmost to make his sure remedy available
to all the world to rid mankind of this fearful plague."[30] Again,
a security guard would not suggest alternate escape routes to
people in a burning building. He would direct the people to
the fire escape designed by the architect. The same is true of
missions. These ideas could be summed up by saying that if
and only if there is no hope for the unevangelized will we have
a compelling motive for missions. "The proper effect of the
doctrine that the knowledge of the gospel is essential to the
salvation of adults . . . is to prompt us to greatly increased
exertion to send the gospel to those who are perishing for lack
of knowledge."[31] James Borland suggests that "to teach any
other way of salvation for the heathen diminishes missionary
zeal and leaves the helpless hopeless."[32]

## 6. The Doctrine of Limited Atonement

Many evangelicals argue that access to salvation cannot be universal on the basis of the doctrine of limited atonement. If Jesus
did not die for every human being but only for those whom God,
in his sovereign election, chose to redeem, then we do not have
to worry at all about salvation being universally accessible.
Loraine Boettner, a five-point Calvinist, states the case well:

> those who are providentially placed in the pagan darkness of
> western China can no more accept Christ as Savior than they

30. Nicole, "One Door and Only One?" p. 3.
31. Hodge, *Systematic Theology*, 2: 648-49. What will happen to those
Christians who do not evangelize? John Gerstner suggests they will perish
along with the unevangelized in hell! See *Baker Dictionary of Theology*, ed.
R. K. Harrison (Grand Rapids: Baker Book House, 1960), p. 264. Dowsett,
in reference to Ezekiel 3:18, says that God considers such people murderers
(*Is God Fair?* p. 62).
32. Borland, "A Theologian Looks at the Gospel and World Religions," *Journal of the Evangelical Theological Society* 33 (March 1990): 11.

can accept the radio, the airplane, or the Copernican system of astronomy, things concerning which they are totally ignorant. When God places people in such conditions we may be sure that He has no more intention that they shall be saved than He has that the soil of northern Siberia, which is frozen all the year round, shall produce crops of wheat. Had he intended otherwise He would have supplied the means leading to the designed end.[33]

## Leading Defenders

### *Augustine*

Augustine, bishop in the north African town of Hippo from A.D. 396 to 430, has exerted an enormous influence on this topic. His ideas on soteriology and the destiny of the unevangelized have cast long shadows throughout church history, particularly among restrictivists. Augustine was well aware that several prominent Christian writers before him, such as Clement of Alexandria and Origen, had espoused wider-hope views, but he pointedly rejected them.

Augustine believed that general revelation brings knowledge of God's nature and ethical demands to all humanity.[34] But he maintained that this knowledge is not sufficient for individual salvation because sin clouds the natural mind and perverts the truth. To be saved, human beings must have explicit knowledge of the Messiah.

Augustine wrote about the question of the unevangelized on several occasions, but his most systematic treatment is found in a letter to Deogratius, in which he responds to the "weighty

33. Boettner, *The Reformed Doctrine of Predestination*, p. 120.
34. See Augustine, *The City of God*, 8.6, 10-12; and *Christian Doctrine*, 2.40. For a study of Augustine's views on general revelation, see Demarest, *General Revelation*, pp. 26-30.

arguments of Porphyry against the Christians."[35] Porphyry
(A.D. 232-304) was an influential neo-Platonic philosopher
whose writings were well known to Augustine. According to
Augustine, he cast the crucial question as follows:

> if Christ declares Himself to be the way of salvation, the Grace
> and the Truth, and affirms that in Him alone, and only to souls
> believing in Him, is the way of return to God, what has become
> of men who lived in the many centuries before Christ came?
> . . . What, then, has become of such an innumerable multitude
> of souls, who were in no wise blameworthy, seeing that He in
> whom alone saving faith can be exercised had not yet favored
> men with His advent? . . . Why, then, did He who is called the
> Savior withhold Himself for so many centuries of the world?

Porphyry was aware that some Christians attempted to meet
his objection by claiming that people before Christ were saved
by faith in the Christ to come. Pagans before Christ, it was
argued, were saved if they turned to the Jewish faith, which
taught about the Christ who was to come. To this Porphyry
said,

> let it not be said that provision had been made for the human
> race by the old Jewish law. It was only after a long time that
> the Jewish law appeared and flourished within the narrow limits
> of Syria. . . . It gradually crept onwards to the coasts of Italy;
> but this was not earlier than the end of the reign of Gaius. . . .
> What, then, became of the souls of men in Rome and Latium
> who lived before the time of the Caesars, and were destitute of
> the grace of Christ, because He had not then come?

In answer to these weighty arguments, Augustine first
points out that Christ is the *eternal* Son of God. "From the

35. For the relevant portions of the letter, see *Nicene and Post-Nicene
Fathers*, series 1, vol. 1, ed. Philip Schaff (1886; reprint, Grand Rapids:
William B. Eerdmans, 1974), pp. 416-18. Subsequent material will be quoted
from this text unless otherwise noted. Augustine recapitulates these same
arguments in chap. 17 of his *Predestination of the Saints*.

beginning of the human race, whosoever believed in Him, and in any way knew Him, and lived in a pious and just manner according to His precepts, was undoubtedly saved by Him, in whatever time and place he may have lived." The people living before the incarnation were saved by the same Savior and the same kind of faith as believers in the New Testament age because they believed in the Savior who was to come. The second point Augustine makes in answer to the question is that "Christ knew that the world was so full of unbelievers in the former ages, that He righteously refused to manifest Himself or to be preached to those of whom He foreknew that they would not believe either His words or His miracles." Christ, in his foreknowledge, knew that most of the human race would not accept him, and so he prolonged the incarnation until there were more people who would accept his gospel.[36] But this is not to say that Augustine believed no people were saved before Christ came. On the contrary, he indicates that many were saved from among both the Israelites and other nations. He asks why we cannot believe that more Gentiles than those mentioned in the Old Testament, like Job, were also saved because the "holy mystery" was revealed to them.[37] He then concludes by describing three classes of human beings: (1) those to whom the gospel was never preached because it was foreknown that they would not believe, (2) those to whom it was preached even though God foreknew they would not believe — these are examples for condemnation — and (3) those to whom the gospel was revealed and who did believe.

Elsewhere Augustine specifically addresses the teaching of the earlier Church Fathers Clement of Alexandria and Origen

36. According to Augustine, the world would still be filled with un-believers if God had not provided the irresistible grace that regenerates the sinner. One is tempted to ask why God has not granted all humans, including those who lived prior to the incarnation, the same grace. Augustine would no doubt respond that this is part of the inscrutable mystery of God's will.

37. This seems to be an important point for Augustine since he mentions it several times. See *The City of God*, 18.47.

that the unevangelized receive an opportunity after death to hear
the gospel and repent. He provides his fullest response in a letter
to Evodius, in the context of an interpretation of 1 Peter 3:19
("He went and preached unto the spirits in prison").[38] Since the
days of Clement of Alexandria it had become popular to understand the descent of Christ into hell in the interval between his
crucifixion and resurrection as an evangelistic mission. While
admitting his perplexity concerning the passage, Augustine suggests that Peter was speaking only of sinners in his own day who
were in the spiritual condition of being in prison. He makes a
number of points to substantiate his case.

First, he asks why Peter says that Christ preached only to
those who were unbelieving in the days of Noah instead of
mentioning all the patriarchs of the Old Testament. Second,
he notes the danger that belief in postmortem evangelization
might simply be wishful thinking. He grants that it is only
natural to view such virtues as "frugality, self-denial, chastity,
sobriety, braving of death in their country's defence, and faith
kept inviolate" among non-Christians as "indications of a certain disposition of mind [that] please us so much that we would
desire those in whom they exist . . . to be freed from the pains
of hell." Nevertheless, he insists that "the verdict of human
feeling [is] different from that of the justice of the Creator."
Third, in anticipation of the criticism that his position implies
that Christ must have descended into hell for no purpose,
Augustine is willing to allow that "some whom He judged
worthy" were, in fact, delivered from hell — but he quickly adds
that it is not "a necessary inference that what the divine mercy
and justice granted to some must be supposed to have been
granted to all." Fourth, although Augustine does not rule out
the possibility that the 1 Peter passage is referring to Christ's
saving work in hell, he does not think it likely; he puts more
stock in the assertion that the descent of Christ delivered the

38. *Nicene and Post-Nicene Fathers*, series 1, vol. 1, pp. 515-20. See also
*The City of God*, 21.13, 17-27.

Old Testament patriarchs not from hell but from "Abraham's bosom," which, he says, is not "a part of hell."

Commenting on 1 Peter 4:6 ("for this cause was the gospel preached also to them that are dead"), Augustine says, "who can be otherwise than perplexed by words so profound as these?" Nonetheless, he goes on to reject three interpretations of this text. First, he says that it cannot refer to purgatorial suffering in the flesh to the end that these sinners might gain heaven, since Peter mentions only those who were living in the days of Noah. Second, Augustine rejects the proposal that it might refer to those who died before the incarnation, who "had sufficient excuse for not believing that which had never been proclaimed to them," on the grounds that "the same excuse is available for all those who have, even after Christ's resurrection, departed this life before the gospel came to them." Third, he rejects the proposal made by some of the Church Fathers that in fact the gospel might be preached in hell to all who had not heard it while alive. In the first place, he says, if this were true, we would have no reason to mourn those who have died without hearing the gospel or to work hard at evangelism; in the second place, if only those who do not hear of Christ before they die have an opportunity to hear after death, then "the gospel ought not to be preached on earth, — a sentiment not less foolish than profane." He concludes that we should "refuse to entertain the thought that the gospel was once preached, or is even to this hour being preached in hell . . . as if a Church had been established there as well as on earth."

Augustine believed that hearing the gospel of Christ was necessary for salvation, and he considered all those dying un-evangelized to be damned to hell. Regarding the numbers of those in heaven and hell, he states that "many more are left under punishment than are delivered from it, in order that it may thus be shown what was due to all."[39] Although this sounds

39. Augustine, *The City of God*, trans. Marcus Dods (New York: Random House, 1950), 21.12.

harsh to modern ears, Augustine believed it should lead those
of us who have been redeemed to give God our sincerest thanks.

### John Calvin

The Reformer John Calvin followed Augustine in many points
of theology, including his views on the destiny of the unevangelized. He deals with the subject in a systematic fashion in his
famous *Institutes of the Christian Religion* (2.6). He begins by
arguing that God's original plan was for humans to learn the
truth about God from general revelation and thus gain eternal
life but that this plan was spoiled by sin. Since all humans are
condemned in Adam, the knowledge of God as Creator is
useless for salvation unless we also learn about Christ. "Surely,
after the fall of the first man no knowledge of God apart from
the Mediator has had power unto salvation."[40] Even though
the name of God was everywhere knowable, "all the heathen,
to a man, by their own vanity either were dragged or slipped
back into false inventions . . . that whatever they had naturally
sensed concerning the sole God had no value beyond making
them inexcusable."[41] He adds that even the wisest of the philosophers corrupted the truth of God. Consequently, Calvin finds
totally ludicrous the statement of his fellow Swiss Reformer
Zwingli that pagans such as Socrates, Aristides, and Cato will
be in heaven:

> all the more vile is the stupidity of those persons who open
> heaven to all the impious and unbelieving without the grace of
> him whom Scripture commonly teaches to be the only door

40. John Calvin, *Institutes of the Christian Religion,* Library of Christian
Classics, vols. 20-21, ed. John T. McNeill, trans. Ford Lewis Battles
(Philadelphia: Westminster Press, 1960), 2.6.1. Subsequent references to this
work are from this edition unless otherwise noted. For a study of Calvin's
understanding of general revelation, see Demarest, *General Revelation,* pp.
50-60.

41. *Institutes,* 1.10.3.

whereby we enter into salvation. . . . Christ answered the Samaritan woman: "You worship what you do not know; we worship what we know; for salvation is from the Jews." In these words he . . . condemns all pagan religions as false. . . . No worship has ever pleased God except that which looked to Christ. On this basis, also, Paul declares that all heathen were "without God and bereft of hope of life."[42]

Calvin also agreed with Augustine that those who lived prior to the incarnation of Christ were saved only by believing in a mediator who was to come.

> Even the Old Covenant declared that there is no faith in the gracious God apart from the Mediator. . . . For this reason I subscribe to the common saying that God is the object of faith, yet it requires qualification. For Christ is not without reason called "the image of the invisible God." This title warns us that, unless God confronts us in Christ, we cannot come to know that we are saved. . . . Apart from Christ the saving knowledge of God does not stand. From the beginning of the world he had consequently been set before all the elect that they should look unto him and put their trust in him.[43]

Furthermore, "it is an indubitable doctrine of Scripture, that we obtain not salvation in Christ except by faith; then there is no hope left for those who continue to death unbelieving."[44]

This is not to say that Calvin believed God limited himself to using human messengers to communicate saving knowledge, however; he held that preaching is the "ordinary dispensation" or means of bringing saving faith but that it should never be used to "prescribe a law for the distribution of his grace."[45] In other words, all those who are *truly elect* can be saved even

---

42. *Institutes*, 2.6.1.

43. *Institutes*, 2.6.2, 4.

44. John Calvin, *Commentary on the Catholic Epistles*, trans. John Owen (Grand Rapids: William B. Eerdmans, 1948), p. 113.

45. Calvin, *Commentary on Romans*, trans. John Owen (Grand Rapids: William B. Eerdmans, 1948), p. 398.

without preaching: God will miraculously send them the message of Christ. According to Calvin, if God had decreed that
a certain person living prior to Jesus was to be saved, then God
saw to it that the individual received the gospel message about
the coming Savior.

Nevertheless, Calvin's emphasis is definitely on the restrictivist side. To prove his point that there is no salvation apart from
knowledge of Christ, he quotes (actually misquotes) 1 John 2:23,
"He that does not have the Son does not have the Father."[46] He
then concludes that all those in other religions (especially the
Turks), "although they proclaim at the top of their lungs that the
Creator of heaven and earth is God, still, while repudiating
Christ, substitute an idol in place of the true God."[47] All such
people, the Turks and the unevangelized alike, will be damned to
hell. God has chosen to make them reprobates, and "they have
been given over to this depravity because they have been raised
up by the just but inscrutable judgment of God to show forth his
glory in their condemnation."[48]

### R. C. Sproul

R. C. Sproul is a contemporary evangelical theologian in the
Calvinist tradition. His book *Reason to Believe* contains a chapter entitled "What about the Poor Native Who Never Heard
of Christ?" in which he does a good job of summing up the
view of many modern evangelicals regarding the destiny of the
unevangelized.[49] He notes that this issue is a chief point of

46. The verse actually reads, "Whoever denies the Son does not have
the Father." John is speaking of those who deliberately and knowingly rejected
Jesus as the Savior. Calvin reads John as saying that one must know about
the incarnate Son of God in order to be saved.
    47. *Institutes*, 2.6.4. See also Calvin's commentary on Acts 17:16-24.
    48. *Institutes*, 3.24.14.
    49. Sproul, *Reason to Believe* (Grand Rapids: Zondervan, 1982), pp.
47-59.

interest among his students and suggests that spiritual compassion stimulates the interest. But he says that the students typically construct their questions within a faulty theological framework. When someone asks about the destiny of the innocent person who has never heard of Christ, says Sproul, it should be noticed that the assumption of *innocence* is incorrect. There are, he contends, no innocent people. All are guilty before God. Citing Romans 1:19-21, he asserts that general revelation is "clear and unambiguous. . . . Man's problem is not that he doesn't know God but that he refuses to acknowledge what he knows to be true. . . . The revelation is sufficient to render man inexcusable."[50] And pagans compound their guilt, he argues, by creating false religions. After citing Romans 1:22-25, Sproul states that "pagan religion is viewed then not as growing out of an honest attempt to search for God, but out of a fundamental rejection of God's self-revelation."[51]

This brings him to the question of the criteria God will use in judging the unevangelized. "The New Testament makes it clear that people will be judged according to the light that they have. . . . They do have a law 'written on their hearts' (Rom. 2:15). . . . Thus if a person in a remote area has never heard of Christ, he will not be punished for that. What he will be punished for is the rejection of the Father of whom he has heard and for the disobedience to the law that is written in his heart."[52] Since all unevangelized will be condemned for rejecting God the Father, whom they know by general revelation, and since the gospel of Christ preached by human messengers (Rom. 10:14-15) is God's only remedy for this sin, it is imperative that the church take up its mandate and evangelize. Otherwise, even larger numbers of unevangelized will be consigned to eternal damnation.

50. Sproul, *Reason to Believe*, p. 52.
51. Sproul, *Reason to Believe*, p. 55.
52. Sproul, *Reason to Believe*, pp. 55-56.

## Evaluation

Restrictivism has special strengths in three areas. First, it provides a solid defense of the particularity and exclusiveness of salvation in Jesus Christ against all forms of latitudinarianism and relativism. Restrictivists rightly object that universalism and modern pluralism often minimize the importance of Jesus. A vibrant christocentrism and emphasis on the historical incarnation of Jesus Christ are essential to the Christian faith, especially in light of the modern temptation to accede to a vague theocentrism. Second, restrictivism rightly emphasizes the act of faith as necessary for salvation. One must have faith in God in order to appropriate the grace he provides. Third, restrictivism provides a strong argument for the importance of evangelism and missions. In today's relativistic world, many are seeking to replace conversion-oriented missions with mere dialogue for better understanding. Dialogue should of course be encouraged, but conversion to Christ must remain the ultimate and primary purpose of missions.

There are many shortcomings to this position, however. Proponents of wider-hope views have produced six basic criticisms, though not every advocate of the wider hope would agree with all six criticisms.

### 1. The Accessibility of Salvation

The cardinal difficulty of restrictivism is its insistence that salvation is not universally accessible; critics maintain that it does not adequately uphold the universal salvific will of God. Does God truly love *all* people enough genuinely to desire that they be saved? Restrictivists would seem to be saying that he does not, since they teach that he has not provided an opportunity for all people to benefit from the redeeming work of the Son. Critics hold that Augustine's response to Porphyry on this point is simply not satisfactory. Porphyry's questions are still with us, they say, and it is time for different answers. If God actually desires all people to be saved (1 Tim. 2:4; 2 Pet. 3:9), then it is reasonable to look for ways in which God might fulfill this desire. It is not enough, say the critics, to argue that Jesus died for everyone but that only some receive an opportunity to be helped by his death. The real issue is whether or not the benefits of the atonement are made available, in some way or other, to every human being.[53]

"The problem," says Clark Pinnock, "is that God cannot save those he would like to save if indeed it is true that there is salvation only where the gospel is preached and accepted."[54] Those who claim both that God desires all to be saved and that all the unevangelized are necessarily damned imply that it is *impossible* for God to save these people. It is the same sort of logic evident in the long-standing Roman Catholic doctrine that it is impossible for God to save unbaptized infants. Why do the same Protestants who declare so confidently that all unevangelized persons will suffer eternal torment recoil in horror when the same is said for unbaptized infants? Do the infants not bear the burden of original sin? Why do restrictivists speak of the great power and will of God in other doctrines but when speaking of the unevangelized prefer to emphasize the power of human sin over the power of God's love? We must not underestimate the capacity of human sin to resist God, but neither must we water down the resourcefulness of God when it comes to achieving his goal of having all people come to know him in a redemptive way.

53. For the argument that restrictivists do not pay adequate attention to the universalist passages of Scripture, see Carl Braaten, *The Flaming Center* (Philadelphia: Fortress Press, 1971), p. 111.
54. Pinnock, "The Finality of Jesus Christ in a World of Religions," in *Christian Faith and Practice in the Modern World: Theology from an Evangelical Point of View*, ed. Mark Noll and David Wells (Grand Rapids: William B. Eerdmans, 1988), p. 163.

## 2. The Role of Christ in Salvation

The second criticism put forth by inclusivists who assume a universally accessible salvation is that restrictivism confuses the ontological necessity of Christ for salvation with our human epistemological necessity of knowing about it. Do texts such as Acts 4:12 ("there is no other name given among men") and John 14:6 ("no man comes to the Father but by me") actually imply that a person must know about Jesus in order to benefit from his work? Many assume they do, but many others would argue that the texts themselves do not say this.[55]

The verse most used in support of restrictivism is Acts 4:12, in which Peter speaks to the members of the Sanhedrin about their need to repent and follow Jesus. The destiny of the unevangelized per se is not at issue here. The context of this passage is the account of Peter's healing of a lame man at the Temple and his subsequent use of the occasion to preach Jesus as the Messiah.[56] The key to understanding this story is the use of the word *onoma* ("name"), which appears seven times in 3:6–4:18. Peter healed the lame man in the *name* of Jesus and then preached Jesus as the resurrected Holy One, the one with divine power and authority (name) to heal (3:12-26). Peter was arrested, and the next day the Council questioned him about the "name" by which he healed the man (4:7). The issue between the leaders and Peter was one of authority.

The expression "in the name of" has its roots in the Old

55. For a discussion of the particularistic-exclusivistic texts in light of the unevangelized, see Charles Garrison, *Two Different Worlds: Christian Absolutes and the Relativism of Social Science* (Newark: University of Delaware Press, 1988), pp. 108-18; and Peggy Starkey, "Biblical Faith and the Challenge of Religious Pluralism," *International Review of Mission*, Jan. 1982, pp. 68-71. Starkey seems to favor pluralism.

56. For helpful studies of this passage, see Irene W. Foulkes, "Two Semantic Problems in the Translation of Acts 4:5-20," *Bible Translator* 29 (1978): 121-25; and Clark Pinnock, "Acts 4:12: No Other Name under Heaven," in *Through No Fault of Their Own*, ed. William Crockett and James Sigountos (Grand Rapids: Baker Book House, 1991).

Testament (Hebrew *beshem*), where it means that the speaker has the commission or authority of the one in whose name he speaks. The Jewish leaders wanted to know the source of the authority by which Peter performed the healing. "Since believers in Yahweh were forbidden to call on any other (supposed) divinity, the question is really an inquiry into the orthodoxy of the apostles as Jewish believers."[57] The Council thought Peter was invoking a foreign deity, a God other than Yahweh the God of Israel. Peter reiterated that it was by the "authority [name] of Jesus" that he healed the man (4:10), but he denied the accusation of heresy and sought to establish his orthodoxy by arguing that it is legitimate to use Jesus' name in connection with divine authority since Jesus is the resurrected Messiah whom God appointed as the "corner stone" (4:10-11). Peter went on to proclaim Jesus not only as the authority (name) who can heal but also as the authority by whom the divinely appointed messianic salvation has come (4:12). Peter insisted that Jesus is the only one with the authority and power to save. The word *sōzein* ("saved") in verse 12 has a double meaning which includes both physical healing and spiritual redemption (4:9-12). Peter's point was that salvation in the *full* messianic sense had come because Jesus of Nazareth is the one God appointed to be the "name" or the source of the prophesied messianic salvation (Ps. 118:22). When Peter said "there is no other name," he meant that salvation (in the full sense) for any human being comes only through Jesus. This was as true for Abraham and Moses as it was for the Sanhedrin.

In using the phrase "no other authority," Peter certainly was making a claim for the finality and exclusiveness of Jesus, but this use hardly settles the issue of whether a person must hear about Jesus in order to benefit from his salvific authority. As Clark Pinnock suggests, Acts 4:12 speaks forcefully about

57. Foulkes, "Two Semantic Problems in the Translation of Acts 4:5-20," p. 122. See also Acts 4:17-18 about the Council's attempts to stop the apostles from speaking in Jesus' name.

the power of Jesus' name to save and heal those who hear and respond to the gospel, but it does not speak to the fate of the unevangelized as such.[58] Restrictivists who claim that it does speak authoritatively on this subject are forcing the text to address an issue that is beyond its scope.

The same is true in many restrictivist treatments of passages in the Gospel of John. In John 14:6, for instance, Jesus teaches his disciples that they truly do know the "way" God wants them to live since they have observed this way of life in Jesus himself and thus have seen the Father (14:9). This text demonstrates that Jesus desires us to come to know him, but the context is silent about the unevangelized. John 3:16 and 18 both refer to the evangelized: those who hear and accept Christ are saved, while those who hear and reject him are condemned. This is likewise true for Mark 16:16. The particularistic passages quoted in defense of the restrictivist claim that all the unevangelized are damned do, indeed, point out the ontological significance of Jesus, but the consensus outside the restrictivist camp is that they do not teach that all must hear of Christ or be forever lost.

Some contend that Acts 11:14 and Romans 10:9-14 clearly teach the necessity of hearing the gospel in order to be saved. In Acts 11 we read that Peter informed the Jerusalem church of his encounter with Cornelius. He reported that the angel had instructed Cornelius to send for Peter so he might "speak words to you by which you will be saved, you and all your household" (11:14). From this some commentators conclude that Cornelius was not saved until he heard about and accepted Christ.[59] If he had died before the arrival of Peter, they contend, he would have spent eternity in hell, since it was only after he accepted Christ that God forgave his sins, purified his heart, and granted him the gift of the Spirit. Only then was

58. Pinnock, "Acts 4:12: No Other Name under Heaven."
59. See John R. W. Stott, *The Spirit, the Church, and the World: The Message of Acts* (Downers Grove, Ill.: InterVarsity Press, 1990), p. 199.

he baptized and publicly brought into the Christian community. After all, R. C. H. Lenski asks, "if his honest pagan convictions had been sufficient, why did he seek the synagogue? If the synagogue had been enough, why was Peter here?"[60]

Three responses can be made in answer to such questions. First, Luther and Calvin are correct when they assert that since Cornelius was a "God fearer," he would have been saved even if he had died before Peter arrived.[61] Those who claim that Cornelius would have been damned to hell if he had died before Peter came overlook the fact that Cornelius was already worshiping the *God* who saves through Jesus Christ. That God was pleased with Cornelius is evident from the fact that his prayers and alms ascended as a "memorial offering" (10:4) and he was "remembered" by God (10:31).[62] Both words have strong theological antecedents in the Old Testament. Furthermore, if worshipers of Yahweh such as Cornelius were not saved until they heard about Christ, then what of all the other worshipers of God in the Old Testament, such as Moses and David? Were they all damned to hell?[63]

Second, Lenski's questions imply that something must have been wrong with Cornelius's faith if God had to work so hard to get the message about Christ to him. But this ignores the fact that the Greek term *sōzō* has the same breadth of meaning as its English equivalent "saved." It is used in the book of Acts to refer

---

60. Lenski, *The Interpretation of the Acts of the Apostles* (Minneapolis: Augsburg, 1961), p. 419.

61. See *Luther's Works*, vol. 26, *Lectures on Galatians*, ed. Jaroslav Pelikan (St. Louis: Concordia Publishing, 1963), p. 210; and Calvin, *Institutes*, 3.17.4.

62. See Lev. 2:2, 9, 16; and Stott, *The Spirit, the Church, and the World*, p. 198.

63. Bruce Demarest claims that a personal relationship with God is mediated *exclusively* through knowledge of Jesus Christ (*General Revelation*, p. 253). Gavin D'Costa argues that "if this exclusivist contention is taken seriously, then it must imply that the revelation of God in Israel's history was either (a) not revelation after all, or (b) a revelation, but somehow inadequate for salvation" (*Theology and Religious Pluralism*, p. 66). If it was inadequate for salvation, then all the Old Testament believers must be in hell.

to physical healing (14:9), making whole (4:9), deliverance from a storm (27:20), a proper relationship with God (15:1), and the fullness of salvation as experienced in a relationship with Christ. It is this last meaning that Luke has in mind here. This is problematic for contemporary evangelicals who tend to use the word *saved* only in the narrow sense of salvation to eternal life beyond the grave. In general, the use of the term *saved* in the evangelical subculture does not reflect its broader usage in the Bible.[64] I believe it would be better to understand the text as indicating that Cornelius was "saved" in the modern evangelical sense before Peter arrived and that he received salvation in its *fullness* when he heard about Jesus. There was nothing categorically wrong with Cornelius's faith; it simply lacked a complete knowledge of the full extent of God's saving love as manifested in Jesus of Nazareth — as was the case with all the Old Testament believers. Cornelius was a "saved" *believer* before Peter arrived, but he became a *Christian* and received the fuller blessings of life in Christ only after Peter came.

Third, it must be remembered that the main point of the story is not that Cornelius as an individual was saved but that Peter and the apostolic church had to come to grips with God's desire to include the Gentiles in the scope of salvation without the prerequisite of a conversion to Judaism. Indeed, if there was anyone who lacked faith in this story, it was Peter, not Cornelius. The Jewish Christians were having an extremely difficult time understanding God's universal salvific will. Peter, following good Jewish practice, did not want to eat the unclean foods or enter the house of a Gentile. The church was not yet multiracial and multicultural, and Gentiles were not welcome in its fellowship. The book of Acts, however, records the great steps *God* took to help the Jewish Christians accept the full inclusion of

64. Like many other biblical terms, *saved* tends to be defined much more precisely by individuals and groups attempting to outline their *own* positions than such terms ever were by the biblical writers. See Vern Poythress, *Symphonic Theology* (Grand Rapids: Zondervan, 1987), pp. 74-75, 94-95.

Gentiles into his grace without undue burdens. The story of Cornelius is meant to inform us of God's desire to include all races in the fellowship of the church, not to teach that until someone is a member of the church and is baptized, he or she is eternally damned. In fact, to argue that the unevangelized are damned is in a sense to commit the same error as the Jerusalem church. In any event, the account in the book of Acts of Peter being sent to Cornelius falls far short of proving the necessity of hearing about Christ for salvation in the narrow evangelical sense.

The same is true of Romans 10. Some believe that Paul asserted the necessity of knowing about Christ for salvation when he said that "if you confess with your mouth Jesus as Lord, and believe in your heart that God raised Him from the dead, you shall be saved" (10:9). But logically this means nothing more than that confession of Christ is *one* sure way to experience salvation: Paul does not say anything about what will happen to those who do not confess Christ because they have never heard of Christ. The text is logically similar to the conditional statement "If it rains, then the sidewalk will be wet." If the condition is fulfilled (if it rains), then the consequent will follow (the sidewalk will be wet). But we cannot with certainty say, "If it is not raining, the sidewalk will not be wet." Someone may turn on a sprinkler, or there may be a pile of melting snow nearby — any number of things besides rain might make the sidewalk wet. It is sometimes argued that since all those who accept Christ are saved, it must follow that *only* those who know about and accept Christ are saved. But this is like arguing that since all Collies are dogs, all dogs must be Collies. The argument is simply fallacious.[65] We

65. Some theologians object to this sort of application of modern logic to the biblical text. They argue that we cannot assume that Paul used the same sort of logic we use, since we know that not all cultures have the same logic. They also point to the fact that "if-then" constructions aren't always meant to function in a strictly logical way in everyday discourse. I certainly agree. But my question is how are we to know whether Paul meant more than what is grammatically or logically implied in his statement? I believe

can be certain the text is telling us that hearing about and coming to know Jesus is one sure way to experience salvation, but we can be just as certain that the text is not explicitly telling us that all the unevangelized are damned.[66]

Moreover, restrictivists commonly overlook Paul's appeal to the creation revelation in Romans 10:18. Quoting the great creation hymn Psalm 19, Paul says that the "gospel" has gone out to all the world. Inclusivists argue that what Paul is saying here is that all who respond to the revelation they have by calling out to God will be saved by Jesus Christ, since calling out to God is, in fact, calling upon the Lord Jesus.

### 3. The Character of General Revelation

The third major criticism of restrictivism concerns the claim that general revelation is sufficient for condemnation but insufficient for salvation. This sort of assertion prompts many to ask, "What kind of God is he who gives man enough knowledge to damn him but not enough to save him?"[67] The kind of God,

---

the burden of proof is on those who posit more meaning in the text than is immediately evident. Surely one needs some sort of additional evidence before asserting that Paul is telling us that all who are ignorant of Christ are for that reason damned. I think we have every right in this instance to ask whether such individuals are in fact finding restrictivist implications in the text only because they are approaching the text with restrictivist assumptions. For a discussion of the application of logic to the Bible, see Paul Helm, "The Role of Logic in Biblical Interpretation," in *Hermeneutics, Inerrancy, and the Bible,* ed. Earl Radmacher and Robert Preus (Grand Rapids: Zondervan, 1984), pp. 839-80.

66. The same is true with regard to Romans 10:13-18. Many restrictivists quote verses 15 and 17 but stop short of verse 18, which declares that all people have heard the "gospel." For a discussion of this passage, see my article "Is Belief in Christ Necessary for Salvation?" *Evangelical Quarterly* 60 (1988): 247-48.

67. Dale Moody, *The Word of Truth: A Summary of Christian Doctrine Based on Biblical Revelation* (Grand Rapids: William B. Eerdmans, 1981), p. 59.

it would seem, who does not truly desire to see all people redeemed. Some have tried to rebut this charge by arguing that if the unevangelized lived up to the light of general revelation, they would be saved, but since Paul says in Romans 1–3 that no one ever does live up to that light, they all deserve eternal damnation. Thus, it is argued, special revelation is necessary for salvation. But Paul also says that all the Jews, who had special revelation, have sinned and that *none* of them seeks God either. In other words, this argument appears to lead to the conclusion that since none of us seeks God, no matter what sort of revelation we have, *all people* are damned to hell.

It seems to me that it would be preferable to view Paul as addressing groups of peoples, both Jews and Gentiles, in the first three chapters of Romans, and as arguing that all have rejected God but that God continues in his love toward all peoples by sending his Son to make atonement for them. By this reading, the type of revelation each group has received is irrelevant to Paul's message of grace. God loves both the Gentiles (who have received only general revelation) and the Jews (who have also received special revelation), and he seeks to save both groups.

Some restrictivists pose a yet more troubling problem by arguing both that the unevangelized are justly condemned for rejecting the light of general revelation and that even a total acceptance of that revelation would still be insufficient for salvation.[68] This is like my telling my daughter that I am angry with her for not washing the dishes and then acknowledging that I would still be angry with her even if she had washed them. By this logic, the unevangelized are truly damned if they do and damned if they don't.

Why is it that I can learn from the created order that I am condemned, but apart from special revelation I cannot be moved by the Holy Spirit to repent and be saved? If an individual's

---

68. This sounds suspiciously like infralapsarianism. This sort of language seems to suggest that people have an opportunity to be saved, whereas in fact it assumes that they do not.

rejection of the truth of general revelation is counted as an
implicit rejection of Jesus, then why is it that an individual's
conviction of sin and desire for God through the leading of the
Holy Spirit are not counted as implicit acceptance of Jesus? Some
object that this would make salvation possible apart from human
evangelism — and yet this does not seem to be a compelling
objection for the many restrictivists who believe that infants who
die will be saved. If infants can be saved through the work of
Christ even though they never hear about Christ, why can
unevangelized adults not be saved in the same manner? If, as the
restrictivists argue, conviction of sin by the Holy Spirit is universal, the fact that the unevangelized "have never heard of Christ is
due not to a failure on their part, as if they were expected to seek
him, but as a failure on the part of the church, which is commanded to seek them. . . . Is it reasonable, is it just, to condemn
the world for the failure of the church?"[69] If not, then the
restrictivist argument must be fundamentally flawed.

Finally, some restrictivists (including Calvin and Hodge)
seem to argue that there is no salvation without assurance of
salvation — that one is not saved unless one knows that one is
saved. As we will see in a later chapter, others contend that it
is possible for an individual to be saved without having an
awareness or assurance of that fact.

### 4. The Boundary of Death

Some adherents of the wider hope challenge the restrictivist
theological control belief that a person's destiny is sealed at
death. Donald Bloesch, for example, believes that it is not
necessarily the case that a person who does not hear about
Christ before he or she dies will be forever lost. The significant
control belief for Bloesch in this instance is the assumption that

69. Peter Cotterell, "The Unevangelized: An Olive Branch from the
Opposition," *International Review of Mission* 77 (Jan. 1988): 132.

people will be condemned to hell only for explicit rejection of Jesus as Lord. If this is true, then all people must be presented with the claims of Christ at some point — if not during their lifetime, then after death.

## 5. The Question of Missions

There are many who reject the restrictivist contention that evangelism and missions are meaningless unless all the unevangelized are necessarily damned to hell. Arguments for the relevance of missions even if there is hope for the salvation of the unevangelized are outlined in Chapter 8.

## 6. Limited Atonement

The doctrine of limited atonement, held by many restrictivists, is seriously problematic. Among the most intractable of its problems are the following two.

First, it raises the perennial question that Bruce Reichenbach has cast as follows: "If he [God] can show irresistible grace to all without harming his omnipotence and goodness, why then does he not?"[70] Is there something deficient about God's distributive justice — that is to say, does God not extend justice to all human beings in the sense of providing an opportunity of salvation for all? If all humans have a fatal disease, and if God is in fact omnipotent and has taken care to provide the medicine to cure the disease through his Son Jesus Christ, then why can he not provide it to all?[71]

70. Reichenbach, "Freedom, Justice, and Moral Responsibility," in *The Grace of God, the Will of Man*, ed. Clark Pinnock (Grand Rapids: Zondervan, 1989), p. 290. Pages 287-99 of this work contain a discussion of the issue of distributive justice in relation to God.
71. The answer provided by advocates of limited atonement lies in their understanding of irresistible grace. If God provided the medicine to all,

Second, it was common for ministers such as Augustine and Calvin to speak of the *massa damnata* as though it pained God not at all to damn anyone. The British philosopher Peter Geach argues that since God does not need the world in any way, "for God a billion rational creatures are as dust in the balance; if a billion perish, God suffers no loss."[72] Does this reflect the love we see as the father publicly disgraces himself by running to meet the prodigal son? Is this the love that searches far and wide for the lost sheep? What kind of love is it when Loraine Boettner asserts that God did not intend to save those in China any more than he intended wheat to grow in Siberia? According to Reformed philosopher Thomas Talbot, this sort of love attributes Satanic qualities to God by suggesting that God merely toys with the damned and does not truly love them.[73] At the very least this doctrine suggests that God does not love the damned with the same kind of redemptive love that Jesus commanded us to show to the world. When Jesus instructs us to love one another as he has loved us (John 13:34), it certainly includes the desire to see redemption brought to the lives of others. But the doctrine of limited atonement tells us that God the Father has no such redeeming love for the damned. In the final analysis, the kind of love the proponents of limited atonement attribute to God is such, said John Wesley, "as makes your blood run cold."[74]

---

then all would be saved. Hence universalism would be true. But universalism is not true, they argue, so God must not provide it to all. This is a legitimate functioning of a control belief, but I find this control belief biblically unacceptable.

72. Geach, *Providence and Evil* (Cambridge: Cambridge University Press, 1977), p. 128.

73. See Talbot, "On Predestination, Reprobation, and the Love of God," *Reformed Journal,* February 1983, pp. 11-15. See also John Piper's reply to Talbot in the April issue and Talbot's response in the June issue.

74. Wesley, quoted in *John Wesley,* ed. Albert Outler (New York: Oxford University Press, 1964), p. 447.

## Historical Bibliography

### *1. Judaism in the New Testament Era*

Judaism before and during the time of the New Testament did not deal specifically with the issue of the salvation of the unevangelized. There was discussion, however, about whether any Gentiles could be saved. There were two main schools of thought on this point in ancient Judaism: one group said there was no hope for the Gentiles, while the other extended great hope for their salvation.

The community at Qumran viewed the Gentiles as God's enemies, and hence held out no hope for them (see E. P. Sanders, *Paul and Palestinian Judaism* [Philadelphia: Fortress Press, 1977], pp. 243-48).

Several apocryphal and pseudepigraphic works rule out hope for the Gentiles. *Jubilees* declares that no Gentiles will be saved (22:20-21). According to 4 Ezra, "the world to come will bring delight to few, but torments to many" (7:48). It is then explained that just as we highly value precious metals such as gold because they are scarce, so God values the redeemed because they are rare (7:49-60). When Ezra asks why God made so many people when only a very few will inherit eternal life, he is told bluntly that "many have been created, but few will be saved" (8:3, also 9:14-22). Sometimes it is stated that salvation is restricted to Israel (*As. Mos.* 10:7) or to those who repent and join themselves to Israel (*Jos. As.* 15:1-11, 8:5, 9:2). In 2 Esdras 8 and 9 we find several analogies to explain why God has created so many people when so few will be saved. Chapter 8 asserts that the earth has lots of clay but not much gold (vv. 2-3) and suggests that just as not all the seeds that are planted sprout, so it is with salvation (41). As a drop of water is to a wave, so are the saved in proportion to the damned (9:20-21).

In Rabbinic Judaism there were those like Rabbi Eliezer, who said, "none of the heathen has any share in the world to come" (Sanders, *Paul and Palestinian Judaism*, pp. 208-9).

## 2. The Early Church through the Middle Ages

Neither Tertullian nor Ambrose (both of whom influenced Augustine) seem to have had any hope for the heathen. Tertullian wrote of how great his joy will be in seeing the great pagan philosophers, poets, kings, and playwrights being tormented in hell (*The Shows*, chap. 30). Ambrose declared that without exception all those who die unbaptized go to hell (*De Abrah.* 2.11). Augustine's views on this issue are best outlined in his letters to Deogratius and Evodius, reviewed in this chapter.

As on so many other issues, Augustine's views influenced significant people such as Pope Gregory the Great (see Ralph Turner, *"Descendit Ad Inferos," Journal of the History of Ideas* 27 [1966]: 177-79). Augustine's viewpoint, however, was modified by several key medieval theologians (on which, see Chap. 5 herein).

The Athanasian Creed, after spelling out correct Christian dogma, flatly states, "this is the Catholic Faith: which except a man believe faithfully, he can not be saved" (art. 44; see also arts. 1-2). For a discussion of the history of interpretation regarding the damnatory clauses of the creed, see chapter 15 of Plumptre's *The Spirits in Prison* (London: Ibister, 1898).

According to Alain of Lille, the Albigensians believed that all people who died before the resurrection of Christ were damned — including John the Baptist (see Turner, *"Descendit Ad Inferos,"* p. 185). Although Alain of Lille makes no direct comment regarding the unevangelized, he thought that the preincarnation pagans needed only the faith of Hebrews 11:6 (so long as they believed in a savior to come), while those living after the incarnation must have explicit faith in Christ (see Turner, *"Descendit Ad Inferos,"* pp. 185-87).

Restrictivism seems to be implicit in the statement of Julian of Norwich that "many creatures shall be damned . . . [men] that dieth out of the Faith of Holy Church, that is to say, they that be heathen men" (see *Revelations of Divine Love,* ed. R. Hudleston [London: 1935], p. xxxii).

Some writers have mistakenly applied to the unevangelized the assertion of Pope Boniface VIII that "for salvation it is absolutely necessary to be subject to the Pope." Boniface was not addressing the "heathen," however; he was attempting to bring under control those seeking to lessen the authority of the papacy.

### 3. Reformation through the Eighteenth Century

Philipp Melanchthon offered no hope for the heathens or adherents to other religions (see *On Christian Doctrine* [New York: Oxford University Press, 1965], pp. 6, 38, 142-43, 167, 191, 212). Although he had little hope for the unevangelized of the New Testament era, Melanchthon did think it plausible that in his descent into hell Christ may have saved "the most distinguished men from all nations, as for example, Scipio, Fabius, and others" (see George Williams, "Erasmus and the Reformers on Non-Christian Religions and *Salus Extra Ecclesiam*," in *Action and Conviction in Early Modern Europe*, ed. Theodore Rabb and Jerrold Seigel [Princeton: Princeton University Press, 1969], p. 353).

For Calvin's views, see his *Institutes of the Christian Religion*, 2.6.1-4.

Thomas Cranmer said, "if we should have heathen parents and die without baptism, we should be damned everlastingly" (cited by Plumptre in *The Spirits in Prison*, p. 170).

In seventeenth-century France, the Jansenists Arnauld and Pascal, resurrecting Augustine, took a restrictivist line (see David Wetsel, "Histoire de la Chine: Pascal and the Challenge to Biblical Time," *Journal of Religion* 69 [April 1989]: 212-15). According to Pascal, God gave the heathen revelation but they distorted it and are blinded by their own sin. Only the biblical revelation can save and only the elect can perceive the truth of the biblical revelation. In the *Pensées*, Pascal declares that the "heathens know not God" (Harvard Classics, vol. 48, ed.

Charles W. Eliot [New York: Collier & Son, 1910], p. 608), that the Greeks and Romans set up false deities (p. 613), and (following Augustine) that belief in the Messiah or at least the Messiah to come is necessary for salvation (pp. 616-17).

Calvin's influence is evident in the Puritans, who for the most part considered the unevangelized to be doomed (see Bruce Demarest, *General Revelation* [Grand Rapids: Zondervan, 1982], pp. 69-71).

Jonathan Edwards viewed the heathen as being without the necessary knowledge for salvation and rejected the idea of a future probation as a "gross absurdity" (see *Works of Jonathan Edwards*, vol. 2 [Carlisle, Pa.: Banner of Truth, 1984], pp. 158-59, 249-53, 515-16). Edwards the Younger agreed with this sentiment (see *That Unknown Country* [Springfield, Mass.: C. A. Nichols, 1888], p. 56).

### 4. The Nineteenth Century

The Princeton theologians A. A. Hodge, Charles Hodge, and B. B. Warfield all followed Calvin's lead on this topic (see A. A. Hodge, *The Atonement* [1867; reprint, Grand Rapids: Baker Book House, 1974], p. 360; Charles Hodge, *Systematic Theology*, vol. 2 [Grand Rapids: William B. Eerdmans, 1940], pp. 646-49; and B. B. Warfield, *Biblical and Theological Studies* [Philadelphia: Presbyterian and Reformed, 1952], p. 350). But Charles Hodge and Warfield disagreed with Calvin on one crucial point, asserting that the number of the saved will greatly outnumber the number of the damned. They reached this conclusion, clearly uncharacteristic of restrictivism, because they believed in the postmillennial doctrine that a tremendous surge of evangelism and conversion will occur in the future. Believing that the future population of the earth will outnumber all the generations that have preceded it, they concluded that in the end more people will be saved than lost.

Enoch Pond maintained that all the heathen are lost (see

"Future State of the Heathen," *Christian Review* 22 [Jan. 1857]: 31-43), and Charles Spurgeon appears to have agreed (see *Spurgeon's Sermons* [Grand Rapids: Zondervan, n.d.], pp. 399-401). Demarest interprets Abraham Kuyper as having held this view (see *General Revelation*, pp. 140-41). And Heinrich Heppe uses the Reformed confessions to support this idea (see *Reformed Dogmatics* [London: George Allen & Unwin, 1950], pp. 539ff.).

## 5. The Twentieth Century

Hendrik Kraemer, a noteworthy missiologist, denied any salvific value in other religions or in general revelation but stopped short of asserting that all of the unevangelized are damned, suggesting that we should leave such determinations in God's hands (see *The Authority of Faith*, ed. W. Paton [London: Oxford University Press, 1939], p. 4). This maneuver has become typical of modern evangelicals who desire to relieve the tension on this issue without paying the theological price.

Louis Berkhof said, "There is no Scripture evidence on which we can base the hope that adult Gentiles, or even Gentile children that have not yet come to years of discretion, will be saved" (see *Systematic Theology* [Grand Rapids: William B. Eerdmans, 1946], p. 693; see also pp. 30-37). Loraine Boettner agreed but added, "we do not deny that God can save some even of the adult heathen people if He chooses to do so. . . . If any such are saved, however, it is by a miracle of pure grace. . . . By an extraordinary method some few of his elect may be gathered from the unevangelized portion" (see *Reformed Doctrine of Predestination* [Grand Rapids: William B. Eerdmans, 1954], pp. 119-20).

Carl Henry believes that everyone who rejects the God of general revelation implicitly rejects Jesus Christ. All people are given some light, but no one lives up to that light, so all of the unevangelized are damned for implicitly rejecting Christ (see *Giving a Reason for Our Hope* [Boston: W. A. Wilde, 1949], pp. 39-43; and *God, Revelation, and Authority,* vol. 6 [Waco, Tex.: Word Books, 1983], pp. 360-69).

Roger Nicole rejects all the wider-hope theories and paints a bleak picture of the destiny of the unevangelized, although he does grant that "ultimately the answer to this question must be left to God" (*Wherever* 4 [1979]: 3-4).

Bruce Demarest follows Boettner in assuming that God may save a few by the extraordinary means of direct special revelation, suggesting that such instances may belong to the "secret things" of God mentioned in Deuteronomy 29:29. But he insists that none can be saved without hearing about Jesus (see *General Revelation,* pp. 250-61).

Missouri Synod Lutherans usually claim no hope for the unevangelized. J. T. Mueller maintained there is salvation only through the sacraments and rejected the idea of an opportunity to be converted after death. Yet he went on to contradict himself when he affirmed that eternal damnation is only for those who explicitly reject Jesus Christ (see *Christian Dogmatics* [St. Louis: Concordia Publishing, 1934], pp. 251, 637). Concordia Seminary, under the direction of J. A. O. Preus, has publicly affirmed that all who die without faith in Jesus are eternally damned (see *A Statement of Scriptural and Confessional Principles,* p. 9; and "Extra Ecclesiam Nulla Salus," *Concordia Theological Quarterly* 15 [July-Oct. 1986]: 151, 162-63).

For other affirmations of the restrictivist contention that all the unevangelized are damned, see the following: J. Ronald Blue, "Untold Billions: Are They Really Lost?" *Bibliotheca Sacra* (Oct.-Dec. 1981): 338-49; Earl Radmacher, "Can Man Be Saved by Light of Nature?" audio recording by Campus Crusade for Christ International, San Bernardino; Mark Shaw, "Is There Salvation outside the Christian Faith?" *East Africa Journal of Evangelical Theology* 2 (1983): 42-62; the Dallas Theological Seminary Statement of Faith, article 7 (few seminaries or denominations unambiguously state this view); Lewis Sperry Chafer, *Major Bible Themes* (Chicago: Moody Press, 1926), pp. 296-97; Jack Cottrell, *What the Bible Says about God the Creator* (Joplin, Mo.: College

Press, 1983), pp. 340-53; Leith Samuel, "The Heathen — Lost?" *HIS*, May 1961, pp. 1-3, 30; Gavin D'Costa, *Theology and Religious Pluralism* (New York: Basil Blackwell, 1986), p. 14; Dick Dowsett, *Is God Really Fair?* (Chicago: Moody Press, 1985); J. Oswald Sanders, *How Lost Are the Heathen?* (Chicago: Moody Press, 1972); Robert Gundry, "Salvation according to Scripture: No Middle Ground," *Christianity Today*, 9 Dec. 1977, pp. 14-16; Henry Thiessen, *Introductory Lectures in Systematic Theology* (Grand Rapids: William B. Eerdmans, 1949), pp. 40, 231; Harry Buis, *The Doctrine of Eternal Punishment* (Philadelphia: Presbyterian and Reformed, 1957), pp. 141-43; Harold Lindsell, *The Christian Philosophy of Missions* (Wheaton, Ill.: Van Kampen Press, 1949), pp. 106-8; Robert Morey, *Death and the Afterlife* (Minneapolis: Bethany House, 1984), pp. 246-55; Gordon Lewis, "The Gospel on Campus," *HIS*, Oct. 1966–Jan. 1967; John Gerstner, "The Fate of the Heathen," in *Baker Dictionary of Theology*, ed. R. K. Harrison (Grand Rapids: Baker Book House, 1960), pp. 263-64; James Borland, "A Theologian Looks at the Gospel and World Religions," *Journal of the Evangelical Theological Society* 33 (March 1990): 3-11; and R. C. Sproul, *Reason to Believe* (Grand Rapids: Zondervan, 1982), pp. 47-59.

# CHAPTER THREE

## *Universalism:*
## *All the Unevangelized Are Saved*

We now turn to a consideration of the position opposite that of restrictivism: universalism. In contrast to the restrictivists, who maintain that all the unevangelized are damned, universalists contend that all the unevangelized will be saved. In this chapter I will mainly be concerned with what could be called "classical" universalism, which affirms the necessity of salvation in Jesus Christ (in terms of both particularity and finality) but nonetheless maintains that all human beings will ultimately be reconciled to God, that none will be eternally damned. Proponents claim that universalism is the only legitimate means by which to harmonize God's universal salvific will with the plight of the unevangelized. Why, they ask, should people be condemned just because they were never able to hear of Jesus?

Universalism became well known in the early church through the writings of Origen but fell into disfavor in medieval times. Interest in universalism began to rise again after the Protestant Reformation. Small streams can be detected as early as 1563, when the Church of England adopted the Thirty-Nine

Articles of Religion, a revision of the Forty-Two Articles of 1553; among the changes was the omission of the earlier article 42, which expressed an opposition to universalism. But it was not until the middle of the eighteenth century that strong currents of universalist thinking began to flow. Since 1800 there has been a tremendous reversal in both Protestant and Roman Catholic circles away from expressions of belief in an eternal conscious punishment of sinners toward expressions endorsing universalism. Outside of evangelicalism, universalism is a very popular theological position.

Although universalists agree that all humans will be saved, they arrive at that conclusion in a considerable variety of ways. The biblical and theological warrants for universalism differ widely depending on the theological orientation of the defender. There are two crucial issues that tend to divide universalists into different categories. The first is the matter of human freedom. Some universalists are determinists, arguing that God's all-powerful will overrides human freedom to bring all people to salvation; Friedrich Schleiermacher is perhaps the best-known proponent of this position. The majority of universalists reject this deterministic view, however, maintaining that eventually all human beings will accept God's gracious offer of salvation of their own free will.

The universalist camp is also divided by the issue of what awaits the unevangelized on the other side of the grave. Some contend that people who are not saved in this life will go to a hell from which they will be given the opportunity to leave. Others contend that all people will be saved without suffering any type of hell. Those who believe that there will be a remedial hell are known as restorationists; those who reject the concept of hell altogether are known as ultra-universalists. Madeleine L'Engle gives expression to the restorationist position when she says that "God's loving concern for his creation will outlast all our willfulness and pride. No matter how many eons it takes, he will not rest until all of creation, including Satan, is reconciled to him, until there is no creature who cannot return his look of love with a joyful response of love."[1] In this chapter the principal focus will be on free-will restorationism, since that is the dominant view among universalists today.

## Key Biblical Texts

The passages used to support universalism fall into five categories. First are those that affirm God's desire to save all people (1 Tim. 2:4, 4:10, 2 Pet. 3:9). Second are those that proclaim the unlimited atonement of Christ (1 John 2:2, Heb. 2:9, Tit. 2:11, 2 Cor. 5:19). Since these first two categories were discussed in Chapter 1, no further comment on them will be made here.

The third group of texts articulates the implications of the universal atoning work of Jesus. Jesus declared, "and I, if I be lifted up from the earth, will draw all men to Myself" (John 12:32; see also 10:16). Paul wrote that just as all things were created in the Son of God, so all things are being reconciled through the Son's "having made peace through the blood of His cross" (Col. 1:16, 20). Far and away the most important passage in this group is Romans 5:12-19. Here Paul draws an analogy between the first and second Adams. The first Adam brought sin, condemnation, and death, but the second Adam, Jesus, brought righteousness, justification, and life. "So then as through one transgression there resulted condemnation to all men, even so through one act of righteousness there resulted justification of life to all men" (5:18).

All universalists argue that universalism is the logical implication of unlimited atonement. Deterministic universalists argue that if the first Adam produced sin and condemnation in all his offspring apart from their choice, then justi-

1. L'Engle, *The Irrational Season* (New York: Seabury Press, 1979), p. 97.

fication to life is produced by the second Adam in all people apart from their choice. Free-will universalists argue that just as all people freely turned away from God (see Rom. 1–2) and so willingly participated in the sin of the first Adam which brought God's condemnation, so all people will freely come to participate in the righteousness of Jesus which brings life. In short, if all are condemned in Adam, all are saved in Christ. All human beings were under the wrath and condemnation of God and thus were vessels "prepared for destruction" (Rom. 9:22). But God did not leave humanity in that state; instead, he has made us "vessels of mercy" through the Son (Rom. 9:23). Consequently, "God has shut up all in disobedience that He might show mercy to all" (Rom. 11:32). No one will finally remain under God's condemnation, say the universalists, because justification will ultimately be applied to all people.

A fourth set of texts refers to the "consummation" of God's plan of salvation in which all people are finally redeemed. The consummation is the event in which all things in heaven and earth are restored to God. Restorationism is sometimes called by its Greek name, *apokatastasis,* from Acts 3:19-21: "repent therefore . . . that He may send Jesus, the Christ appointed for you, whom heaven must receive until the period of restoration of all things about which God spoke by the mouth of his holy prophets from ancient time."

Universalists usually cite Paul as the New Testament writer who saw most clearly the salvation of all people in the consummation. In Philippians Paul mentions the obedience of Jesus and then declares, "therefore also God highly exalted Him, and bestowed on Him the name which is above every name, that at the name of Jesus every knee should bow, of those who are in heaven, and on earth, and under the earth, and that every tongue should confess that Jesus Christ is Lord, to the glory of God the Father" (2:9-11). Universalists maintain that this text explicitly affirms the final restoration of all created beings, since confessing Jesus as Lord entails salvation.

The final passage in this category used to support universalism, and the favorite of universalists, is 1 Corinthians 15:22-28:

> For as in Adam all die, so also in Christ all shall be made alive. But each in his own order: Christ the first fruits, after that those who are Christ's at His coming, then comes the end, when He delivers up the kingdom to the God and Father, when He has abolished all rule and all authority and power. For He must reign until He has put all His enemies under His feet. The last enemy that will be abolished is death. For He has put all things in subjection under His feet. But when He says, "All things are put in subjection," it is evident that He is excepted who put all things in subjection to Him. And when all things are subjected to Him, then the Son Himself also will be subjected to the one who subjected all things to Him, that God may be all in all.

Restorationists interpret this text as saying that all people will be given life in Christ; it may take longer for some than for others, but eventually all will come into the kingdom of Christ, and there will no longer be any enemies to the kingdom of God, only loyal subjects. When this occurs, then Christ will have achieved his goal, and God will be "all in all."

A final group of texts refers to damnation and separation. These passages speak of two classes of people, the saved and the lost, the sheep and the goats. Universalists do not ignore such texts but interpret them in a way consistent with what they see as the overriding theme of the New Testament brought out in the passages cited above.[2]

---

2. Evangelicals have long accused universalists not only of ignoring the damnation texts but even of rejecting them outright in favor of the universalistic texts. N. T. Wright argues that universalists are attempting "*Sachkritik,* the criticism (and rejection) of one part of scripture on the basis of another" ("Towards a Biblical View of Universalism," *Themelios* 4 [Jan. 1979]: 55). Nigel Cameron asserts that universalists destroy the authority of the Bible by using "some texts as the basis for the criticism of others" ("Universalism and the Logic of Revelation," *Evangelical Review of Theology* 11 [Oct. 1987]: 332). He adds that this sort of maneuver sets human reason above the biblical

Universalists deal with the texts that refer to eternal
damnation in a variety of ways. First, they demonstrate that
these texts are not as numerous as commonly believed. John
Hick suggests that there are extremely few texts that clearly
speak of *eternal* damnation, while the more numerous passages
referring to postmortem rewards and punishments are quite
general and do not explicitly indicate eternal damnation.[3] He
argues that the notion of *eternal* condemnation is read into
Jesus' teaching in many parables but that there are in fact only
two passages in the gospels that, strictly speaking, refer to
eternal loss. The first is the parable of the sheep and the goats

text. This sort of criticism is not entirely groundless. Some universalists —
John Hick, for example — do at times practice *Sachkritik* or flatly reject certain
biblical texts. And Nels Ferré essentially argues that while the New Testament
does teach both universalism and eternal damnation, universalism is more
consistent with the emphasis of the New Testament as a whole (see *The
Christian Understanding of God* [New York: Harper, 1951], p. 244).

But evangelicals must not ignore the human element in the interpretive
process. On the one side, I. Howard Marshall has insightfully pointed out
how even evangelicals practice a form of *Sachkritik* (see "An Evangelical
Approach to Theological Criticism," *Themelios* 13 [April 1988]: 79-85). On
the other side, Hick denies the charge that he is rejecting the teaching of
Jesus: "Are we however in all this saying, presumptuously, that Jesus thought
that some men will be damned but that the Christian theologian can know
better?' No, we are not saying this" (*Death and Eternal Life* [London: Collins,
1976], p. 250); Hick does not believe the historical Jesus taught eternal
damnation. Restorationists would respond that all of us are interpreting the
biblical text, and we must theologize when so doing. Furthermore they would
turn the accusation of *Sachkritik* around on the evangelicals who use the
damnation texts to criticize and overshadow the universalistic texts. The pot
should not call the kettle black! It is certainly a form of theological criticism
when evangelical Calvinists argue that the passages that assert God's desire
to save all human beings cannot mean what they seem to mean since (1) if
God desired all to be saved then all would be saved (universalism), and (2) the
Bible is clear that universalism is not true, so (3) God must not truly desire
all to be saved. As J. I. Packer puts it, "to say that Christ died for everyone
logically leads to universalism" (see Terry Miethe, "The Universal Power of
the Atonement," in *The Grace of God, the Will of Man*, ed. Clark Pinnock
[Grand Rapids: Zondervan, 1989], p. 75).

3. Hick, *Death and Eternal Life*, pp. 243-45.

which concludes, "and these will go away into eternal punishment, but the righteous into eternal life" (Matt. 25:46).[4] The other is Mark 3:29: "whoever blasphemes against the Holy Spirit never has forgiveness, but is guilty of an eternal sin." Some universalists are willing to admit that even Paul taught eternal separation when he wrote that those who do not obey the gospel "will pay the penalty of eternal destruction, away from the presence of the Lord and from the glory of His power" (2 Thess. 1:9).

Having made these concessions, universalists typically proceed to argue that these references to eternal damnation must be seen in their proper contexts or settings. Jesus and Paul utilized the strong language regarding eternal loss in order to bring individuals to a commitment to God. They were calling for a serious decision, and the nature of their existential preaching required graphic imagery to portray the importance of the choice.[5]

A third line of argument used to interpret the damnation or limited-salvation texts draws on a distinction between the nature of these texts and the universal salvation texts. Universalists grant that the New Testament writers commonly spoke of the human race as divided into two classes of people, the saved and the lost. Paul, for instance, wrote that "the word of the cross is to those who are perishing foolishness, but to us who are being saved it is the power of God" (1 Cor. 1:18).[6] But they hold that the "two-group" language in the New Testament is not ultimate: the consummation texts speak of one

4. Contrary to John Robinson's assertion that universalists base nothing on the fact that the word *eternal* here *(aiōnios)* does not always mean "everlasting" (see *In the End God* [New York: Harper & Row, 1968], p. 131), some universalists (e.g., Charles Chauncy) do make this point in interpreting the verse.

5. See Nels Ferré, *The Christian Understanding of God,* p. 245; and Hick, *Death and Eternal Life,* pp. 248-49.

6. For other Pauline texts which refer to "limited" salvation, see M. Eugene Boring, "The Language of Universal Salvation in Paul," *Journal of Biblical Literature* 105 (June 1986): 269, 277.

group of people, not two, in the eschaton. M. Eugene Boring argues that Paul's language of one group and two groups must be interpreted in light of the metaphors of God as king and judge respectively.[7] The judge image is tied to the necessity of faith for salvation and the punishment, condemnation, and separation that will ensue if this condition is not met. The king image, on the other hand, is associated with the teaching that God's lordship will be unconditionally met through his grace. The two metaphors have different purposes and contexts, says Boring, and neither must be subordinated to the other; Paul must be allowed to use the different images for his different purposes so that both remain fully true.

> The limited salvation statements proceed from, and conjure up, the image of God-the-judge and its corollary, human responsibility. Without these statements, the affirmation of universal salvation could only be heard as a fate; evangelism loses something of its urgency. . . . The universal-salvation statements proceed from, and conjure up, the image of God-the-king, who finally extends his *de jure* gracious reign *de facto* to include all his creation. Without *these* statements, Paul's affirmations of a salvation limited to Christian believers must be heard as affirming a frustrated God who brought all creation into being but despite his best efforts could only salvage some of it.[8]

Restorationists grant that the God-as-judge metaphor does point to damnation and separation, but they argue that these punishments are only temporary. The concept of eternal damnation is hyperbolic, they say, a rhetorical device aimed at producing faith in the hearers. They contend that the God-as-king metaphor points to the fact that God's kingdom will eventually be unified in eternity, that grace will become the only reality and all people will come under the lordship of Jesus

7. See Boring, "The Language of Universal Salvation in Paul," 269-92. He surveys the ways in which various scholars (e.g., Bultmann, E. P. Sanders, C. H. Dodd, J. C. Beker) handle both sets of texts in Paul.

8. Boring, "The Language of Universal Salvation in Paul," p. 291.

Christ.[9] In actual practice universalists do subordinate the God-as-judge metaphor to the God-as-king metaphor and interpret the universal profession of the lordship of Christ as equivalent to universal salvation. Ernest Best argues that those who interpret Philippians 2:9-11 as suggesting that some individuals may be consigned to hell and there be forced to acknowledge the lordship of Christ without hope of salvation are operating "with a wrong conception of victory; for a man to stand on another's neck and to compel him to confess he has been vanquished is not a victory compatible with the God of the cross."[10] Restorationists assert that, properly interpreted, the New Testament affirms the final reconciliation of God's creatures.

## Theological Considerations

The theological arguments put forth in favor of universalism center on the nature of God — in particular, on the divine attributes of love, omnipotence, eternality, and justice.

### Sovereign Love

The first two attributes, omnipotence and love, are usually discussed together and referred to as sovereign love. Universalists assume that God loves all people and desires the reconciliation of his creatures. "The God of the New Testament is not half-saving, half-punishing: he is the God of salvation. . . . If he can save all men, then he *will* save all men."[11] Nels Ferré handles this issue

9. See Boring, "The Language of Universal Salvation in Paul," pp. 274-92; and Hick, *Death and Eternal Life*, p. 249.

10. Best, *The First and Second Epistles to the Thessalonians,* Harper's New Testament Commentaries (New York: Harper & Row, 1972), p. 368.

11. William Dalton, *Salvation and Damnation* (Butler, Wis.: Clergy Book Service, 1977), p. 81.

as part of the problem of evil: "the logic of the situation is simple. Either God could not or would not save all. If He could not He is not sovereign; then not all things are possible with God (Matt. 19:26). If He would not, again the New Testament is wrong, for it openly claims that He would have all to be saved (1 Tim. 2:4). Nor would He be totally good."[12] But what of human freedom? Does God force salvation upon us whether we want it or not? On this question universalists are divided into the free-will camp and the determinist camp.

Deterministic universalism has its roots in the Calvinist tradition. In America universal salvation based on Calvinistic foundations was made popular by the English immigrant John Murray (1741-1815) and continued in a modified form in the preaching of the famous Boston minister Hosea Ballou (1771-1852).[13] Perhaps the most influential advocate of deterministic universalism was the famed German theologian Friedrich Schleiermacher (1768-1834). By the late eighteenth century the Calvinistic teaching of the double decree (God chooses some for heaven and chooses most for hell) was deeply rooted on American soil. The doctrines of unconditional election, irresistible grace, and eternal punishment in hell were commonly accepted in a straightforward fashion, and hence it was assumed that the biblical statements about God's desire to save all must not be interpreted literally.[14] Universalists similarly affirmed the doctrines of unconditional election and irresistible grace but then proceeded to affirm God's universal salvific will rather

12. *Evil and the Christian Faith* (Freeport, N.Y.: Books for Libraries Press, 1971), p. 118.

13. See *Universalism in America: A Documentary History*, ed. Ernest Cassara (Boston: Beacon Press, 1971), pp. 10-24.

14. A prevailing means of resolving the dilemma involved the assertion that God has both a secret will and a revealed will. He tells humanity that he desires to save all of us, but secretly (actually) he does not. For a critique of this idea, see Randall Bassinger, "Exhaustive Divine Sovereignty: A Practical Critique," in *The Grace of God, the Will of Man*, ed. Clark Pinnock (Grand Rapids: Zondervan, 1989), pp. 198-203.

than the idea of divine retribution and hence concluded that the texts about an eternal hell must not be interpreted literally. This line of thought coheres well with the classical notion of God's sovereignty — namely, that he can guarantee the final outcome of any course of events since he does not take risks. The human will is no obstacle when the will of the Omnipotent desires to redeem all humanity.

Schleiermacher argued for a single predestination by which all people would be saved through God's omnipotent grace. In arriving at this conclusion, he rejected two crucial doctrines: limited atonement and conditional election. He argued that Jesus died for all people, and since there can be no favoritism or caprice in God, all people must be elected in Christ. He repudiated the Arminian idea of conditional election based on human faith on the grounds that it would make salvation a matter of works rather than grace. He also rejected the argument that God elects certain individuals because he foresees that they will have faith. This idea would mean that there was an element of conditionality in God's determination, said Schleiermacher, but God is absolutely unconditioned.[15]

Contemporary theologian Langdon Gilkey concurs with Schleiermacher on this point: "There can be no dual destiny in this hope . . . no ultimate division between persons who are sheep and persons who are goats . . . if the divine power is to be ultimately sovereign and the divine love the ultimate quality of that power. Orthodox Calvinism was correct in its supralapsarian emphasis. . . . So long as there is a dual destiny, faith is a merit that saves."[16] Although this strain of universalism has had many adherents, its downplay of human freedom has led many universalists to propose a version that does not deny authentic freedom.

15. See Schleiermacher, *The Christian Faith*, 2 vols., ed. H. R. Mackintosh and J. S. Stewart (New York: Harper & Row, 1963), 2: 539-60, 720-22.
16. Gilkey, *Reaping the Whirlwind* (New York: Seabury Press, 1981), p. 298.

John Hick draws out the antinomy of divine sovereignty and human freedom in the following way. "On the one side is the omnipotent divine love intending man's salvation. If that divine intention is never fulfilled, then God is not after all the sovereign lord of his own universe: he is a limited God. . . . On the other side is our human freedom. If man is saved against his will . . . then . . . God would have turned the human thou into an it."[17] Hick argues that all people will freely choose to be reconciled to God because "God has so made us that the inherent gravitation of our being is towards him."[18] Building on Augustine's famous remark that our hearts will be restless until they find their rest in God, Hick argues that God has created us in such a way that our inner drives seek God of necessity. Given God's gracious and patient love, all humanity will eventually seek the realization of this inner drive in him.

Nels Ferré, who made restorationism a central part of his theology, also argued that universalism and human freedom are compatible. On the one side Ferré places God's sovereign love. "He wants all to be saved, and His wants are never vain."[19] "The saving Love is sovereign Lord and God knows which acts and operations should be produced or prevented, and He knows how to direct every action and operation to its end, so that nothing upsets his plans."[20] On the other side he places human freedom. All humans must confront God's love, and hence "no one can be saved until he understands and accepts God as holy love."[21] He attempts to reconcile both sides with the restorationist idea that God will patiently work even after we die to reclaim us. He admits that "sin is too stubborn and freedom too real for easy victory. . . . Yet certainly Christ will not fail."[22]

17. Hick, *Death and Eternal Life*, p. 243.
18. Hick, *Death and Eternal Life*, p. 251.
19. Ferré, *Evil and the Christian Faith*, p. 117.
20. Ferré, *The Christian Understanding of God*, p. 247.
21. Ferré, "Universalism: Pro and Con," *Christianity Today*, 1 March 1963, p. 24.
22. Ferré, *Christ and the Christian* (New York: Harper, 1958), p. 247.

"There are no incorrigible sinners; God has no permanent problem children."[23] On one occasion he asserted that "in the afterlife God will put the screw on hard enough to make men want to change their ways,"[24] but elsewhere Ferré softens his tone and suggests that this victory of God will come through patient persuasion, not by command or force.[25]

Ferré is confident that God can guarantee the final salvation of all humanity because he is infinite and his "freedom is not limited by the freedom of His creatures."[26] In fact this does not serve to resolve the contradiction of affirming both God's omnipotence and human freedom — and apparently Ferré is aware of this as well, for he subsequently argues that human logic is too limited to resolve the issue but that God is infinite and is not bound by the constraints of human logic as we are. He predicts that in the end God will actualize a transcendent logic that will permit all humans to submit to God freely.[27] If God cannot operate on a different logic, says Ferré, then he must be finite.[28]

## God's Eternal Persistence

The third attribute of God on which restorationists rest their arguments is divine eternality. Since God's love cannot be limited by our earthly time, there will be countless eons in the afterlife in which he might finally achieve his plan of universal redemption. We cannot escape God's persistent love in time or space. As the psalmist says, "Where can I go from Thy Spirit?

23. Ferré, *The Christian Understanding of God*, p. 229.

24. Ferré, quoted by J. I. Packer in "All Men Won't Be Saved," *Eternity* 16 (Nov. 1965): 44.

25. Ferré, *The Universal Word: A Theology for a Universal Faith* (Philadelphia: Westminster Press, 1969), p. 258.

26. Ferré, *The Christian Understanding of God*, p. 111.

27. Ferré, *The Christian Understanding of God*, p. 22.

28. Ferré, *The Christian Understanding of God*, p. 247.

Or where can I flee from Thy presence? If I ascend to heaven, Thou art there; If I make my bed in Sheol, behold, Thou art there" (Ps. 139:7-8).

Restorationists argue that the notion that human destinies are eternally fixed at death is a medieval accretion and not biblically supported.[29] If it were the case, then God's love would be limited by time. But God is infinite, and so his redemptive love cannot be limited by our temporal rejections. However, this introduces another question: If there are future opportunities to accept God's grace after death, will there also be opportunities to reject that grace even after we have accepted it? John Hick agrees with Origen that there will indeed be such opportunities. But both agree that sometime in eternity all people will be redeemed, never to fall or reject God again.[30] No creatures will ever be so alienated from or hateful of God that they will be beyond salvation. No persons have ever existed who can eternally spurn God's love.[31]

### The Justice of God

Universalists contend that God's justice must be understood as an expression of his love. Love is the central attribute in the nature of God. It must not be subsumed or even placed alongside his justice as it has been in traditional theology. This view of the nature of God radically transforms the understanding of the nature and purposes of hell. The transformation is clearly evident in the development of New England theology.

There were three main purposes for hell in the mindset of eighteenth-century New England. These were made popu-

29. See John Robinson, *In the End God*, pp. 43-44.
30. See Hick, *Death and Eternal Life*, p. 258. See also Boring, "The Language of Universal Salvation in Paul," p. 278.
31. So says Dalton, *Salvation and Damnation*, p. 82.

lar in the preaching of Jonathan Edwards and Samuel Hopkins.[32] An understanding of these purposes is important for grasping the development of universalism in relation to the concept of divine justice. First was the idea of "infinite sin." The argument is that since God is infinite, any sin against God is an infinite sin and so deserves infinite punishment in hell. Second was the idea that God damns most people to hell for *his* glory. Third was the notion that an awareness of the reality of eternal punishment serves the "public welfare" by keeping the masses from immorality.[33]

New England universalists attacked all three of these ideas as inconsistent with the Christian understanding of God and sin. They argued that only an infinite being could sin infinitely. Since humans are finite, we can only commit finite sin, and a just God would not infinitely punish a finite sin. The idea that God damned people to hell for his own glory was upheld by its Calvinist defenders, but popular sentiment on this issue was clearly with the universalists. What kind of God would take delight in creating people just to punish them eternally? Preachers such as Edwards responded that God's wisdom is beyond our understanding, but most people rejected such arguments because they made God seem much less loving than themselves. And the restorationists also had a ready response to the argument that a belief in hell is necessary to prevent lawlessness: they themselves affirmed a belief in the reality of hell, and they believed that their understanding of its nature might help to preserve public order more effectively

32. See Joseph Haroutunian, *Piety versus Moralism: The Passing of New England Theology* (Hamden, Conn.: Archon, 1964), pp. 132, 142, 150; and Cassara, *Universalism in America*, chap. 1.

33. From the sixteenth through the eighteenth centuries, universalism was often kept as a "secret doctrine" by ministers who feared how the members of their congregations might behave if they preached universalism openly. See Richard Bauckham, "Universalism: A Historical Survey," *Themelios* 4 (Jan. 1979): 50.

than the traditional Calvinist understanding. Since all people sooner or later will partake of life-changing salvation, the restorationists argued, they might as well do it now and avoid suffering after death.

The restorationist understanding of the nature and purpose of hell is radically different from that of the restrictivist tradition. Restorationists view hell not as a place of mere retributive punishment but as a remedial and pedagogical place of transformation. They draw on Irenaeus's vision of "life as pilgrimage," in contrast to Augustine's vision of life as the context for a single decision of eternal consequence.[34] The pilgrimage motif comports with an understanding of divine justice as a part of the overall framework of God's plan of universal salvation. All of human existence, before and after death, is seen in the light of a great pilgrimage toward God. No one will be forced into heaven, and no one will enter heaven who is incapable of enjoying it. For those who spurn God's love, there is hell, but "hell at any time can be turned into purgatory if it is accepted and used."[35]

So restorationists do not object to the reality of hell. The sticking point for them is rather the concept of an *eternal* hell. If hell were eternal, they argue, then there would be an ultimate dualism in the universe — God and evil.[36] Since God's justice demands the eradication of evil, evil cannot be eternal. Why would God torture people in hell eternally if there were no opportunity for repentance and reconciliation? The existence of an eternal hell would not only raise questions about God's power and justice but would have the practical

34. See Owen Norment Jr., "Chauncy, Gordon, and Ferré: Sovereign Love and Universal Salvation in the New England Tradition," *Harvard Theological Review* 72 (July-Oct. 1979): 303.

35. Michael Paternoster, *Thou Art There Also: God, Death and Hell* (London: SPCK, 1967), p. 155.

36. See John Baillie, *And the Life Everlasting* (London: Oxford University Press, 1934), pp. 240-45.

effect of preventing those in heaven from experiencing complete bliss. Schleiermacher argued that if eternal damnation existed, eternal bliss could not, since the awareness of those suffering in hell would ruin the blessedness of those in heaven.[37] Ferré agrees: "heaven can be heaven only when it has emptied hell."[38]

If all this is true, then why should hell be preached? First to inform people that no one who rejects God's grace will get off easy. Second, "to preach to sinners that all will be saved will not reach them on their level of fear and hate of God. . . . They must be told: repent or perish!"[39] Hell is real even if not eternal.[40]

If the unevangelized will in fact receive their opportunity for salvation after this life, then why should anyone bother with missions now? Universalists respond that just because we can trust God to work things out in the future life does not mean we should shirk our responsibilities in this life to show others "a more excellent way." Furthermore, "the work of Jesus Christ is the only point in history where the characteristics of God [as love and wisdom] are concretely demonstrated and revealed."[41] Informing our fellow human beings about the love of Jesus will help bring them into God's family sooner.

In summary, the key ideas upon which universalism is based are the unlimited atonement of Christ, God's universal salvific will, and the sovereign love of God.

37. Schleiermacher, *The Christian Faith*, 2: 721.

38. Ferré, *Evil and the Christian Faith*, p. 119.

39. Ferré, "Universalism: Pro and Con," p. 24.

40. Ferré says that those who preach an eternal hell do so because they want to gain control over people (*The Christian Understanding of God*, p. 234). John Baillie argues that those who profess a belief in the reality of an eternal hell actually *want* it for others out of vindictiveness. He claims that if the doctrine had been developed in light of what the proponents themselves deserved, they would have arrived at different conclusions (*And the Life Everlasting*, p. 241).

41. W. B. Easton, "Christ's Atonement and the Non-Christian," *Theology Today* 20 (April 1963): 75.

## Leading Defenders

### Origen

The third-century Church Father Origen lived in Alexandria, Egypt, an important center of intellectual activity in his day. He was one of the brightest and best-read early Christian writers. He was also one of the first prominent Church Fathers to argue for universalism.[42] Origen understood that some would judge his ideas heretical, and so he put forth his views cautiously and without dogmatism.[43] Despite such precautions, he later came under condemnation for a number of his teachings, among which was his advocacy of universalism.[44] Nevertheless, his restorationist views remained influential in the history of the church.

Origen defended the Christian faith against several important critics. His restorationist ideas developed in part as a

42. This assessment is based on the received version of Origen's *De Principiis (First Principles)*, the volume in which he most fully develops his universalist views. It should be noted that the original Greek text of this work has largely been lost to us. The closest thing we have to an authoritative text is a translation prepared by Rufinus 150 years after the fact. Scholars maintain that Rufinus took significant liberties with the original text in translating it, however, and hence it may be that this Latin edition does not always accurately reflect Origen's views.

43. See Origen, *De Principiis*, 1.6.1. Subsequent references are to the version appearing in *The Ante-Nicene Fathers*, vol. 4, ed. Alexander Roberts and James Donaldson (1885; reprint, Grand Rapids: William B. Eerdmans, 1979), and will be made parenthetically in the text.

44. It is a matter of debate who condemned Origen's teachings and by what authority, as well as when and why they were condemned. It is a point of special controversy whether Origen was specifically condemned for his teaching on final restoration or for his views on the person of Jesus Christ. See Philip Schaff, *Nicene and Post-Nicene Fathers*, second series, vol. 14 (1899; reprint, Grand Rapids: William B. Eerdmans, 1979), pp. 316-17. E. H. Plumptre doubts that Origen was condemned for universalism by any legitimate authority (*The Spirits in Prison* [London: Ibibster, 1898], pp. 141-42). E. Pusey believes that Origen was condemned for restorationism by several authorities (*What Is of Faith as to Everlasting Punishment* [Oxford: James Parker, 1880], pp. 129-53).

defense against the charge by the Valentinian heretic Candidus that Christianity contained an ultimate dualism — God and Satan.[45] Origen argued that Christianity contains no dualism, that God is supreme. Hence it cannot be that both God and Satan reign eternally in their respective realms, and so he rejected the notion of an eternal hell, teaching instead that all spiritual beings will finally become obedient servants in God's kingdom. He explains his ideas most fully in his *First Principles*.

He believed that . . . "the goodness of God, through His Christ, may recall all His creatures to one end, even His enemies being conquered and subdued. For thus says holy Scripture, 'The LORD said to my Lord, Sit Thou at My right hand, until I make Thine enemies Thy footstool'" (*De Prin.*, 1.6.1). All spiritual creatures will be saved since all will be "subject to Christ" (1 Cor. 15:25). A key dictum for Origen is that "the end is always like the beginning," which means that since all creation was originally subject to God, all creation will return to its original adoration of God.[46] Consequently, rebellion against God is only temporary. Those who have fallen from grace have not fallen irrecoverably but will be "restored to their condition of happiness . . . that this order of this human race . . . , in the future world, or in ages to come, when there shall be the new heavens and new earth, spoken of by Isaiah . . . , may be restored to that unity promised by the Lord Jesus [John 17:20-21] . . . and the Apostle Paul [Eph 4:13]" (*De Prin.*, 1.6.2).

Origen even speculates about the possibility that the restoration of all free creatures will extend to the Devil and his angels. He notes the possibility that such beings may have changed their natural free will into a nature which never desires repentance (*De Prin.*, 1.6.3). Although he encourages his read-

45. See Alan Fairhurst, "Death and Destiny," *The Churchman* 95 (1981): 313.

46. For other background beliefs that shape Origen's universalism, see Jerry Walls, "Universalism in Origen's First Principles," *Asbury Seminarian* 36 (April 1981): 3-13.

ers to decide for themselves about the salvation of Satan, he expresses his own belief that it will happen. "For nothing is impossible to the Omnipotent, nor is anything incapable of restoration to its Creator" (*De Prin.*, 3.6.5). Origen did not believe, however, that God will annul the freedom of spiritual beings and force them into submission. He maintained that all free beings will, of their own free will, be reclaimed by God's love (*De Prin.*, 1.6.3).

Origen held that the restoration process may come slowly for some but that God is long-suffering and so will bring it to pass (*De Prin.*, 3.1.13, 3.6.6). To accomplish his goal, God will use instruction and punishment after death. Punishment in hell, says Origen, is always for the purpose of redemption (2.5.3).[47] As physicians give remedies to the sick in order that they may recover their health, so God deals with sinners. "The fury of God's vengeance is profitable for the purgation of souls. . . . The punishment . . . by fire, is understood to be applied with the object of healing" (*De Prin.*, 2.10.6).

Origen also believed that, once healed, a person might again fall from grace. In fact, he believed that there is a sort of two-lane highway between heaven and hell. Once in heaven, individuals still possess free will and hence may choose to sin, in which case they would have to leave heaven for a while. He suggested that this process of fall and return might go on countless times for some people and not at all for others. Some souls are so ordered toward God that they will always choose to love God and never need remedial punishment. The soul is on a pilgrimage or voyage to the promised land, and God's ultimate goal for everyone is perfection.[48] Some individuals reach perfection upon death, while others need periods of pur-

47. Origen asserts that Scripture speaks of the torments of hell "in order to terrify those who cannot by any other means be saved from the flood of their sins" (*Contra Celsus*, 5.15).

48. See Celia Rabinowitz, "Personal and Cosmic Salvation in Origen," *Vigiliae Christianae* 38 (Dec. 1984): 324-25.

gation. In the end, however, all people will freely be brought to perfection, and then there will no longer be any need of purgations. Then, "when death shall no longer anywhere exist, nor the sting of death, nor any evil at all, then verily God will be 'all in all'" (*De Prin.*, 3.6.3).[49] According to Origen, individuals can attain personal salvation anytime in this life or after death, but the *apokatastasis* (restoration) is the time when salvation is realized cosmically and collectively, when all creatures are united with God.[50]

### Charles Chauncy

According to Joseph Haroutunian, "by the year 1796 disbelief in endless damnation had assumed alarming proportions" in New England.[51] The writing of Boston clergyman Charles Chauncy was extremely influential in bringing this about. Soon after the Great Awakening, which brought hellfire vividly into people's minds, Chauncy and other Calvinists began to doubt the doctrine of eternal damnation.[52] But it was not until 1784 that he published a major work supporting a restorationist version of universalism — *The Mystery Hid*

49. Also see *De Principiis*, 2.3.7, 3.1.21, and 2.3.3.
50. See Rabinowitz, "Personal and Cosmic Salvation in Origen," p. 327.
51. Haroutunian, *Piety versus Moralism*, p. 152.
52. Haroutunian points out that the theological stage was set for a controversy about hell since there had been erosions of assent to the doctrines of original sin and total depravity (*Piety versus Moralism*, p. 134). Universalism in America also has roots in the Brethren and Baptists of pietistic persuasion, on which see James Alexander, "Universalism among the Early Brethren," *Brethren Life and Thought* 32 (Winter 1987): 25-32. Cassara documents a number of other influences that contributed to the rise of universalism in America: the Enlightenment, deism, Unitarianism, Jeffersonian democracy, and American optimism about humanity (*Universalism in America*, chap. 1). On Chauncy's legacy, see Owen Norment, "Chauncy, Gordon, and Ferré: Sovereign Love and Universal Salvation in the New England Tradition," *Harvard Theological Review* 72 (July 1979): 285-304.

*from Ages and Generations, Made Manifest by the Gospel —
Revelation; or, The Salvation of All Men the Grand Thing Aimed
at in the Scheme of God, as Opened in the New Testament
Writings, and Entrusted with Jesus Christ to Bring into Effect.*[53]
Most of the book (238 pages!) is taken up with "scriptural
proofs" and answers to objections.[54] Chauncy's support for
universalism can be summarized in five arguments.

First he documents biblical support for the doctrine of
unlimited atonement and for God's universal salvific will. "If
God *desires the salvation of all,* and Christ died that this *desire*
of God might be complied with, is it credible that a *small portion*
of men only should be saved in *event?*" (*Mystery,* p. 168). His
key text is Romans 5:12-21.

His second argument concerns the nature of God. Since
God is all-powerful, all-wise, and all-merciful, he can and will
save all people. Nothing could prevent such a God from achieving
his ends! "Shall we set up *man* in opposition to *God,* and say that
his *foolishness* and *obstinacy* are overmatch for the infinite wisdom,
knowledge, and power of God?" (*Mystery,* pp. 167-68). He finds
it ridiculous to accuse an omniscient God of creating people he
knew would be finally impenitent (*Mystery,* pp. 2-3). If humans
can outwit God and remain rebellious forever, then they must be
smarter and more powerful than God.

Third, he regards hell as temporary and disciplinary. All
people will sooner or later be reconciled to God. Those who
are reconciled in this life go directly to heaven upon death;
those who refuse God's grace now must undergo the "second
death," wherein they will suffer the pains of hell (*Mystery,* pp.
90-91). Fear of the second death should keep people from
thinking they can continue in their evil ways without repenting.
Heaven is only for those who can enjoy God, so no one will

53. Subsequent citations of this volume will be taken from the reprint
edition produced by Arno Press (New York, 1969) and will be cited
parenthetically in the text.
54. For an account of the Calvinistic response to Chauncy, see
Haroutunian, *Piety versus Moralism,* pp. 140-52.

enter heaven "till they are all cured of their moral depravity, and formed to a meetness for heaven" (*Mystery*, p. 10). Hell has utility value in that it serves God's larger purpose of bringing all to salvation, which he will accomplish through moral and rational means consistent with human freedom.

His fourth argument concerns the nature of human sin. He rejects the concept of "infinite sin" as an affront to God. Sin, he says, "is the fault of a *finite creature*, and the effect of *finite* principles, passions, and appetites. To say, therefore, that the sinner is doomed to *infinite misery* for the *finite* faults of a *finite* life, looks like a reflection on the *infinite justice*, as well as goodness, of God" (*Mystery*, pp. 319-20).[55]

Chauncy's fifth theological argument focuses on Jesus as victor over sin and death. Jesus came to destroy the work of the devil (1 John 3:8). Was he not successful? Chauncy indicates that Paul's assertion that all things will eventually be subject to Christ (1 Cor. 15:24-29) convinced him of the validity of universalism. He argues that the text will be fulfilled not at the second coming of Christ but only after the second death is destroyed (*Mystery*, pp. 208-9). In reference to the victory of Jesus on the cross, he wrote, "it cannot but reflect great dishonor on him to suppose, that the *Devil* . . . should *finally* get the better of him, by effecting the *everlasting damnation* of the *greater part* of those whom he came from heaven on purpose to *save*" (*Mystery*, pp. 324-25). How can it be said that the Devil and his kingdom will be destroyed if millions of the Sons of Adam will continue in rebellion for all eternity? If that is so, then "Adam has done *more hurt* than Christ has done *good*," which is clearly contrary to the teaching of Romans 5:12-19 (*Mystery*, p. 87).

55. Chauncy goes on to argue that it would not be fair for God, the impartial judge, to reward the good with infinite happiness and the wicked with infinite misery when the difference between good and wicked people is often very slight. I would suggest that this reveals a weakness in his understanding of the gospel.

## John A. T. Robinson

An important defender of universalism in the twentieth century is John A. T. Robinson, a bishop of the Church of England. In his book *In the End God* he presents a case for restorationist universalism that draws upon the arguments of earlier universalists but stands apart as an excellent popular treatment because of his lucid logic and accessible prose.[56]

Robinson traces the essence of the debate over universalism back to the New Testament itself, which he claims teaches both *apokatastasis* and punishment for the impenitent. He surveys and rejects three possible solutions to this problem that have have been popular in the church. The first is the Calvinist view of the double decree, which he rejects out of hand, asserting that God has only one decree: to save all people. The second response is that it is impossible for us to say whether there will be a universal restoration. Robinson argues that the New Testament does not say universalism *may* happen but that it *will* happen. Finally, he examines the dominant view that God will be "all in all" despite the damnation of many. He believes that this view, though popular in the church, actually contains an incorrect view of God, that it contradicts the divine attributes of omnipotence, love, and justice. He maintains that in God love and justice are identical, and this precludes the possibility of a purely retributive hell. This is not to say that God's love is a sentimental weakness that accommodates the frailties of his sinful creatures, however; to the contrary, God hates evil. But his love and justice are expressed in a steadfast determination to pursue and achieve salvation for all people. And, as eternal

56. For his review of the chief universalist arguments, see chapters 10 and 11 of *In The End God* (New York: Harper & Row, 1968). Subsequent references to this work will be made parenthetically in the text. For more of his treatment of the issues, see Robinson, "Universalism — Is It Heretical?" *Scottish Journal of Theology* 2 (1949): 139-55, and his reply to Thomas Torrance on pp. 378-80. See also Robinson, *On Being the Church in the World* (Philadelphia: Westminster Press, 1960), pp. 130-33.

punishment would contradict God's love, so it would contradict his omnipotence, since it would constitute "a concession to a power outside himself" (*In the End God,* p. 117). If eternal damnation were to become a reality, says Robinson, "God would simply cease to be God" (*In the End God,* p. 118).

Robinson's arguments for universal restoration center on the divine attributes rather than on any proposal of human worthiness, since he contends that humanity deserves hell. But he does indicate that two biblical teachings about human beings are essential to a proper view of universalism: (1) God has created men and women as free creatures, and (2) he demands a faith decision from all.

With respect to the matter of human freedom, Robinson argues that God's omnipotence does not swallow creaturely freedom but works with it until all people freely accept his redemption. Nevertheless, human freedom must never be thought stronger than God's omnipotent love. "May we not imagine a love so strong that ultimately no one will be able to restrain himself from free and grateful surrender?" (*In the End God,* p. 122). Robinson makes clear his answer by arguing that the burden of biblical evidence leaves us with only two alternatives: we must either find some way to reconcile God's omnipotent love with his damnation of at least some people or there must be some way to reconcile universalism with human freedom. Since the first alternative is clearly impossible — if any power could prevent God from universal restoration, then he would not be almighty — we must conclude that universalism does not contradict human freedom. Since God cannot fail, it must be the case that all human beings will freely be restored.

Robinson also stresses the reality of hell and the need for a decision in response to God's love. When the Lord Jesus was asked whether only a few are saved, he did not answer the question but instead called for a faith decision on the part of the audience (Luke 13:23-24). All must make this decision, but it is not specified that they must do so in this life. Robinson asserts that the notion that our destinies are sealed at death is a Hellenistic intrusion into theology and has no biblical warrant (*In the End God*, pp. 43-44). God's strong love will work through countless ages until all are reconciled. This does not, however, lessen the seriousness of hell. From the point of view of the person making the decision, hell is a reality. But from God's point of view "hell is an ultimate impossibility" (*In the End God*, p. 130). God's nature prohibits the existence of an eternal hell. "In a universe of love there can be no heaven which tolerates a chamber of horrors" (*In the End God*, p. 133).

## Evaluation

Classical universalism meets the tests of evangelical orthodoxy to the extent that it characterizes sin as rebellion from God, asserts that grace is necessary for salvation, and holds Jesus Christ as the highest expression of that grace. Universalism has met a felt need by providing an alternative to the restrictivist belief that God desires the salvation of only a few and the damnation of most of the human race for his glory. Furthermore, restorationists have brought to the attention of the church a biblical theme long ignored — the idea that God's punishments are redemptive rather than merely retributive or even vindictive, as has sometimes been suggested. It is for these reasons, I believe, that universalism has been so warmly embraced in the Christian community. When people are asked to choose between the extremes of the harsh, unloving God of restrictivism and the loving God of universalism, it is not difficult to understand why universalism seems so attractive.[57] But this is a false dilemma; we are not forced to choose between

57. Edward Pusey agrees; see *What Is of Faith as to Everlasting Punishment?* (London: Oxford University Press, 1880), p. 8. John Stuart Mill is but one example he cites of people who were turned away because of the harshness of the Calvinistic doctrines. See Mill's *Autobiography* (New York: Bobbs-Merrill, 1957), pp. 27-28.

these extremes. The universalist claim that universalism is the only option that can harmonize God's universal salvific will and the plight of the unevangelized is easily rebutted. All that is required for harmonization is that salvation be universally accessible. Still, it is with some regret that I reject the arguments for universalism. My heart longs that the doctrine be proven correct. But I find a number of problems with universalism, in particular two associated with the biblical evidence and two of a theological nature.

### 1. Universalism vs. Universally Accessible Salvation

One problem with the universalist arguments lies in the fact that the passages so often cited in its support provide less evidence for universalism itself than for universally accessible salvation, the complete objective reconciliation of Christ, or the final supremacy of God's kingdom.[58] Universalists typically do not distinguish between objective and subjective reconciliation. They do not make the distinction implicit in the assertion that although Calvary was for all, salvation is only for believers. In Romans 5:12-19 Paul brings out both elements. He asserts that Jesus' act of righteousness produced justification of life for "all people" — by which he means "Jews and Gentiles alike," without distinction. That is to say, salvation is available to all people regardless of race or geography. But beyond establishing the universal accessibility of salvation, there remains the issue of whether an "act of faith" is necessary to appropriate it. In Romans 5:17 Paul appears to be saying that the salvation provided by Christ must be subjectively appropriated by faith: "those who receive the abundance of grace and of the gift of righteousness will reign in life through the One, Jesus Christ."

58. For a good discussion of the universalist texts in this regard, see N. T. Wright, "Towards a Biblical View of Universalism," *Themelios* 4 (Jan. 1979): 54-58.

Rudolph Bultmann has noted with respect to this text that the "participle *lambanontes* implies a condition: if, or so far as, they receive."[59] This is a consistent theme in Paul's epistles. Nevertheless, even if we interpret this text as saying "If you believe then you will be saved," we still cannot infer any pronouncement about those who do not believe. The conditional element in Romans 5:17 does not settle the matter by itself. Appeal must be made to the control belief that an act of faith is necessary for salvation. I stand with those who have adopted this control belief, but I concede that those who reject it will not be persuaded on this point.

Texts such as 1 Timothy 2:4 instruct us about God's universal salvific will, not universalism. The immediate context concerns the instruction to pray for all people — even those persecuting the church — since Christ died for all people and God desires the redemption even of those who hate Christ and persecute the church (as Paul once did).

The statement that one day God will be "all in all" (1 Cor. 15:28) is a promise that the present order will not remain as it is but will be brought under God's subjection. At the consummation, "all people, the godly and ungodly, and all angels, the good and the bad, will be compelled through the person and work of Christ to recognize God as the One and Only."[60] But there is no clear indication here that all will finally be saved.

## 2. The Reality of Hell

A second difficulty for proponents of universalism lies in the fact that some New Testament writers did teach an eternal hell. Jesus spoke of "eternal punishment" (Matt. 25:46). He also

59. Bultmann, *Theology of the New Testament*, 2 vols., trans. Kendrick Grobel (New York: Scribner's, 1951), 1: 303.
60. Peter Toon, *Heaven and Hell: A Biblical and Theological Overview* (New York: Thomas Nelson, 1986), p. 194.

taught about the sin against the Holy Spirit which is never forgiven "in this age or in the age to come" (Matt. 12:32) since it is an "eternal sin" (Mark 3:29). The so-called "hard sayings" of Jesus are all in the synoptic Gospels and Q. The various attempts by universalists to escape this fact are exegetically unconvincing.[61] The warnings in Hebrews and the pastoral epistles reflect the warnings of Jesus. Paul wrote to the Thessalonians that when the Lord Jesus is revealed from heaven, God will deal "out retribution to those who do not know God and to those who do not obey the gospel of our Lord Jesus. And these will pay the penalty of eternal destruction, away from the presence of the Lord and from the glory of His power" (2 Thess. 1:8-9).[62] Such passages referring to God's final judgment offer no hope for the reconciliation of those who ultimately reject God's grace. To claim that no such people have ever existed does not correspond well with these texts.

A similar problem is evident with respect to Eugene Boring's distinction between two-group language reflecting the present state of affairs in which God rules as judge and one-group language reflecting the future state of affairs in which God will rule as king. Second Thessalonians uses two-group language in cosmic and eschatological terms. Paul used two-group language to speak of the ultimate division whereby some will spurn God's love forever; he viewed the divine punishment for such rejection as an unfortunate eternal reality, not merely a present condition. Universalists such as Boring and Robinson use the distinction between God as judge and God as king in a subtle way to arrive at universalism. They say that the metaphors of God as judge and king must be given equal status and

61. See Bauckham, "Universalism: A Historical Survey," p. 52; and Toon, *Heaven and Hell*, p. 190. Some modern universalists have adopted the strategy of dismissing these sayings by attributing them to the limitations of Jesus' apocalyptic background.

62. For a list of texts in Paul's writings that teach limited salvation, see Boring, "The Language of Universal Salvation in Paul," p. 269n.1 and p. 277.

neither subordinated to the other, but in fact they themselves subordinate the judge metaphor to the king metaphor. They inevitably smuggle the idea of salvation out of God as judge and into God as king.[63] Furthermore, they claim that the God-as-king metaphor implicitly precludes the possibility of anyone's refusing God's grace on the grounds that this would imply a weak king. But this reflects a questionable understanding of the nature of God's kingship. The Bible depicts God as a very unusual king, one willing to suffer because of and for his subjects. The Old Testament prophets note that God's people repeatedly disobeyed him and rejected his grace. What sort of king would allow this to go on for centuries? Only a very unusual king, a king without precedent in the Babylonian and Egyptian cultures, a king who will not force his love upon his subjects even if that means he must allow them to spurn him eternally.

### 3. Divine Love and Human Freedom

Traditional criticisms of universalism assert that ultimately it allows divine power to swallow up human freedom. But most of those who bring these criticisms agree with universalists that "the will of the omnipotent is always undefeated," that God cannot be frustrated or fail to achieve his desired goals. If this is in fact the case, we are faced with just three possibilities: (1) God chooses all for damnation, (2) God chooses all for salvation, or (3) God chooses some for heaven and some for hell. There are no Christian advocates of the first option; this leaves only universalism on the one hand and the Calvinist "double decree" on the other. If we operate on the premise that God desires the salvation of all humans, we must conclude that the double decree is false and hence that universalism is true.

63. See Boring, "The Language of Universal Salvation in Paul," pp. 285, 290.

The problem here is that both universalists and double-decree Calvinists define omnipotence as God's ability to get whatever he wants: there is nothing God cannot do. This corresponds exactly to the traditional problem of evil: Can God make free creatures and guarantee they will never sin? No! That would involve a contradiction, since one aspect of freedom (defined as the ability either to do something or not — libertarian) is the impossibility of guaranteeing the outcome. This is the customary "free-will defense." But universalists, Calvinistic predestinarians, and many non-Christian philosophers claim that is exactly what God can do. They all believe that God does not take risks, that he can guarantee outcomes even if he grants freedom to some creatures.[64] Universalists argue that if God always gets his way, then there will only be one group of people in the afterlife — the redeemed. Calvinists claim that God always gets what he desires, and he elects some for eternal damnation and others for eternal life. Atheistic philosophers argue that if God always got his way, there would be no sin or evil in the first place, and since there is sin and evil, they conclude that God cannot exist.

To attempt to escape from the logic of the argument as Ferré does, by claiming God is not bound by human logic and hence he is not faced with a dilemma here, is to break the rules

64. For more on this, see Jerry Walls, "Can God Save Anyone He Will?" *Scottish Journal of Theology* 38 (1985): 155-72. Contemporary analytic philosophy provides a potential solution here through what is known as "possible worlds" theory. The agument might be made that God could create any number of worlds in which all people sin, and among these possible worlds there might be one in which eventually all people respond positively to Jesus Christ of their own free will. It would be God's decision whether actually to create such a world, and yet were he to do so, human freedom would not be compromised by his action. This approach is clearly not without its problems, however. For one thing, if it were possible for God to create such a world and yet he chose not to create it, we would be faced with a more serious problem of evil than before. Furthermore, I maintain that the sort of divine foreknowledge implied by this theory is inconsistent with a biblical understanding of God.

of the theological game. Theology is a human enterprise and must be played within the rules of human understanding. If Ferré's argument is permissible, then any theological proposition is permissible, and none is refutable. Theologians could construct any sort of arguments they liked, regardless of their contradictions, and simply claim that God is not bound by human logic. Their assertions would cease to have any real meaning.

The major difficulty with the universalist, Calvinist, and atheist views is their concept of God. It is my contention that all three views build on an idea of God that is foreign to what we find in the Bible. The Bible presents us with a God who makes himself vulnerable by creating creatures who have the freedom to reject him.[65] This God takes risks and leaves himself open to being despised, rejected, and crucified. The God of the Bible is not a deity of raw power but a Creator and Sovereign who nonetheless suffers with, because of, and for his creatures. For those with this view of God, Robinson's assertion that "God would cease to be God" if he didn't save all people loses its force. For those who perceive God as the "defenseless superior power" who in grace makes himself vulnerable rather than as an absolute dictator whose every whim is satisfied, the universalist argument is significantly less compelling. The vulnerable God of the Bible whose will is not always fulfilled (Matt. 7:21) will not cease to be God if his desire to redeem all is not universally fulfilled. The universalists do make a valid point in arguing that it would pain God if any of his creatures chose hell, and hence that he would suffer forever if eternal damnation were a reality. But is it not possible that God might be willing to accept such suffering as the price of being a God of vulnerable love, the God of the Bible?

The universalist conception of human freedom and divine

65. For a more complete elaboration of this point, see my essay "God as Personal," in *The Grace of God, the Will of Man*, ed. Clark Pinnock (Grand Rapids: Zondervan, 1989), pp. 165-80.

omnipotence is problematic on a number of other counts as well. To the extent that universalism based on divine omnipotence diminishes the vitality of human freedom, it destroys the personal, I-Thou relationship God desires. "In such a procedure the actual historical particularity of every choice as a free movement disappears, and necessity takes its place — no matter how hard one may try to avoid it."[66] Furthermore, Ferré, Hick, and Robinson all *claim* God can bring about the reconciliation of all free creatures but they never plausibly demonstrate *how* this can be if the creatures remain forever free. And if, as they suggest, human freedom entails the possibility that individuals will continue to fall from grace and return to hell in the afterlife, how can it be guaranteed that there will ever come a time when all people will cease to turn away from God and hell will be done away with?

A more crucial failure of universalists in connection with free will involves the "mystery of iniquity." They typically underestimate the irrationality of sin. Sin does not make sense, even to God (Jer. 3:7). If Plato was correct in asserting that "to know the truth is to do the truth," then the problem of sin could presumably be solved through education. God, the master teacher, would not have any failing students. But sin is irrational. There is no good reason to sin, no good reason for not trusting God. Sin is not a problem to be solved but a mystery to be challenged by gracious love. The fact that it is essentially irrational opens the door to the possibility that even God must suffer with it, that he may not be able to guarantee that all people will finally accept his love. To those who do not want any part of God's love, who say No to Jesus, he gives what they most desire — the opportunity to be themselves, enslaved forever by the horrible freedom they have demanded.[67]

66. Thomas F. Torrance, "Universalism or Election?" *Scottish Journal of Theology* 2 (1949): 313.

67. See C. S. Lewis, *The Problem of Pain* (New York: Macmillan, 1962), pp. 118-28.

## 4. The Purpose of Divine Judgment

One of the significant reasons for the popularity of the universalist position in the Christian community is the fact that it is perceived to offer alternatives to less tenable positions. For example, many people view universalism as less objectionable than the assertion that a loving God would eternally torture any of his creatures in hell.[68] And yet the Bible seems to provide substantial warrant for the concept of divine retributive justice. It seems clear that a sound understanding of divine judgment and the purpose of hell is important for our assessment of the validity of the universalist argument.

I believe any understanding of God's justice must be tied to a faith in his love for his creatures. I believe that the primary purpose of divine judgment is redemptive. When God judges, he is seeking repentance and reconciliation. And yet true justice cannot simply overlook perpetual rebellion. I believe the biblical evidence suggests that eventually, after enduring much suffering, God brings to a close the opportunity for redemption and exercises retributive justice. But I would quickly add that God's retribution is not anything like vindictiveness; rather, it involves bringing forth the consequences of our evil choices. Those who remain impenitent to the end receive the justice they desire: they are removed from the presence of the Lord. He will not force anyone from his presence, but in the end he will accede to those who refuse his offers of redemption, who perpetually

68. I think it is plausible to say that the picture of a loving God offered by universalists becomes more attractive as the picture of a cruel God serving as a sort of proprietor of hell becomes more horrible. The Bible offers no support for the picture of a God who delights in the torture of sinners. Stephen Davis gives evidence of a better grasp of the scriptural evidence when he defines hell as "separation from God as the source of true love, joy, peace, and light. It is not a place of agony, torment, torture, and utter horror (here I am opposing the lurid and even sadistic pictures of hell envisioned by some Christian thinkers). But there is no deep or ultimate joy there and I believe its citizens are largely miserable" ("Universalism, Hell, and the Fate of the Ignorant," *Modern Theology* 6 [Jan 1990]: 178).

rebel against him. The purpose of the eternal hell is to bring about the end of the rebellion.[69] Although I believe that hell involves retributive justice, I agree with Stephen Travis that "both heaven and hell are best spoken of not as reward and punishment for the kind of life we have lived, but as the logical outcome of our relationship to God in this life. . . . And hell, we may say, is not a punishment for turning one's back on Christ and choosing the road that leads to destruction. It is where the road leads."[70]

## Excursus on Radical Pluralism

Some of the more prominent universalists have become radical pluralists who no longer hold to the particularity and finality of salvation only through Jesus Christ. Radical pluralists do not believe that Christianity is the one true or even the highest religion in which the other major religions find their fulfillment; they believe that all religions are valid and none may truthfully claim supremacy. They urge Christians to move from a Christ-centered faith that excludes other people to a God-centered faith

69. Some suggest that God may bring about the end of eternal rebellion not through eternal punishment but through an absolute cessation of existence. Proponents of this doctrine of annihilationism contend that it not only obviates the problems associated with the universalist response to the issue of perpetual human rebellion against God but also removes the objection that an eternal hell would imply an ultimate dualism. Evangelicals are increasingly coming out in favor of annihilationism. See, for example, John R. W. Stott and David Edwards, *Evangelical Essentials* (Downers Grove, Ill.: InterVarsity Press, 1988), pp. 314-20; and Clark Pinnock, "The Destruction of the Finally Impenitent," *Criswell Theological Review* 4 (Spring 1990): 243-59. For a historical survey and bilbical defense, see Edward Fudge, *The Fire That Consumes: A Biblical and Historical Study of Final Punishment* (Houston: Providential Press, 1983). And for a treatment of some New Testament scholars who maintain that Paul did not teach eternal conscious punishment, see Boring, "The Language of Universal Salvation in Paul," p. 281n.36.

70. Travis, "The Problem of Judgment," *Themelios* 11 (Jan. 1986): 54.

that includes others by claiming that all religions are acceptable. It is not enough, say pluralists, to say all people will be saved in the lifeboat of Christ; we need to affirm that all people already have their own lifeboat and don't need another one.

Writers such as Nels Ferré and John Hick began as classical universalists affirming the finality of Jesus but later moved into pluralistic waters.[71] A considerable number of universalists have moved in this direction during the twentieth century, developing syncretistic theologies. They typically begin by abandoning the singular importance of Christ, then the finality of the Christian faith, and sometimes even the worship of God.[72] This is not to say that this sort of declension is new to the theological scene, however. The nineteenth-century German theologian David Strauss argued that if knowledge of Christ were necessary for salvation, then Jesus could not be the universal savior (since not all have heard of him) and Christianity could not be necessary for salvation.[73] The poet Alexander Pope anticipated such ideas when he wrote his "Universal Prayer":

> Father of all, in every age
>   In every clime, adored
> By saint, by savage, or by sage,
>   Jehovah, Jove, or Lord.

In the same spirit, John Hick has written that "all salvation — that is, all creating of human animals into children of God — is the work of God. The different religions have their different names for God acting savingly towards mankind."[74]

---

71. See Nels Ferré, *The Universal Word: A Theology for a Universal Faith* (Philadelphia: Westminster Press, 1969), pp. 158, 170-71; and John Hick, *An Interpretation of Religion* (London: Macmillan, 1989).

72. See Cassara, *Universalism in America*, pp. 39-42.

73. Strauss, *Dogmatik*, 1: 264-71; 2: 148, cited by Stewart Salmond in *The Christian Doctrine of Immortality*, 5th ed. (Edinburgh: T. & T. Clark, 1913), p. 374.

74. Hick, *The Myth of God Incarnate* (London: SCM Press, 1977), p. 181.

Radical pluralists reject two key Christian beliefs. The most crucial of these is the particularity and finality of Christ. In his book *No Other Name?* Paul Knitter, a leading pluralist, rejects the principle "that belief in the normativity, finality, unsurpassability of Christ forms an essential part of the Christian message."[75] He asserts that pluralists "can endorse a theocentric theology of religions, based on a theocentric, nonnormative reinterpretation of the uniqueness of Jesus Christ."[76] Wesley Ariarajah, writing for the World Council of Churches, maintains that Jesus never claimed to be God, that he simply preached a gospel of acceptance by God, and that the New Testament writers made Christianity christocentric instead of theocentric.[77] John Hick calls this shift from a Jesus-centered model to a God-centered model a "Copernican revolution" in theology that "involves a shift from the dogma that Christianity is at the center to the realization that it is *God* who is at the center, and that all the religions of mankind, including our own, serve and revolve around him."[78] In this scheme Christianity is but one locus of truth and one way of worshiping God. Hinduism, Islam, Buddhism, Taoism, and all other religions revolve around the same God as all the planets in our solar system revolve around the same sun.

A second key belief of classical Christian thought revised by radical pluralists is the authority of the Bible. Pluralists at best regard the Bible as but one revelation among many and at worst as a wholly human book. They maintain that it is useful within the Christian community but has no binding authority. The ultimate criteria of truth are dialogue with other religions

75. Knitter, *No Other Name? A Critical Survey of Christian Attitudes toward the World Religions* (Maryknoll, N.Y.: Orbis Books, 1985), p. 143.

76. Knitter, *No Other Name?* p. 200.

77. Ariarajah, *The Bible and People of Other Faiths,* Risk Series, no. 26 (Geneva: World Council of Churches), pp. 21-31.

78. Hick, *God and the Universe of Faiths* (New York: St. Martin's Press, 1973), p. 131. See also chapter 2 of his book *God Has Many Names* (Philadelphia: Westminster Press, 1982).

and whatever else fosters acceptance and inclusion. Knitter calls this a "new model" of truth that will help free the church from its "Latin captivity."[79] He calls for a rejection of the old criteria, which he says fostered exclusion. Today we need criteria of truth that will help the religions of the world relate to, listen to, and accept each other. In such an approach the highest court of appeal cannot be the Bible or any other purported source of divine revelation; instead, we must turn to natural religion.[80]

Hick and others have ventured onto pluralistic ground largely in reaction to the difficulties of traditional theology which presents a harsh and exclusive God who condemns most of the human race to hell as a matter of course. "Is it credible that the loving God and Father of all men has decreed that only those born within one particular thread of human history shall be saved?" asks Hick. "Is not such an idea excessively parochial, presenting God in effect as the tribal deity of the predominantly Christian West?"[81] Hick also talks about how his personal encounters with Muslim, Hindu, and Sikh worshipers helped produce the Copernican revolution in his own thinking.[82] It is not enough to say all will be saved through Jesus Christ, he argues; all people will be saved in their own way. Hick views all the attempts to broaden the scope of God's universal love within the context of the Christian faith itself (such as those discussed in Part 3 of this work) as "small print to the old theology" and "artificial theories" that cannot hope to cope with the facts of God's world.[83]

79. Knitter, *No Other Name?* pp. 217-23.
80. For Hick's construction of criteria for evaluating truth claims, see chaps. 5-6 of *God Has Many Names,* and chap. 20 of *An Interpretation of Religion: Human Responses to the Transcendent* (New Haven: Yale University Press, 1989).
81. Hick, *The Myth of God Incarnate,* p. 180.
82. See Hick, "Is There Only One Way to God?" *Theology* 85 (Jan. 1982): 4-7.
83. Hick, *The Myth of God Incarnate,* p. 180. See also chap. 2 of *God Has Many Names.* Knitter agrees with him on this point; see *No Other Name?* p. 117.

But how true do Hick and other radical pluralists themselves remain to the facts of God's world? I have three broad objections to their work.

## 1. The Pitfalls of Radical Reinterpretation

The other major religions contain no true parallel to the Christian doctrine of the incarnation.[84] Attempts to draw exact parallels between Jesus and avatars or divine incarnations in Oriental religions are based on a misunderstanding of the Oriental worldview. These religions simply do not have the same understandings of creation, God, sin, and salvation that provide the framework for the Christian understanding of the incarnation of Jesus. Hick has to engage in a fundamental reinterpretation of the Christian understanding of the incarnation as myth in order plausibly to assert that it does have parallels in other religions. In his latest works, Hick reinterprets all religions (though in my opinion his reconstruction of Christianity is far more radical than his reconstruction of the Eastern religions) in an effort to place them all within the same framework as mythological responses to "the Real." In doing so, however, he is not treating the religions according to their own self-understanding — one of the generally accepted requirements for interreligious dialogue — but is imposing a framework on all religions and then standing in judgment on them.

## 2. Who Is God? What Is Salvation?

While the reconstruction that Hick and other pluralists have undertaken is radical, there is arguably a sense in which it is not radical enough. The problem lies in their asserting both that God

84. See Stuart Hackett, *Reconstruction of the Christian Revelation Claim* (Grand Rapids: Baker Book House, 1984), pp. 250-53.

will save all people and that all religions are valid ways of salvation. If the words "God will save" are to have any meaning, they must have a particular content. When Hick and Knitter claim that *God will save* all, do they have a Christian understanding of God and salvation in mind? If so, then they are not true pluralists: they are smuggling in a Christian conception and making it definitive. If not, then what exactly do they mean? If they are genuinely including Hinduism or Buddhism, then they are radically altering the Christian understanding of the assertion that "God will save," since these nontheistic Eastern religions posit a nonpersonal God who cannot *do* anything and a nonindividualistic existence after death that is quite different from the Christian conception of personal, individual survival of death.

Similarly, the assertion that "God loves all people" has drastically different meanings in the contexts of different religions. It seems quite clear on the face of it that the character of the love from a personal God would be quite unlike that from an impersonal God. Will any definition of love satisfy the pluralists? Gavin D'Costa has suggested that "if the Copernican revolution requires a *God* of love at the center for its initial coherence, then surely, however interesting and illuminating the insights from non-theistic religions, in the final analysis they cannot be said to be as true or as appropriate to the divine reality."[85] And Clark Pinnock asks, "How can one relegate Jesus to the margins and still keep the God he reveals in the center? After all, Jesus is the main reason we picture God as a loving Person wanting to reconcile the world in the first place. Other religions do not teach this particular concept of deity."[86] Pluralists such as Hick remove the God of Christianity via the front door with much fanfare only to smuggle him quietly in the back door, and it is for this reason that they are not success-

85. D'Costa, *Theology and Religious Pluralism* (New York: Basil Blackwell, 1986), p. 38.
86. Pinnock, "Toward an Evangelical Theology of Religions," *Journal of the Evangelical Theological Society* 33 (Fall 1990): 363.

ful in completing the revolution from a christocentric to a theocentric theology.[87]

Both Hick and Knitter have realized this and have since moved from advocating theocentrism to advocating a much more vague "soteriocentrism," to viewing the basic thrust of every religion in terms of the attempt to liberate people from oppression and injustice and bring about "the kingdom and its justice."[88] In this mode of thought, according to Knitter, orthopraxis is authoritative over orthodoxy. And instead of saying, "the God of love will save all people," Hick, who now prefers the term "the Real" to "God," would say, "all religions may be evaluated on the basis of their appropriate or inappropriate responses to the Real."[89] An appropriate response is one that fosters a move from self-centeredness to Reality-centeredness. Yet Hick continues to believe that the "divine attitude" toward the world is one of *agape* and to speak of "God's will." Such terms make sense, of course, only within a personalistic conception of ultimate reality. Hick still has a ways to go in order to expunge the remnants of theocentrism from his theology. After all, any number of religions (not to mention such quasireligions as nihilism and secular humanism) reject the premise that there is a divine being, much less that this being loves us in any significant sense.

The move beyond theocentrism is beset by other problems as well. Pertaining to the concept of "salvation" as liberation or as appropriate responses to the Real, how does one decide what responses are "appropriate" or what constitutes a valid definition

87. For a fuller critique of theocentric pluralism, see S. Mark Heim, "Thinking about Theocentric Christology," *Journal of Ecumenical Studies*, Winter 1987, pp. 1-16.

88. See Knitter, "Toward a Liberation Theology of Religions," in *The Myth of Christian Uniqueness: Toward a Pluralistic Theology of Religions*, ed. John Hick and Paul Knitter (Maryknoll, N.Y.: Orbis Books, 1987), pp. 178-200. See also Hick, *An Interpretation of Religion: Human Responses to the Transcendent* (New Haven: Yale University Press, 1989); and "Straightening the Record: Some Response to Critics," *Modern Theology* 6 (Jan. 1990): 187-95.

89. See chap. 19 of *Interpretation of Religion*.

of liberation? How are we to derive a normative definition of "kingdom justice"? What authority will determine what is correct orthopraxis? On what grounds is self-centeredness condemned? Why is nihilism an inappropriate response to the Real? It does not seem that all religions would agree on the answers to such questions. Moreover, in the move beyond theocentrism, has not the term "Real" been watered down to the point that it lacks any significant content? Does not Hick's conception run into the same problem of ineffability as does Plotinus's "One"? If no definition can be given of the Real, then we cannot speak meaningfully about it. If the Real has no predicates, then Feuerbach's question returns: "Does it exist?" If we attempt to go to Hick's God, we must commit ourselves to silence or at least be willing to admit that we cannot make any true or false assertions about the Real. In any event, we cannot appeal to any normative criteria for adjudicating between the truth claims of various religions concerning "appropriate" responses to the Real.[90] Though Hick wants to avoid relativism, it is not at all clear how he can do so, given his presuppositions.

### 3. The Criteria for Truth

Knitter's desire to avoid relativism seems as problematic as Hick's. Knitter proposes the adoption of a "new model" of truth, asserting that our ultimate criterion for determining the truth of a proposition should be a determination of whether it helps us to accept and relate to others. Why should we accept this criterion for truth? Knitter says we should do so because it will help us accept and relate to others! The argument itself, then, is circular, but beyond this it seems somewhat self-contradictory as well, in the extent to which it implicitly excludes other criteria

90. For a fuller consideration of these points, see Peter Byrne, "John Hick's Philosophy of World Religions," *Scottish Journal of Theology* 35 (1982): 293-98.

of truth. The new model of truth is, in fact, quite unaccepting of the entire Western tradition. Is this not exclusivism in pluralistic clothing?[91]

\* \* \*

In outlining these weaknesses in the arguments of the radical pluralists, I am not suggesting that they have no legitimate criticisms of exclusivistic forms of Christian theology. Evangelicals have for too long been unwilling to learn from other cultures and religions.[92] We have been overly ethnocentric in our approach to missions, worship, and theology. But it is too much to ask that we solve the problem by sacrificing the finality of Jesus Christ at the altar of religious dialogue. A belief in the triumph of God's grace as manifested in Jesus is essential to the Christian faith. Moreover, it is altogether possible to affirm both the finality of Christ and God's universal salvific will and still have a positive approach to other religions.[93] Orthodox christology does not entail a restrictive soteriology.

91. Knitter's new model of truth is self-contradictory on a very fundamental level. As vigorously as it promotes inclusivistic "both-and" thinking, it rejects traditional Christian "either/or" thinking on the grounds that it is exclusivistic. But does this rejection of either/or thinking not itself compromise the essence of the inclusivist argument? In what sense is it truly inclusive if it rejects so significant a tradition of thought? Indeed, it could be argued that the logic of the new model of truth ultimately leads to solipsism.

92. I find it odd that evangelicals are so willing to make use of the latest insights of educational theory, psychology, and marketing but are hesitant to find truth in other religions. Why do they accept the assertion that God works to transform cultures and movements (such as the civil rights movement) but reject the idea that God may be at work in other religions? Are not all institutionalized forms of religion a mixed bag of good and evil? For an evangelical approach to dialogue with other religions, see chap. 7 of Vinay Samuel and Chris Sugden's *Sharing Jesus in the Two Thirds World* (Grand Rapids: William B. Eerdmans, 1983).

93. There are many examples of orthodox evangelical openness to other religions. Russell Aldwinckle is well informed regarding the details of Oriental religions; see *Jesus — A Savior or the Savior?* (Macon, Ga.: Mercer Uni-

## Historical Bibliography

### 1. Judaism in the New Testament Era

The pseudepigraphic work *The Testament of Simeon* contains what some consider to be a reference to universalism — "he [the Messiah] will save all the gentiles and the tribe of Israel" (7:2).

### 2. Early Church through the Middle Ages

Clement of Alexandria, Origen's teacher, taught a restorationism based, in part, on the descent of Christ into hades and the preaching of the apostles in hell after Christ (*Stromata* 6.6).

The outstanding fourth-century theologian Gregory of Nyssa followed Origen in teaching restorationism. God is the great goldsmith and physician, he wrote, who will purify and heal every rebellious creature (see *Nicene and Post-Nicene Fathers*, series 2, vol. 5, ed. Philip Schaff [1892; reprint, Grand Rapids: William B. Eerdmans, 1954], pp. 444, 452, 483, 495-96).

Theodore of Mopsuestia and Diodore of Tarsus along with several other lesser names of the day were universalists (see Plumptre, *The Spirits in Prison* [London: Isbister, 1898], pp. 140-41).

Gregory of Nazianzen considered universalism an open question, but he seems to have preferred the idea of an eternal hell (*Orations*, 40.36).

After Augustine, universalism fell into disfavor and was

---

versity Press, 1982). S. Mark Heim does an excellent job of answering the common objections to interreligious dialogue and also provides a helpful typology in *Is Christ the Only Way?* (Valley Forge, Pa.: Judson Press, 1985). Gavin D'Costa examines pluralism, exclusivism, and inclusivism in *Theology and Religious Pluralism*. E. C. Dewick demonstrates that the church has always included representatives of both restrictive and accepting stances toward other religions; see *The Christian Attitude to Other Religions* (London: Cambridge University Press, 1953).

rarely seriously considered again until after the Reformation. The lone exception was John Scotus Erigena, in the ninth century, who viewed the torments of hell as a metaphor for an evil conscience (*The Divine Nature* 5.29).

### 3. The Reformation through the Nineteenth Century

According to Richard Bauckham, "a few sixteenth century Anabaptists and Spiritualists, notably John Denck, and a few of the most radical religious thinkers of the English Interregnum, notably Gerrard Winstanley and Richard Coppin, were universalists" ("Universalism: A Historical Survey," *Themelios* 4 [Jan. 1979]: 50). Bauckham also notes that in seventeenth-century England, some Cambridge Platonists such as Peter Sterry and Jeremiah White were restorationists, and in the eighteenth century the devotional writer William Law popularized universalism. The universalism of some of the radical Pietists influenced some of the early Brethren, who helped bring it to America (see James Alexander, "Universalism among the Early Brethren," *Brethren Life and Thought* 32 [Winter 1987]: 25-32).

In America the first published universalist tract was *Everlasting Gospel* by George Klein Nicolai under the pseudonym Paul Siegvolck in 1753, but it was preachers such as John Murray, Charles Chauncy, and later Hosea Ballou who made universalism attractive to Americans (see chap. 1 of *Universalism in America: A Documentary History*, ed. Ernest Cassara [Boston: Beacon, 1971]).

In the nineteenth century, significant German universalists were Friedrich Schleiermacher (*The Christian Faith*, vol. 2, ed. H. R. Mackintosh and J. S. Stewart [New York: Harper & Row, 1963], pp. 539-60, 720-22) and Albrecht Ritschl (*The Christian Doctrine of Justification and Reconciliation*, ed. H. R. Macintosh and A. B. Macaulay [Clinton, N.J.: Reference Book Publishers, 1966], pp. 125-39).

F. D. Maurice and F. W. Farrar were significant English

universalists, although their intent was not so much to defend universalism as to oppose extreme Calvinism and the concept of eternal punishment (see Bauckham, "Universalism," p. 51).

For more extensive discussions of universalists during this period, see the following: D. P. Walker, *The Decline of Hell* (London: Routledge and Kegan Paul, 1964); Geoffrey Rowell, *Hell and the Victorians: A Study of the Nineteenth Century Theological Controversies concerning Eternal Punishment and the Future Life* (Oxford: Clarendon Press, 1974); the bibliography by Ezra Abbot in W. R. Alger's *A Critical History of the Doctrine of a Future Life*, 3rd ed. (New York: W. J. Widdleton, 1878); the bibliography in the article on universalism in the *Evangelical Dictionary of Theology*, ed. Walter Elwell (Grand Rapids: Baker Book House, 1984); Cassara, *Universalism in America;* and Alan Seaburg, "Recent Scholarship in American Universalism: A Bibliographical Essay," *Church History* 41 (Dec. 1972): 513-23.

### 4. The Twentieth Century

Universalism has been affirmed by such notable modern figures as John Baillie (*And the Life Everlasting* [London: Oxford University Press, 1934], pp. 237-45), William Barclay (*William Barclay: A Spiritual Autobiography* [Grand Rapids: William B. Eerdmans, 1977], pp. 65-68), William Temple *(Nature, Man and God* [London: Macmillan, 1951], pp. 414-17), Nels Ferré (*The Christian Understanding of God* [New York: Harper, 1951], chap. 9; and *Evil and the Christian Faith* [Freeport, N.Y.: Books for Libraries, 1971], chap. 12), Paul Tillich (*Systematic Theology,* vol. 3 [Chicago: University of Chicago Press, 1963], pp. 406-19), the Roman Catholic William Dalton (*Salvation and Damnation* [Butler, Wis.: Clergy Book Service, 1977]), John Hick (*Death and Eternal Life* [London: Collins, 1976], chap. 13), Langdon Gilkey (*Reaping the Whirlwind* [New York: Seabury Press, 1981], pp. 296-99), Gordon Kaufman (*Systematic Theology* [New York: Scribner's, 1968], pp. 305-6, 471-72),

M. Eugene Boring ("The Language of Universal Salvation in Paul," *Journal of Biblical Literature* 105 [June 1986]: 269-92), and John A. T. Robinson (*In the End God* [New York: Harper & Row, 1968], chaps. 10-11).

Another group of twentieth-century theologians believes universalism is a genuine possibility that we ought not deny even though we cannot affirm its truth dogmatically. They hope for the final salvation of all human beings but do not believe there is enough evidence to substantiate it as a theological dogma.

Karl Barth taught that all people are elect in Christ. He maintained that preaching the gospel only discloses what is already true of them — namely, that they are reconciled to God. Barth also holds that God is free, however, and that he does not have to be eternally patient with us and save everyone (see *Church Dogmatics*, 4 vols. [Edinburgh: T. & T. Clark, 1936-69], 4/3: 461-78).

Emil Brunner argued that the law/gospel, judgment/ grace, damnation/universalism biblical texts must be understood not as "things" (empirical objects) but as relational truths. One side or the other of these is subjectively true of *us* depending upon our relationship to God. However, since *God's* holiness is identical with his love, we can have confidence that in the end grace will bring all people safely through the judgment (see *Dogmatics*, vol. 3 [Philadelphia: Westminster Press, 1962], pp. 415-24; and *Eternal Hope* [Philadelphia: Westminster Press, 1954], pp. 170-84).

Jacques Ellul argues for predestinarian universalism when he says, "We are not free to decide and choose to be damned" (*What I Believe*, trans. Geoffrey Bromiley [Grand Rapids: William B. Eerdmans, 1989]: 192).

Other advocates of hopeful universalism include the following: John Macquarrie, who concedes that annihilation may become a reality for some but hopes for universalism (*Principles of Christian Theology*, 2d ed. [New York: Scribner's, 1977], pp. 361-67); Hans Küng, who agrees with Barth (*On Being a Chris-*

*tian* (Garden City, N.Y.: Doubleday, 1976], pp. 369-70, 395);
Hans Urs Von Balthasar (*Dare We Hope That All Men Be Saved?*
trans. David Kipp and Lothar Krauth [San Francisco: Ignatius
Press, 1988], p. 213); G. C. Berkouwer (*The Return of Christ*
[Grand Rapids: William B. Eerdmans, 1972], pp. 387-423);
Brian Hebblethwaite (*The Christian Hope* [Grand Rapids: Wil-
liam B. Eerdmans, 1984], pp. 192-94, 217-18); Karl Rahner
(*Foundations of Christian Faith* [New York: Seabury Press,
1978], pp. 443-44); Vernard Eller (*The Most Revealing Book of
the Bible* [Grand Rapids: William B. Eerdmans, 1974], pp.
188-205); and Helmut Thielicke (*The Evangelical Faith*, vol. 3
[Grand Rapids: William B. Eerdmans, 1982], pp. 453-56).

# PART THREE

*Salvation as Universally Accessible*

# CHAPTER FOUR

## *The Wider Hope*

We have seen that both restrictivism and universalism are in their own ways incompatible with the key premises of God's universal salvific will and the finality of Jesus. Now we turn to a consideration of a variety of positions located between these two ends of the spectrum. All of the positions discussed in Part 3 of the book affirm that God, in grace, grants every individual a genuine opportunity to participate in the redemptive work of the Lord Jesus, that no human being is excluded from the possibility of benefiting from salvific grace. The views differ regarding the nature and timing of the opportunity for salvation — specifically, on the issues of whether people must be aware that their salvation is in Jesus Christ and whether the opportunity for salvation is given only before physical death or also after death.

All of these "wider hope" views are defined in part by their opposition to certain universalist and restrictivist assumptions. For example, proponents of the wider hope reject the restrictivist assertion that it is enough to maintain that all people have an opportunity to be saved if they never sin. Salvation is not genuinely universally accessible, they say, unless all people have an opportunity of being redeemed by God's

grace after they have sinned. Paul declares that "while we were
yet sinners, Christ died for us" (Rom. 5:8). They insist that we
must emphasize the cosmic implications of the incarnation and
atonement of Jesus in seeking the salvation of the ungodly.
Confessing *Jesus* as *the* Savior does not entail our denying the
universal aspects of his work. Jesus came to save the world. The
particular and the universal must be held together. The crucial
issue is the way in which these two truths are to be applied to
the question of the unevangelized. On this Christians have
never agreed. In Part 3 I examine a variety of answers propounded by Christians throughout the history of the church.

Some further development, beyond that mentioned in
Chapter 1, of the rationale for universally accessible salvation
may be helpful. Proponents of universally accessible salvation
find a wealth of evidence in support of their position in the
Bible.[1] The opening chapter of Genesis begins with the creation of male and female in the image of God and the pronouncement of God's blessing upon them (1:26-28). Genesis
portrays God as working with all humanity and not merely
with the Israelites. As the story unfolds, humanity sins against
God, but in the midst of judgment (the curse), God finds an
opportunity for issuing a promise of future deliverance (Gen.
3:15). The promise that a seed of the woman will crush the
serpent's head has cosmic implications, since it promises to
affect every area of life touched by sin. God chose not to leave
humanity in a state of fear and alienation but to seek our
redemption. This same theme of promised blessing arising
from the midst of judgment appears in the story of Noah.
After the flood, God enacts a "cosmic covenant" that includes
a promise of universal blessing (Gen. 9:8-19). The covenant
he made with Noah and his sons, of which the rainbow was

---

1. For further delineation of the following points, see Richard Drum-
mond, *Toward a New Age in Christian Theology* (Maryknoll, N.Y.: Orbis
Books, 1985), pp. 5-7; and Walbert Bühlmann, *God's Chosen Peoples*, trans.
Robert Barr (Maryknoll, N.Y.: Orbis Books, 1982), pp. 11-56.

the sign, extends to all humanity, since the whole human race descends from these sons (Gen. 9:19).

God continued with his plan of redemption by deciding to initiate the fulfillment of his universal salvific will through the particular descendants of Abraham. "But even the particularity or narrower ethnic scope of this call and covenant with Abraham is specifically stated to be effected only for a universal restorative purpose, that 'by you all the families of the earth will bless themselves' (Gen. 12:3; cf. Gen. 18:18; 22:18; 26:4; 28:14)."[2] The covenant with Abraham did not abrogate the older covenants; rather, it developed and articulated God's universal redemptive plans more fully. Furthermore, the election of Abraham and his descendants should not be understood to mean that particular people were chosen for heaven while others were overlooked. To the contrary, the Israelites were elected for earthly service. God chose to bring the universal Savior, the Lord Jesus, into the world through this people. God's desire to bless *all* the families of the earth through Abraham is proclaimed as having been fulfilled in Jesus of Nazareth by the New Testament writers. The salvific intention of God is universal and is derailed by neither race nor geography. The God who called Abraham is the same God who desires all people to be saved (2 Pet. 3:9). The "savior of all men" (1 Tim. 4:10), who "desires all men to be saved" (1 Tim. 2:4), is the same God who created all humanity and promised to bless them. The God who came to Eve after she had sinned and promised her a seed who would crush the serpent's head is the same God who "has shut up all in disobedience that He might show mercy to all" (Rom. 11:32). God has not left the human race to fear and alienation but has provided redemption through his beloved Son.

God so loved the whole world that he sent his Son, Jesus, who died for the ungodly. As we read in Isaiah 55:8, this is a God whose ways are not our ways. Isaiah is not referring to any sort of metaphysical or mysterious way in which God is

2. Drummond, *Toward a New Age in Christian Theology,* p. 6.

not like us. Rather, God is not like us, declares Isaiah, because he is willing to *forgive* people who have terribly hurt and rejected him. God calls on the wicked people to return to him, "for He will abundantly pardon" (Isa. 55:7).

This unusual "way" of God is illustrated in the Exodus narrative, where God seeks the salvation of Pharaoh even though he was brutally oppressing the people of Israel. Pharaoh had declared that he did not know this God named Yahweh of whom Moses spoke (Exod. 5:2). So the God of Israel sought, through the plagues, to get Pharaoh to "know" him (Exod. 7:5, 17, 8:10). The Hebrew word *yada* ("know") here carries with it the idea of relational and redemptive knowledge, not mere cognition of abstract and insignificant pieces of information. Yahweh, the God of Israel, wanted Pharaoh and the Egyptian people to experience his truth and life-giving grace. The plagues were designed to show the uselessness of the Egyptian deities.[3] By demonstrating the impotence of the Egyptian gods, Yahweh sought to free Pharaoh and the Egyptians from this burden and grant them the opportunity to turn to him — the Creator and Redeemer. In other words, God was trying to evangelize Pharaoh and the Egyptians![4] This is quite different from what I would expect to read in the text, since I would not desire the salvation of such a king. On the contrary, I would think he should be assassinated! But the God of Israel and the Father of our Lord Jesus is different in that he patiently seeks Pharaoh's salvation. His ways are not our ways.

This same point is brought out in the book of Jonah, where we read that God desired the redemption of the Assyrian

3. See John Davis, *Moses and the Gods of Egypt* (Grand Rapids: Baker Book House, 1971), pp. 84-128; and Nahum Sarna, *Exploring Exodus* (New York: Schocken Books, 1987), pp. 78-80.

4. For an excellent treatment of this idea, see Roger Forster and Paul Marston, *God's Strategy in Human History* (Minneapolis: Bethany House, 1973). For a treatment in essential agreement with the idea, see Walter Kaiser, "Exodus," in *Expositor's Bible Commentary,* vol. 2 (Grand Rapids: Zondervan, 1990), p. 345.

people, who had treated the people of Israel with great cruelty. The prophet Jonah, however, did not want such people redeemed; he wanted them destroyed. I am like Jonah in that I would like to see justice and judgment brought down upon such inhumane people; I would not want them evangelized. God's ways are truly not our ways.

That God is not like us in this regard is the point of such parables as that of the prodigal son (which might better be called the parable of the loving father).[5] In this parable the younger son indicates that he wishes his father were dead so he could have his portion of the inheritance. Any self-respecting Jewish father would have disowned such a son and thrown him out. But the father in the parable has long-range hopes of redemption. When the son returns, the father again does what no self-respecting Jewish father would have done — he runs to meet him! And when the older son insults the father by refusing to enter the house and demanding that the father come outside to meet him, the father again ignores the insult and goes out to seek a reconciliation. In the same way, our unusual God loves his children, including those whom we may consider particularly ungodly. The church is still struggling to understand this great theme of the Bible.

God's extraordinary love is coupled with a distributive justice that seeks the welfare of those most easily exploited and ignored in society (widows, orphans, and aliens). These two attributes combine to provide the powerful image of a God who desires the highest well-being of every person. The God revealed in the Bible shows grace to all people and desires all to participate in the redemptive process (1 Tim. 2:4). He does not have to show such grace. He does so freely. In light of these observations, I do not feel it unreasonable to conclude that the

5. For an insightful discussion of the importance of the cultural background for understanding this parable, see Kenneth Ewing Bailey, *Poet and Peasant: A Literary-Cultural Approach to the Parables in Luke* (Grand Rapids: William B. Eerdmans, 1976), pp. 158-206.

motivation for developing theories that explore universally accessible salvation in relation to the unevangelized rests solidly on the major themes of the Scriptures.[6]

There are some misunderstandings about universally accessible salvation and the wider hope that are worthy of attention. Some restrictivists have a difficult time grasping the difference between universally accessible salvation and universalism.[7] Other evangelicals ask whether one can believe in the "wider hope" without eventually slipping into universalism, whether hope for the unevangelized might not become a "Trojan horse for universalism within the orthodox tradition."[8] Obviously it is possible that some individuals who presently support universally accessible salvation might reject it in favor of universalism, just as some Lutherans might convert to Roman Catholicism. But the *position* of universally accessible salvation will never become universalism, just as consubstantiation will never become transubstantiation. Universally accessible salvation is not identical with universalism and never will be, just as a C sharp will never become an E flat, or pink become red.

Some critics argue that wider-hope theories are not explicitly taught in the Bible. I would respond in the first place by saying that I do not consider this a particularly telling criticism, since a number of the church's important doctrines (e.g., the hypostatic

6. There are those who reject this conclusion, however. For example, at the "Evangelical Affirmations" conference, J. I. Packer suggested that proponents of universally accessible salvation have been influenced more by the "American value of fairness" than by reliance on biblical evidence in adopting their position — though I am then not sure how he would account for the non-American affirmations of universally accessible salvation throughout church history.

7. Millard Erickson initially distinguishes between the two but then attempts to discredit certain views of universally accessible salvation (e.g., Clark Pinnock's) by subtly associating them with universalism (see "Is Universalistic Thinking Now Appearing among Evangelicals?" *United Evangelical Action* 48 [Sept. 1989]: 6).

8. Nigel Cameron, "Universalism and the Logic of Revelation," *Evangelical Review of Theology* 11 (Oct. 1987): 324.

union of Jesus' human and divine natures in one person) are not explicitly taught in the Bible. Wider-hope positions are theological explanations based on major themes and particular passages of Scripture. I think it can also be reasonably argued that the construction of a wider-hope position parallels Paul's attempt to extend salvation to the Gentiles even though there was little explicit teaching about that in the Old Testament.

Paul's understanding of Jesus as the glorified Messiah and the fact that there was no single Jewish view concerning the salvation of Gentiles drove him "to formulate a distinct theory of universal salvation which really has no precedent."[9] Paul argued against the Judaizers that Jesus was Lord and Savior of all and hence that the Gentiles were not to be excluded from God's love. Along the same lines, proponents of universally accessible salvation in Jesus argue against those who would automatically damn the unevangelized. Our situation is somewhat parallel to the Council of Jerusalem (Acts 15). At that historic meeting, the leaders of the apostolic church decided to allow Gentiles into the church with less restrictive requirements than had previously been accepted by the Jewish Christians. I believe we need to return to this more cosmopolitan and inclusive stance of the apostolic church, that we should boldly uphold universally accessible salvation. The specific contours of this belief remain an open question in the church. In subsequent chapters we will look at some of the views that have been adopted.

## Historical Bibliography

Before concluding this chapter, I would like to mention some of the individuals and confessions that have expressed support for the wider hope in general but have taken no stand on any

9. Barnabas Lindars, "The Old Testament and Universalism in Paul," *Bulletin of the John Rylands University Library* 69 (Spring 1987): 512-13.

particular theory covered in Part 3. This historical survey differs from those in other chapters in that it is not comprehensive and discusses creeds and confessions sometimes used against advocates of the wider hope.

### 1. Rabbinic Judaism, Arnobius, and the Athanasian Creed

Some Jewish rabbis entertained great hope for the salvation of many Gentiles. E. P. Sanders notes that "the view of R. Joshua that the righteous of all nations (that is, of all non-Jews) would inherit the world to come became the accepted view of the Synagogue" (*Paul and Palestinian Judaism* [Philadelphia: Fortress Press, 1977], p. 147; see also pp. 206-12). The belief became common among the rabbis that Gentiles would be admitted to heaven on the basis of the Noachic covenant (see *The Encyclopedia of Religion and Ethics*, 12 vols., ed. James Hastings [New York: Scribner's, 1908-26], 11: 147-48).

The fourth-century Christian writer Arnobius shared the belief in the wider hope but did not say how God's grace is made universal. While rejecting universalism (on the grounds that it violates human free will) and acknowledging that there is no certain answer regarding the unevangelized, he nevertheless asserts that "the Lord's compassion has been shown to them, too, and the divine kindness has been extended to all alike; they have been preserved, have been delivered, and have laid aside the lot and condition of mortality" (*Against the Heathen* 2.63, in *The Ante-Nicene Fathers*, vol. 6, ed. Alexander Roberts and James Donaldson [1887; reprint, Grand Rapids: William B. Eerdmans, 1971], p. 458).

Some writers cite the restrictive clauses of the Athanasian creed (written ca. A.D. 500) in opposition to the wider hope. The first three clauses read: "Whosoever will be saved: before all things it is necessary that he hold the Catholic Faith: which Faith except every one do keep whole and undefiled: without doubt he shall perish everlastingly. And the Catholic Faith is

this: That we worship one God in Trinity, and Trinity in Unity."
But it is worth noting that the exclusions in these clauses are
addressed pointedly to those heretics and schismatics within
Christendom who were modifying or rejecting the doctrine of
the Trinity. The creed was not addressed to the unevangelized.

## 2. The Reformation through the Nineteenth Century

Martin Luther is sometimes interpreted as believing that all
the unevangelized are damned. The Smalkald Articles in the
*Book of Concord,* for instance, state, "in these matters, which
concern the external, spoken Word, we must hold firmly to the
conviction that God gives no one his Spirit or grace except
through or with the external spoken Word which comes before"
(§8). But the context in which this statement appears is important. In the next sentence, Luther writes, "thus we shall be
protected from the enthusiasts — that is from the spiritualists."
Luther is addressing the problem of "the spiritualists," not the
question of the unevangelized. The same is true in his Larger
Catechism (nos. 45 and 56): he is discussing issues of Christendom and the papacy, not the unevangelized.

Pointing to selected passages from Luther's commentary
on Galatians, Bruce Demarest also gives the impression that
the Reformer held out no hope for the unevangelized (*General
Revelation* [Grand Rapids: Zondervan, 1982], pp. 45-49). It is
true that in his commentary on Galatians 3:2 and Romans 1:21
Luther says that all people have a natural knowledge of God
but instead of worshiping God they turn to idols. It is also true
that Luther considered preaching and the sacraments to be vital
means of grace.

Moreover, some scholars have inferred a restrictivist in-
clination on Luther's part from his disagreements with Erasmus
(see, e.g., *Inquisitio de Fide: A Colloquy by Desiderius Erasmus
Roterdamus,* 2d ed., ed. Craig R. Thompson [Hamden, Conn.:
Archon Books, 1975], pp. 111-13; and George Williams,

"Erasmus and the Reformers on Non-Christian Religions and *Salus Extra Ecclesiam,*" in *Action and Conviction in Early Modern Europe,* ed. Theodore Rabb and Jerrold Seigel [Princeton: Princeton University Press, 1969], pp. 337-53). Luther repudiated Erasmus's semipelagianism and accused him of holding ancient pagans such as Cicero in too high esteem (see *The Bondage of the Will,* trans. J. I. Packer and O. R. Johnston [Westwood, N.J.: Fleming H. Revell, 1957], pp. 121-22; and Luther's letter to Spalatin of 19 October 1516, in vol. 48 of *Luther's Works,* ed. Gottfried G. Krodel [Philadelphia: Fortress Press, 1963], pp. 23-26).

Luther followed the lead of Augustine in declaring that the virtues and learning of the ancient pagans fell short of Christian virtues and truth. He suggested that although they made the best of their free will, they came up short when compared to the gospel revelation. It is faith in Christ that creates godly virtue, he says, and a "virtuous" person without Christ does not merit grace.

In the end, however, none of this evidence convincingly establishes that Luther was a restrictivist. In none of the Luther material cited above does Luther specifically deal with the unevangelized. When he does refer to famous pagan writers such as Cicero (and he does so with high praise!), Luther never declares that they are damned in hell. And this despite the fact that Luther was not one to mince words!

Part of the difficulty in interpreting Luther arises from the fact that he was not concerned with providing a systematic formulation of his thought. In this way as in others, he was no Calvin. Luther's writings were occasional, and he sometimes contradicted himself, or at least failed to carry through the logical implications of certain of his beliefs. Such was the case when he spoke of the unevangelized. He seldom addressed the topic of the unevangelized, since he believed the great commission had been fulfilled and "no one has any longer such a universal apostolic command" (see Carl Braaten, *The Flaming Center* [Philadelphia: Fortress Press, 1977], p. 15). But on those admittedly rare occasions when Luther does specifically mention the unevangelized, he sounds quite hopeful. In his Romans commentary of 1515, for example, he says, "original sin God could forgive [the unevangelized] (even though they may not have recognized it and confessed it) on account of some act of humility towards God as the highest being that they know. Neither were they bound to the Gospel and to Christ as specifically recognized, as the Jews were not either. Or one can say that all people of this type have been given so much light and grace by an act of prevenient mercy of God as is sufficient for their salvation in their situation, as in the case of Job, Naaman, Jethro, and others" (*Luther's Works*, vol. 25, ed. Jaroslav Pelikan [St. Louis: Concordia Publishing, 1972], p. 181).

In a letter he wrote around the year 1522, Luther addressed the issue of whether a person who dies without faith can be saved. He is dogmatic in insisting that God saves no one apart from faith, but he adds, "it would be quite a different question whether God can impart faith to some in the hour of death or after death so that these people could be saved through faith. Who would doubt God's ability to do that? No one, however, can prove that he does do this." In other words, if any are saved in this way, they are still saved by faith. "Otherwise every sermon, the gospel, and faith would be vain." In this letter Luther openly rejects universalism, but his major concern is to prohibit idle speculation on difficult questions by those who are spiritually immature (see *Luther's Works*, vol. 45, ed. Helmut Lehmann [Philadelphia: Fortress Press, 1968], pp. 51-55).

In the end, I think it fair to conclude that Luther was at least open to the question of the salvation of the unevangelized. It is less clear whether he could be considered an advocate of universally accessible salvation. It is worth noting, however, that in the letter mentioned above, Luther refers to 1 Timothy 2:4 and says it is God's will that all be saved. Moreover, on one occasion "Luther went so far as to consign Cicero to his place in paradise" (see H. G. Haile, *Luther: An Experiment in Biography* [New York: Doubleday, 1980], p. 326; see also Philip Watson, *Let God Be God*

[New York: Epworth Press, 1947], p. 93). And he sometimes flirted with the idea that the preaching of Christ in hell effected the salvation of some unevangelized (see *The Encyclopedia of Religion and Ethics*, 4: 656; and *The Evangelical Dictionary of Theology*, ed. Walter Elwell [Grand Rapids, Baker Book, 1984], p. 314). At the very least, then, I think it implausible to contend that Luther opposed the wider hope.

Scholars have suggested that several Reformed confessions can be interpreted as opposing the wider hope, but, as in the case of the Athanasian Creed, a consideration of the audience to whom these documents are addressed is important for understanding their intent in this regard. It is true that none of these confessions can be said to support the wider hope, but in my opinion it is equally true that none of them specifically rules it out.

The Second Helvetic Confession of 1566 became, on the issue of salvation outside the church, the model that other Reformed confessions followed. Section 17 states that "none can live before God who do not communicate with the true Church of God, but separate themselves from the same. For as without the ark of Noah there was no escaping . . . without Christ, who in the church offers himself to be enjoyed of the elect, there can be no certain salvation." This clause was specifically addressed to those who "separate" from the "true" church, not to the unevangelized. The very next paragraph, in fact, indicates that this statement should not be interpreted as suggesting that God cannot save those who are outside the "true" church. "For we know that God had some friends in the world that were not of the commonwealth of Israel." Moreover, elsewhere in the confession the distinction is made between the "usual" and unusual means of divine illumination. The normal means is human preaching of Christ, but "we know . . . that God can illuminate whom and when he will, even without the external ministry" (1.7).

Article 18 of the Thirty-Nine Articles of the Church of England (1571) states, "they also are to be had accursed, that presume to say, that every man shall be saved by the law or sect which he professeth, so that he be diligent to frame his life according to that law, and the light of nature. For Holy Scripture doth set out unto us only the name of Jesus Christ, whereby men must be saved." Although this anathema is sometimes assumed to be ruling out all hope for the unevangelized, it does not in fact do so. The article begins with a rejection of the specific teaching of certain individuals that all religions lead to salvation. It is almost certainly directed against specific Anabaptists who were teaching that rejection of Jesus as Savior would not result in damnation (see Edgar Gibson, *The Thirty-Nine Articles of the Church of England* [London: Methuen, 1898], pp. 489-90). Furthermore, it could also be directed against the early forms of Deism based solely on natural religion (see E. H. Plumptre, *The Spirits in Prison* [London: Ibister, 1898], pp. 185-87).

The Westminster Confession takes a similar tack. "Elect infants, dying in infancy, are regenerated and saved by Christ through the Spirit, who worketh when, where, and how he pleaseth. So also are all other elect persons, who are incapable of being outwardly called by the ministry of the Word" (10.3). This allows for the salvation of some unevangelized, but on the other hand, the writers do specifically rule out the idea that "people not professing the Christian religion, be saved in any other way whatsoever, be they never so diligent to frame their lives according to the light of nature and the law of that religion they do profess" (10.4). Again, however, what is being opposed here is the belief that all religions are valid ways of approaching God.

William Shedd found enough latitude in the wording in these confessions to allow for an affirmation of the wider hope; he even went so far as to claim that Reformed theologians in the late nineteenth century generally interpreted them as hopeful concerning the salvation of the unevangelized (see *Dogmatic Theology*, 3 vols. [New York: Scribner's, 1888-94], 2: 706-8). The Church of Scotland's Declaratory Act of 1879 says that "while none are saved except through the mediation of Christ . . . it is not required to be held that . . . God may not extend his grace to any who are without the pale of ordinary means, as it may seem good in his sight" (§4). For other figures of this era who supported the wider hope, see Plumptre, *The Spirits in Prison*, chapter 2.

### 3. The Twentieth Century

The Anglican National Congress held in Nottingham, England, in 1977 wrestled with this issue, and it is clear from the statement they produced that British evangelicals are divided on it. Under the heading "salvation" it reads, "though the Bible excludes the hope of universal salvation, it envisages the presence in glory of a countless multitude of the redeemed. We are not fully agreed, however, as to the ultimate extent of salvation. . . . Jesus Christ is the only name given by God by which Man must be saved. Therefore, if there are people who are saved without hearing the name of Christ, they are saved only on the basis of his work." This statement expressly rules out universalism and a "second chance" after death for those who have heard the gospel, but it does not rule out the possibility of evangelization after death for the unevangelized (see *The Nottingham Statement* [Cover Wallop, Hampshire: BAS Printers, 1977], p. 15).

The Lausanne Covenant, influential in evangelical circles, does not rule out all wider hope views even though it does reject the same two ideas rejected in the Reformed confessions surveyed above. "We recognize that all men have some knowledge of God through his general revelation in nature. But we deny that this can save, for men suppress the truth by their unrighteousness. We also reject as derogatory to Christ and the gospel every kind of syncretism and dialogue which implies that Christ speaks equally through all religions and ideologies" (§3). The signers of the covenant all affirmed the finality of Christ but could not agree regarding the fate of the unevangelized (see Colin Chapman, "The Challenge of Other Religions," *World Evangelization* [Jan. 1990]: 17).

A recent attempt by some evangelicals at a statement concerning the unevangelized also ended in disagreement. The "Evangelical Affirmations" were produced by a conference at Trinity Evangelical Divinity School in May 1989 (see *Evangelical Affirmations*, ed. Kenneth Kantzer and Carl Henry [Grand Rapids: Academie, 1990], pp. 27-38). The statement on the person of Christ reads as follows: "without Christ and the biblical gospel, sinful humanity is without salvation and is left to create its own 'gospels'" (§1). This section is directed against both radical pluralists and cults. Section 9 addresses the issue of the unevangelized more directly: "we affirm that only through the work of Christ can any person be saved and resurrected to live with God forever. Unbelievers will be separated eternally from God. Concern for evangelism should not be compromised by any illusion that all will be finally saved (universalism)." Though this section affirms the particularity of Christ and rejects universalism, it does not rule out universally accessible salvation. The issue was discussed, but the conferees could not agree on the issue.

John R. W. Stott, a major voice in contemporary evangelicalism, recently came out in favor of the wider hope. He refuses, however, to state *how* the unevangelized may be saved, and that is why I am mentioning him here. He writes, "I have never been able to conjure up (as some great Evangelical missionaries have) the appalling vision of the millions who are not only perishing but will inevitably perish. On the other hand . . . I am not and cannot be a universalist. Between these extremes I cherish the hope that the majority of the human race will be saved. And I have a solid biblical basis for this belief" (see David Edwards and John R. W. Stott, *Evangelical Essentials: A Liberal-Evangelical Dialogue* [Downers Grove, Ill.: InterVarsity Press, 1988], p. 327). David Edwards had accused the Lausanne Covenant of ruling out hope for the unevangelized, but Stott, one of the principal authors of the Covenant, insists that it does not. He surveys numerous wider-hope theories, expressing his openness to some and his disinclination to accept others. Though attracted to the view that salvation may be possible apart from evangelization (outlined in Chap. 7 herein), he says the most Christian stance is to acknowledge that we cannot know the *method* God will use in saving most of the human race.

### 4. Extra Ecclesiam Nulla Salus

Before leaving this historical survey, mention should be made of the well-known formula *extra ecclesiam nulla salus* ("outside the church there is no salvation"). The formula is often cited in support of the argument that the church has traditionally believed that all unevangelized are damned. Such an interpretation, however, will not withstand historical investigation. The phrase was first used by Origen and later by Cyprian, neither of whom used it in connection with the unevangelized but rather in reference to separatists or "adulterers" who had forsaken the mother church or who had departed from the ark of salvation.

There have been two primary interpretations of the phrase. The first, and strictest, asserts that unless one is a formal member of the Roman Catholic Church one cannot be saved. After the time of Constantine, a noticeable shift occurred in the church with respect to the inclusion or exclusion of differing viewpoints. The concern for the unity of the Empire led to a corresponding concern for the unity of the church. But whereas the unity had previously been viewed primarily as inward and relational, it now came to be viewed primarily in terms of conformity to specific creeds and other tests that could be publicly verified and controlled. The imperial state church became an important agency for maintaining imperial political control (see Richard Drummond, *Toward a New Age in Christian Theology* [Maryknoll, N.Y.: Orbis Books, 1985], p. 41). Augustine's restrictivism was a natural outgrowth of the new emphasis on external tests for unity. Augustine's pupil Fulgentius of Ruspe went even further than his teacher, defining the *extra ecclesiam* in such a way as to place all pagans, Jews, schismatics, and all infants (even the unborn) who die without baptism outside the visible church and hence under sentence of eternal punishment. The Fourth Lateran Council in 1215 and Pope Boniface VIII in his bull *Unam Sanctam* followed these restrictivist lines. The Council of Florence (1438-45) followed Fulgentius quite explicitly: "those not living within the Catholic Church, not only pagans, but also Jews, heretics, and schismatics cannot become participants in eternal life, but will depart 'into everlasting fire which was prepared for the devil and his angels,' unless before the end of life the same have been added to the flock" (see Henry Denzinger, *The Sources of Catholic Dogma* [St. Louis: B. Herder, 1957], p. 230).

Alongside the restrictivist definition there existed the second interpretation, which is in accordance with the church's magisterium. It too holds that actual membership in the Catholic Church is necessary for salvation, but this does not entail that all the unevangelized are damned, since allowances are made for the possibility that individuals might be invisible or implicit members of the true church. The *New Catholic Encyclopedia* (15 vols. [Washington: Catholic University of America Press, 1967]) states that "those . . . who through invincible ignorance are excluded from such membership can nevertheless be saved if they have supernatural faith and are in the state of sanctifying grace. . . . Although juridically speaking they are 'outside' *(extra)* the Catholic church and formally not its members, yet in a vital sense they are 'inside' *(intra)* . . . invisible members of the Catholic church" (5: 768).

This more inclusive understanding of the scope of God's grace developed to a large extent during the Middle Ages. From Augustine came the idea that grace is dispensed by the church through the sacraments. From Prosper of Aquitaine came the assertion that God genuinely desires the salvation of all people. To reconcile these two ideas, theologians developed the ideas of the "baptism of desire" and "implicit faith": God would consider people baptized and members of the true church even if they had never heard of Jesus Christ, so long as they responded in faith to his grace as it was manifested to them. To this end, proponents of this view maintained that an act of faith in response to God's grace is essential for salvation. In this way, they affirmed both universally accessible salvation and the necessity of membership in the church. After surveying the views of several medieval theologians on both sides of the issue, Craig Thompson concludes that, "in the judgment of some of the greatest medieval theologians, acceptance of 'Nulla salus extra Ecclesiam' need not be inconsistent with confidence that a Socrates could be saved" (see *Inquisitio de Fide: A Colloquy by Desiderius Erasmus Roterdamus*, 2d ed., ed. Craig R. Thompson [Hamden, Conn.: Archon Books, 1975], p. 110). Nevertheless, the ambiguity of the phrase continued to spawn debate between those who claimed hope for the "infidels" and those who did not.

Long before Vatican I (1869), the majority of Roman Catholic scholars taught a more lenient position. At Vatican I, as well as in standard Catholic theology texts of the period, there were significant discussions of the *extra ecclesiam*, and the wider-hope interpretation was the most popular (see R. P. Greenwood, "Extra Ecclesiam Nulla Salus," *Theology* 76 [Aug. 1973]: 417-18). The encyclical *Mystici Corporis* of Pope Pius XII (1943) and a letter of the Holy Office to the Archbishop of Boston (1949) concerning a priest who taught the stricter interpretation of the phrase set the stage for the adoption of a wider-hope position at Vatican II (1962-65).

For helpful studies of the history and interpretation of the phrase, see Greenwood's article "Extra Ecclesiam Nulla Salus." Joseph Fenton gives a more restrictive interpretation on the grounds that he does not want the phrase emptied of meaning, but he does not rule out the wider hope; see *The Catholic Church and Salvation: In the Light of Recent Pronouncements by the Holy See* (Westminster, Md.: Newman, 1958). John King does a masterly job of recounting the various interpretations within their historical contexts in *The Necessity of the Church for Salvation in Selected Theological Writings of the Past Century* (Washington: Catholic University of America Press, 1960). Calvin Eichhorst reviews the positions of Fenton, Hans Küng, and Karl Rahner in "From Outside the Church to Inside: Toward a Triumph of Grace in Catholicism," *Dialogue* 12 (Summer 1973): 190-96. Robert Wilken discusses both Catholic and Protestant interpretations in "The Making of a Phrase," *Dialogue* 12 (Summer 1973): 174-81. And Hans Küng argues that the phrase should be rejected since it has been emptied of meaning; see *The Church* (New York: Doubleday, 1976), pp. 403-11.

# CHAPTER FIVE

## *Universal Evangelization — before Death*

In this chapter I survey three variations of the view that salvation is universally accessible through evangelization before death. The first view is that God sees to it that all individuals who seek him will in fact receive the gospel. The second view is that all people have an evangelistic encounter with Christ at the moment of death. The third view is that God will judge the unevangelized on the basis of how they would have responded had they heard the gospel.

These three views have two control beliefs in common. First, they maintain that in order to be saved, people must be evangelized and accept the gospel or at least be judged by God on the basis of how they would have responded had they heard. There is no salvation apart from a response to the preaching of the cross. Second, they agree that a person's final destiny is sealed at death. There is no opportunity to accept Christ after death.

There are also two points on which these views do not agree. Some proponents of the views maintain that there is no salvation apart from *human* messengers, while others hold that God may use angels or direct illumination for evangelization. There is also disagreement about whether every single individual is actually evangelized or whether only the opportunity for universal evangelization exists. Those who say that only the opportunity exists believe that those who are never presented with the gospel did not desire to hear it, that if they had desired it, God would have made certain that they had received it.


## God Will Send the Message

The first view we will be looking at is that God sees to it that all unevangelized persons who seek him will, in one way or another, be exposed to the gospel of Christ so they can make a decision. The idea that God would send the message to the unevangelized did not become popular until the later Middle Ages. The guiding principle was that no one would be damned to hell without an opportunity for salvation. Since the medieval Scholastics believed that most of the world had been evangelized, the question arose concerning the fate of those few who yet remained outside the sphere of human preaching. Would such people be damned without hearing about Christ? The great medieval theologian Thomas Aquinas said No. God will send the message of the gospel to them. No one is damned without the opportunity of being saved.

Proponents of this view believe that God ensures that the gospel is directed to those who are searching for the truth but that these individuals are not saved until they hear and believe the word of Christ. Some proponents of this view believe that God sends the message only through human agents, while others believe that God may send it through dreams or angels. Furthermore, some proponents of this position claim that God universally sends the gospel message to every unevangelized person, while others believe that only the opportunity of receiving the message is universal. The former believe that all people are actually evangelized with the gospel, while the latter do not.

## Key Biblical Texts

The book of Hebrews informs us that whoever would draw near to God "must believe that He is, and that He is a rewarder of those who seek Him" (11:6). God is pleased with such people because they exercise faith in him. In fact, God searches for those people who will worship him (John 4:23). When he senses a person searching for him, he sends the gospel message by one means or another. Several examples from biblical history are usually cited in support of this claim. The Ethiopian eunuch was seeking God, so God sent Philip to him to proclaim the word of Christ (Acts 8). In Acts 10 we read that the Roman centurion Cornelius was searching for the true God, so God used a vision to direct him to send for the apostle Peter. Peter came and proclaimed Christ to him. Philip and Peter are examples of human preachers used by God. Some scholars point to the stories of Abimelech (Gen. 20), Nebuchadnezzar (Dan. 2), and Ananias (Acts 9:10) in support of the assertion that God also uses dreams, visions, and angels to send his message. And others contend that God may also use the Bible itself, apart from any preacher, for evangelism.

## Theological Considerations

There are four closely related theological ideas that support this position.

1. *General revelation is insufficient as a vehicle for salvation.* Norman L. Geisler asserts that "natural revelation is sufficient only to reveal the moral standard for man, but . . . it is not sufficient for man's salvation."[1] Though general revelation is given *to* all people, say the proponents of this view, it cannot bring about salvation.

1. Geisler, *Options in Contemporary Christian Ethics* (Grand Rapids: Baker Book House, 1981), p. 32.

2. *Explicit knowledge of Christ is necessary for salvation.* Special revelation is given *for* all people in order to bring about reconciliation with God. Having cited John 3:18, Robertson McQuilken argues that "it is those who believe *on Christ* — not simply those who, through their encounter with creation and their own innate moral judgment, believe in a righteous creator — who receive eternal life."[2] Thomas Aquinas echoed these sentiments when he said that everyone since the time of the incarnation must "believe explicitly the general articles, such as that God is triune, that the Son of God was made flesh, died, and rose from the dead."[3] If a person responds to the light he or she has, God will send the message so the individual can believe on Christ and be saved.

There is disagreement, however, regarding how the message of Christ is sent. McQuilken says, "of course, [God's] method for sending this light is a human messenger."[4] Others hold that while human preachers appear to be God's ordinary means for evangelism, he also uses nonhuman agents as messengers — albeit rarely. J. Oliver Buswell Jr. approvingly quotes the Leiden *Synopsis* (1581) as follows: "God does not always supply the two methods of calling possible to himself (i.e. outward and inward calling), but calls some to him only by the inner light and leading of the Holy Spirit without the ministry of his outward Word. This method of calling is of course *per se* sufficient for salvation, but very rare, extraordinary, and unknown to us."[5]

Aquinas took a much more generous view. He believed

2. McQuilken, *The Great Omission* (Grand Rapids: Baker Book, 1984), p. 44.

3. Aquinas, *The Disputed Questions on Truth*, vol. 2, trans. James McGlynn (Chicago: Henry Regnery, 1953), p. 262 (q.14, a.11). See also *Summa Theologica*, II, 2, q.2, a.7; and *In Three Sentences*, dist. 25, q.2, a.2. Thomas also says that baptism is absolutely necessary for salvation (*ST,* III, q.65, a.4) but that this requirement can be satisfied *in voto* (through baptism by desire).

4. McQuilken, *The Great Omission*, p. 49.

5. Buswell, *A Systematic Theology of the Christian Religion*, vol. 2 (Grand Rapids: Zondervan, 1963), p. 161.

the world had been thoroughly evangelized by his day and that there were only a handful of people in the world who remained unevangelized, those "brought up in the forest or among wild beasts."[6] For such people, he wrote, "it pertains to divine providence to furnish everyone with what is necessary for salvation, provided that on his part there is no hindrance. Thus, if someone so brought up followed the direction of natural reason in seeking good and avoiding evil, we must most certainly hold that God would either reveal to him through the internal inspiration what had to be believed, or would send some preacher of the faith to him as he sent Peter to Cornelius (Acts 10:20)."[7]

Aquinas was here following the lead of his famous teacher, Albert the Great, who claimed that this was the common view of his day.[8] Albert had written that "theologians in general teach that it is impossible that a man, who performs adequately all in his power to do to prepare himself, should not receive a revelation from God, or instruction from men who have been themselves inspired, or some sign of a Mediator. And I believe that to be true because of the Providence of God, Who prepares equally His benefits for all, and presents them to all, provided that we be ready to receive them."[9]

The sixteenth-century Dutch theologian Jacobus Arminius followed the medieval Scholastics on this point. He asked, "What peril or error can there be in any man saying, 'God converts great numbers of persons, (that is, *very many*), by the internal revelation of the Holy Spirit or by the ministry of angels'; provided it be at the same time stated, that no one is converted except by this very word."[10]

6. Aquinas, *The Disputed Questions on Truth*, q.14, a.11.

7. Aquinas, *The Disputed Questions on Truth*, q.14, a.11.

8. See T. P. Dunning, "Langland and the Salvation of the Heathen," *Medium Aevum* 12 (1943): 49.

9. Cited by Dunning in "Langland and the Salvation of the Heathen," p. 49.

10. Arminius, *The Writings of James Arminius*, 3 vols., trans. James Nichols (Grand Rapids: Baker Book House, 1956), 1: 331.

3. *No one seeks God apart from the influence of grace.* Arminius believed that no human could believe the truth or do good (seek God) unaided by divine grace.[11] He argued that when people confess themselves to be in great need, it is evidence that God has already shown grace and will grant further grace to assist them toward salvation. Buswell believed that this work of the Holy Spirit is universal. "By its universality I mean that, although I cannot cogently prove it from the Scripture, I postulate that the convicting work of the Holy Spirit is absolutely universal to the entire human race in all ages and in all areas."[12] He maintained that the convicting work of the Spirit is sufficient to bring about the search for God and that God will provide what is needed for salvation once a person begins looking for him. "To him who responds," says McQuilken, "more light will be given."[13] If people seek God by responding to the light they have and the prompting of the Holy Spirit, God will send the message of Christ to them. If no such message is sent, it is proof that they were not seeking God. If people reject the revelation they have, then damnation rests solely on their shoulders.

4. *No one receives an opportunity for evangelism after death.* All proponents of this view affirm that the ultimate destiny of the individual is fixed at death. Once people are in hell, they are always in hell. Aquinas, for instance, taught that the medieval practice of praying for the dead was pointless, that there could be no effective intercession for those in hell.[14]

### A Leading Defender: Thomas Aquinas

As we have seen, Aquinas believed that there was only a handful of people who remained unevangelized in his day, and con-

11. See *The Writings of James Arminius*, 1: 322-27.
12. Buswell, *Systematic Theology*, 2: 160.
13. McQuilken, *The Great Omission*, p. 47.
14. Aquinas, *ST,* supplement to the third part, q.71, a.5.

sequently he did not give a great deal of attention to formulating a view concerning their destiny. Nevertheless, his ideas on the subject are clear enough to give us a sense of his position.[15]

Several control beliefs common to the Middle Ages shaped Aquinas's views regarding the unevangelized (and the views of many Catholics and Protestants after him).[16] He believed that all people are condemned because of both original sin and (if they live long enough) actual sin.[17] He also held that an "act of faith" is a necessary condition of salvation for adults.[18] Third, he maintained that all who are damned to hell are damned of their own fault, that no one who seeks God will fail to receive the opportunity for salvation.[19] But this opportunity must include supernatural revelation. Aquinas makes a significant distinction between the laity and the clergy in this regard. He grants lay believers a great margin of error concerning the doctrines they must believe for salvation. He also puts Gentiles who lived before the time of Christ in the category of the laity, suggesting that people who lived before the incarnation could be saved only if they had some sort of vague knowledge of God's desire to save them. Laypeople living after the incarnation, on the other hand, must believe in Jesus Christ and the Trinity in order to be saved, although their understanding of these doctrines does not have to be as refined as that of the clergy.[20] Fourth, although baptism is necessary for salvation, the "baptism by desire" may suffice. Fifth, Aquinas believed that God desires that all people be saved but that not all will

15. Helpful studies of Aquinas on the unevangelized may be found in Ricardo Lombardi, *The Salvation of the Unbeliever,* trans. Dorothy White (Westminster, Md.: Newman, 1956); and Ladislaus Boros, *The Mystery of Death,* trans. Gregory Bainbridge (New York: Herder & Herder, 1965).

16. Dunning discusses four of the control beliefs in the following list; see "Langland and the Salvation of the Heathen," pp. 46-47.

17. Aquinas, *ST,* III, q.52, a.5.

18. Aquinas, *ST,* III, q.68, a.1; and *In Three Sentences,* dist. 25, q.2, a.1.

19. Aquinas, *Disputed Questions,* q.14, a.11.

20. Aquinas, *ST,* II, 2, q.2, aa.3-8.

be saved. Finally, he ruled out any notion of an opportunity for repentance after death. He specifically asserted that when Christ descended into hell, he did not effect the release of any souls there.[21] A person's destiny is sealed at death.

On the basis of these control beliefs, Aquinas explains how the "unevangelized" before and after the incarnation were saved. He concedes that some preincarnation Gentiles may have been saved without having received illumination regarding the coming Messiah. "If, however, some were saved without receiving any revelation, they were not saved without faith in a Mediator, for though they did not believe in him explicitly, they did, nevertheless, have implicit faith through believing in divine providence, since they believed God would deliver mankind."[22] Some scholars have taken this statement as an indication that Aquinas believed that the postincarnation unevangelized can be saved without direct revelation from God. There are, however, two reasons to reject such an interpretation. First, although he was willing to concede that some preincarnation Gentiles might have been saved apart from direct revelation, Aquinas says, "it is likely that the mystery of our redemption was revealed to many Gentiles before Christ's coming, as is clear from the Sibylline prophecies."[23] That is to say, he believed that most preincarnation Gentiles were informed of the mystery of Christ through special revelation provided by angels.[24] Second, although he grants that some postincarnation people may attain baptism and church membership only "implicitly," Aquinas insists that such people must have "explicit faith" in Christ and the Trinity. That is to say, he believed that God will send the message of Christ to anyone who responds to his prevenient grace.

21. Aquinas, *ST,* III, q.52, a.6.
22. Aquinas, *ST,* II, 2, q.2, a.7.
23. Aquinas, *Disputed Questions*, q.14, a.11; and see *ST,* II, 2, q.2, a.7.
24. Aquinas, *ST,* I, 2, q.98, a.5. Here Aquinas acknowledges his indebtedness to Pseudo-Dionysius's *Celestial Hierarchy* 9.4.

## Historical Bibliography

### 1. Middle Ages through the Reformation

According to T. P. Dunning, most of the theologians from the twelfth through the fifteenth centuries endorsed the concept of the wider hope through universal sending of the message (see "Langland and the Salvation of the Heathen," *Medium Aevum* 12 [1943]: 45-54).[25] Harking back to Augustine, Hugh of St. Victor and St. Bernard set about to determine the absolute minimum of truths that the act of faith must embrace. They agreed that a person has to believe in God's existence and providence (Heb. 11:6) and have an implicit faith in a mediator (as Abraham did, John 8:56) in order to be saved. Alexander of Hales (1180-1245) sums up the position of many medieval theologians when he says of an unevangelized person that "if he does what is within his power, the Lord will enlighten him with a secret inspiration, by means of an angel or a man." This became the formula for many of the medieval Scholastics, including Peter Lombard, Albert the Great, St. Bonaventure, Giles of Rome, Aquinas, the poet William Langland, Duns Scotus, Surandus, Denis the Carthusian, Thomas of Strasbourg, St. Bernardine of Siena, Gabriel Biel, and Francisco Suarez (see Dunning, "Langland and the Salvation of the Heathen," pp. 45-54; Ralph Turner, "*Descendit ad Inferos:* Medieval Views on Christ's Descent into Hell, and the Salvation of the Ancient Just," *Journal of the History of Ideas* 27 [1966]: 173-94; and Ricardo Lombardi, *The Salvation of the Unbeliever*, trans.

---

25. It should be noted that Dunning does not address the issue of the distinction between people living prior to and after the incarnation, and hence in discussing the positions of a number of medieval theologians he does not specify whether they believed in a universal sending of the message to the postincarnation unevangelized. He does assert that Augustine endorsed such a sending, but he is wrong on this point. Augustine only went so far as to say that God could grant divine illumination to anyone he wanted (see Chap. 2 herein).

Dorothy White [Westminster, Md.: Newman, 1956], p. 232). Langland does seem to have leaned toward inclusivism, however (see his *Piers the Plowman*, trans. J. F. Goodridge [Baltimore: Penguin Books, 1966], pp. 124, 149-50).

Dante's *Divine Comedy* contains much in the way of summation concerning both medieval theology and Greek and Roman learning. His views on the unevangelized are no different. Basically his writing reflects the dominant view of the day, that salvation is universally accessible. But interpretation of this work is complicated by the fact that it is written as allegory: one must be careful about pressing the imagery too far. Moreover, some church authorities were somewhat suspicious of his high esteem for ancient pagan learning, and this may have prevented him from saying everything he truly believed about the ancients (see the introduction by Archibald MacAllister to *The Inferno*, trans. John Ciardi [New York: Mentor, 1954], XIV-XXI; all subsequent citations are from this translation).

In *The Inferno* Dante describes the outermost circle of hell where there is "untormented sadness" (no bliss, but no torment either). Here we find "limbo," containing infants who died unbaptized and without knowledge of the Trinity. Also present in this limbo are many of the "noble pagans" such as Virgil, Homer, Ovid, Hector, Socrates, Plato, Aristotle, Euclid, and Averrhoes (Canto 4). Dante asks his guide through hell if any have ever left hell for paradise. He is told that when Jesus descended into hell he removed the saints from Old Testament times such as Adam, Abel, Abraham, and David. They were delivered because they believed the special revelation about the coming Messiah. When he moves on to survey purgatory, which is unlike hell in that all in purgatory ultimately enter heaven, he makes an interesting remark about Cato of Utica, who killed himself rather than lose his freedom. He was originally in Limbo but was summoned from that domain of hell to be guardian of purgatory (Canto 1). It is not clear, however, whether Cato eventually makes it to heaven (see Ciardi's *The Purgatorio*, pp. 37-38).

In *The Paradiso* (Canto 19) Dante directly addresses the question of God's justice in relation to the unevangelized.

> A man is born in sight
> of Indus' water, and there is none there
> to speak of Christ, and none to read or write.
>
> . . . He dies unbaptized and cannot receive
> the saving faith. What justice is it damns him?
> Is it his fault that he does not believe?

Dante's guide responds:

> To this high empery
> none ever rose but through belief in Christ,
> either before or after his agony.

Dante thus asserts that explicit knowledge of Christ is necessary for the salvation of those who have lived both before and after the incarnation. Yet this principle does not entail that all the unevangelized are damned, for in Canto 20 he places some noble pagans in heaven! He writes of Ripheus the Trojan who, according to Dante, received a vision of Christ a millennium before the incarnation. God apparently was willing to send the message to him. He also tells of Trajan, an unevangelized individual who was commonly assumed by Dante's contemporaries to have been saved. Legend had it that Pope Gregory I had prayed so fervently for Trajan that God pardoned him. In his account of the story, Dante indicates that Trajan was removed from hell and restored to his body long enough to be converted to Christ. It is interesting to note, however, that the author of *The Golden Legend* gives a more orthodox account of Trajan's salvation. (On this and the question of why only these two "noble heathen" are mentioned by Dante as being saved, see Dunning's "Langland and the Salvation of the Heathen," pp. 53-54.)

Dante concludes his discussion of salvation for the unevangelized by saying,

Mortals, be slow to judge! Not even we
who look on God in heaven know, as yet,
how many he will choose for ecstasy.

Jacobus Arminius (1560-1609) acknowledges his indebtedness to the medieval Scholastics on this issue. He was also
aware of the controversy Zwingli created by assigning pagans
such as Socrates places in heaven. Arminius says that if any
such pagans are in heaven, then they "must have been instructed
concerning their salvation by the Holy Ghost or by angels,"
since there is little chance they ever saw the Scriptures. Arminius believed many people were converted in this way (see
*The Writings of James Arminius*, 3 vols., trans. James Nichols
[Grand Rapids: Baker Book House, 1956], 1: 322-32).

## 2. The Twentieth Century

In his book *The Great Omission* (Grand Rapids: Baker Book,
1984), Robertson McQuilken responds to what he characterizes
as the five major excuses people give for not getting involved
in world evangelization. One of these, he says, is that people
believe there must be a way of salvation other than hearing and
receiving Christ before death. He proceeds to survey and reject
various wider-hope theories. Although he does affirm universally accessible salvation, he probably would not welcome being
classified as a proponent of the wider hope. I am placing him
in this category because he says that if people seek God, God
will send the message to them by *human* agents. He interprets
the fact that not many missionaries have experiences such as
Philip's in the New Testament as evidence that on the whole
people do not seek God. This leads to a curious tension, if not
an inconsistency, in his position.

McQuilken declares that as many as two hundred million
nonevangelicals may have saving faith, but that still leaves, by
his estimate, ninety percent of the human race destined for hell
(p. 40). He believes that the unevangelized will be condemned

for rejecting the revelation they have. So, although he grants that God may send the message, he does not believe this happens very often. On the face of it, it would seem that he should be classified as something of a restrictivist who believes that the unevangelized are damned except in extremely rare instances. But McQuilken's position is further obscured by another statement he makes on this issue. "How does one respond in a Japanese village when a new convert inquires, 'What about my ancestors?'" he asks. "My response is simple: I am not the judge. 'Will not the judge of all the earth do right?' (Gen. 18:25)" (pp. 49-50). What are we to make of this curious citation of Genesis 18:25, a text commonly interpreted as offering hope for the unevangelized? Perhaps it is simply a matter of his desiring, as a missionary, to provide an answer that sounds hopeful, in order not to hinder the reception of the gospel message. Nevertheless, it seems to me to be in clear contradiction of his stated position, which is that all must hear the gospel from human agents or be forever lost.

Other advocates of universally accessible salvation through universal sending include J. Oliver Buswell Jr. (*A Systematic Theology of the Christian Religion,* vol. 2 [Grand Rapids: Zondervan, 1963], pp. 158-65), Norman Geisler (*Options in Contemporary Christian Ethics* [Grand Rapids: Baker Book House, 1981], p. 32), Wesley Gustafson ("The Heathen — Damned?" *HIS,* March 1951, pp. 6-9), Earl Radmacher (*Can Man Be Saved by Light of Nature?* [San Bernardino: Campus Crusade for Christ International, n.d.], audiocassette), Robert Lightner (*Heaven for Those Who Can't Believe* [Schaumburg, Ill.: Regular Baptist Press, 1977], p. 44), and David Dewitt (*Answering the Tough Ones* [Chicago: Moody Press, 1980], pp. 62-65). This is also the view of some Thomistic Roman Catholics. Ricardo Lombardi, writing shortly before Vatican II, suggested that some form of special revelation is necessary for salvation. He argued that God will either send the message by internal illumination or that enough of the "original revelation" given by God and dispersed throughout the world's peoples, however fragmentary and distorted, is sufficient for salvation (*The Salvation of the Unbeliever* [Westminster, Md.: Newman, 1956]).

## Universal Opportunity at Death

The idea that the unevangelized will be given an opportunity to be saved at the moment of death is primarily Roman Catholic. Known as the "final option" theory, it became well known in the late nineteenth century and still has adherents today.[26] Though Vatican II did not adopt this position, it is still tenable in the Roman Catholic community.

In essence, proponents of the final option theory hold that *all* people will have an encounter with Jesus Christ at the moment of death and have an opportunity to exercise saving faith in him. Several ideas distinguish this view. First, it entails absolute universal evangelization: every single individual hears about the work of Christ, even those who are already Christians. Second, this evangelistic encounter occurs at the moment of death, when the soul is separating from the body — not after death, when the person's destiny is presumed to be sealed. Proponents of the theory maintain that the moment the soul is being separated from the body is the first time in an individual's existence that he or she has the ability to make a fully free personal act. This fully free act is similar to the decision the angels made — in full knowledge of the truth, unhindered by any constraints. The soul is fully awake and aware of the seriousness of the situation. At this moment the soul ceases to

26. No less a light than John Cardinal Henry Newman endorsed the final-option theory; see Alan Fairhurst, "Death and Destiny," *The Churchman* 95 (1981): 324n.75. Some contemporary Catholics reject Karl Rahner's "anonymous Christianity" in favor of the final-option theory on the grounds that the latter conforms better to traditional Catholic doctrine; see Joseph NiNoia, "The Universality of Salvation and the Diversity of Religious Aims," *World Mission* 32 (Winter 1981-82): 4-15.

act in a changeable way and acts rather with an unchangeable intent toward a particular end. Hence, the decision made at this moment is irreversible. The final distinguishing characteristic is that prior choices we have made deeply influence but do not determine our final decision. We may choose to confirm the way we have lived or we may reject it.[27]

## *Theological Considerations*

Proponents of this view readily admit that it is not found in Scripture. They argue that it is a theological hypothesis that does the best job of accommodating a number of the Roman Catholic Church's traditional doctrines, including the following:

1. A person's destiny is sealed at death (following Tertullian and Cyprian), so there is no opportunity after death for conversion.
2. Jesus Christ is the only Savior, and there is no saving faith apart from knowledge of Jesus' life and work and the Trinity.
3. Salvation is defined as personal fellowship with Jesus Christ.
4. Jesus died for all people, and God desires the salvation of all people.
5. An act of faith is necessary for salvation.[28]

Since Jesus is the only means of salvation and God desires the salvation of all, the final-option theory proposes that all have an encounter with Christ at the moment of death wherein the individual's final destiny is sealed. Those who accept Christ thereby receive genuine salvation — a personal relationship with Jesus.

---

27. There are those who modify this to say that no one can live a life totally devoid of faith and convert at the last moment. They hold that the final choice is simply the culmination of all the previous choices made during one's earthly existence. See *The New Catholic Encyclopedia*, vol. 4 (Washington: Catholic University of America Press, 1967), p. 694.

28. For more Roman Catholic doctrines with which the final-option theory comports well, see Roger Troisfontaines, *I Do Not Die*, trans. Francis Albert (New York: Desclee, 1963), p. 180n.41.

Proponents of the final-option theory contend that it has several other advantages as well. For one thing, it provides for a truly universal evangelization. There is no need for reliance on problematic concepts of implicit faith, baptism by desire, or anonymous Christianity. All people will have to make the ultimate choice of following or spurning Christ in full knowledge of the truth. A second advantage is that "no man reaches life everlasting in the state of original sin, for either that sin is erased by an act of love or it is replaced by personal sin."[29] Ladislaus Boros, a well-known defender of the final-option theory, says of a person at the time of his encounter with Christ that "if he makes a negative decision, he sets himself up . . . in rebellion against God, and exacerbates his state of *original* sin by an *actual* sinfulness personally accepted and fully exercised."[30] Anyone condemned to hell is condemned for rejecting Jesus Christ.

Another significant advantage of the final-option theory is that it provides a better answer than the older notion of limbo to the question of salvation for infants and mentally incompetent people who die. Boros argues that the church used the concept of limbo (a postmortem state in which people suffer no pain but no bliss either) to arrive at a lenient position for those who die unevangelized: "in the limbo hypothesis we have the really decisive and successful challenge made to the zealots of damnation."[31] He faults the limbo hypothesis, however, for suggesting the possibility that any sort of hell, which by definition involves eternal separation from God, could fail to involve pain. This he finds ridiculous. Moreover, he contends that the final-option hypothesis better fulfills the true intent of the limbo hypothesis inasmuch as it suggests a means by which *all* people, including infants and mentally incompetent persons, are enabled to make their own conscious decisions about God. Infants are endowed

29. Troisfontaines, *I Do Not Die*, p. 175.
30. Boros, *The Mystery of Death*, trans. Gregory Bainbridge (New York: Herder & Herder, 1965), p. 128.
31. Boros, *The Mystery of Death*, p. 111.

with spirit, and this spirit is made fully awake at the moment of death. "In death the infant enters into the full possession of its spirituality, i.e. into a state of adulthood. . . . The result of this is that no one dies as an infant, though he may leave us in infancy."[32] All human beings come, at the moment of death, to a point of development whereby they are enabled to make either an act of faith for salvation or an act of sin for damnation.

Critics might ask if it would not be better to wait until death to make a decision. Proponents of the final-option theory say No, for "who can assure me that I *will wish* to change my stand later?"[33] It would be dangerous for people to think that all the decisions they have made against Christ in this life will have no influence on them when the final option is presented. "The final decision is in part determined by the preparatory decisions taken during the course of a lifetime. It does, indeed, offer the possibility of correcting at the end all the decisions of a whole lifetime, but the complete re-directing of a whole life's fundamental orientation must always be looked on as an extreme case in the order of probability, a real one no doubt, but one which, because it is an extreme case, cannot be taken into account existentially."[34] We should not be so foolish as to think we can develop lifestyles and attitudes of disobedience to Christ now and then easily reverse them at death.

## Middle Knowledge

Despite the fact that few people have ever heard the term "middle knowledge," it refers to a view not infrequently propounded by scholars and laity alike. Middle knowledge is the name given to a special type of knowledge attributed to God's

---

32. Boros, *The Mystery of Death,* p. 110.
33. Troisfontaines, *I Do Not Die,* p. 179.
34. Boros, *The Mystery of Death,* p. 97.

omniscience.[35] It is called middle knowledge because it is understood to stand between two other types of divine knowledge. Proponents of this view hold that God has three types of knowledge: (1) he knows all the possibilities of what *could* happen in any state of affairs, (2) he knows all that *would* happen in any state of affairs if one of the conditions were different in any way, and (3) he knows all that *will* actually happen. The traditional view of God's omniscience holds that he knows everything that could happen and everything that will happen. Advocates of middle knowledge argue that God's omniscience also encompasses knowledge of everything that *would* happen if something were changed. For instance, if God has middle knowledge, then he knows what I would have had for breakfast this morning had there been no eggs in the refrigerator. I may not know whether I would have had oatmeal or corn flakes, but God knows which one (if either) I would have chosen. Advocates of middle knowledge break into two schools of thought when it comes to the question of the unevangelized.

The first group holds that God will save those unevangelized persons who would have accepted Christ had they had the opportunity of hearing the good news of salvation. Donald Lake says that "God knows who would, under ideal circumstances, believe the gospel, and on the basis of his foreknowledge, applies that gospel even if the person never hears the gospel during his lifetime."[36] Brethren evangelist George

---

35. For an introduction to and defense of middle knowledge, see William Craig, *The Only Wise God: The Compatibility of Divine Foreknowledge and Human Freedom* (Grand Rapids: Baker Book House, 1987). Arminius believed God had such knowledge but he did not apply it to the subject of the unevangelized. See *The Writings of James Arminius*, 1: 248.

36. Lake, *Grace Unlimited*, ed. Clark Pinnock (Minneapolis: Bethany, 1975), p. 43. Evert Osburn concurs; see "Those Who Have Never Heard: Have They No Hope?" *Journal of the Evangelical Theological Society* 32 (Sept. 1989): 368. Though the arguments for this position are principally drawn from God's omniscience, reference is sometimes made to Jesus' statements that the cities of Tyre, Sidon, and Sodom would have repented had they witnessed the sorts of miracles he performed in Galilee (Matt. 11:21-23).

Goodman asks, "What if an omniscient God, seeing that [the unevangelized] take a true attitude to the light they have, is able to see that had the Greater Light, the True Light, been given to them, they would have rejoiced in the light? Does the fact that the light never reached them prevent the outflow of His grace to them?"[37] Both Goodman and Lake believe that God's salvation is universally accessible and that those unevangelized who would have accepted Christ had they heard about him will be saved by him even though they remain ignorant of him.

A second group that affirms the idea that God possesses middle knowledge contends that he does not use it to save any unevangelized persons. They contend that God desires the salvation of every individual and that he supplies sufficient grace for every individual to be saved but that no one can be saved apart from hearing about Christ from a human agent. For all practical purposes, this position is identical to the "God will send the message" view examined above. Since most people have not received the word of Christ by human missionaries "we must admit," claims William Craig, a proponent of this view, "that the vast majority of persons in the world are condemned and will be forever lost."[38] This sounds harsh, but Craig contends that those who are condemned have no one to blame for their damnation but themselves: "our salvation is in our own hands."[39] They might have been saved if only they had desired it, for then God would have sent a missionary to tell them about Christ. But instead of desiring the truth, they rejected the light of general revelation. "Why," asks Craig, "did God not supply special revelation to persons

37. Goodman, cited by J. Oswald Sanders in *How Lost Are the Heathen?* (Chicago: Moody Press, 1972), p. 62.
38. Craig, "No Other Name: A Middle Knowledge Perspective on the Exclusivity of Salvation through Christ," *Faith and Philosophy* 6 (April 1989): 176. Craig does concede that in some rare cases God might extend salvation to individuals who never heard of Christ.
39. Craig, "No Other Name," p. 186.

who, while rejecting the general revelation they do have, would have responded to the gospel of Christ if they had been sufficiently well-informed concerning it? There are no such persons. . . . For God in His providence has so arranged the world that anyone who would receive Christ has the opportunity to do so."[40] If people die without hearing about Christ, it is because God knew they would not believe in Christ even had they heard. God is justified in not sending the message necessary for salvation to the vast majority of humanity because he knows they would not have accepted Christ had they been evangelized.

The concept of middle knowledge is used in a couple of ways, then — both to allow for the salvation of the unevangelized and to rule it out. Though both positions affirm universally accessible salvation, the former is more in line with the wider hope, while the latter has more in common with restrictivism. Whereas Goodman and Lake believe people can be saved apart from hearing about Christ, Craig believes this quite unlikely. Another interesting difference between these opposing uses of middle knowledge is that Goodman and Lake appear to suggest that an act of faith is unnecessary for salvation. Their position seems to imply that a person could be saved without any sort of commitment or act of trust in God. All that is needed is the knowledge *God* has that they would have committed themselves to Christ had they been evangelized. Salvation of the unevangelized is thus totally dependent on God's foreknowledge and completely independent of human will. Craig, on the other hand, maintains that no one is saved without an act of faith in Christ.

40. Craig, "No Other Name," p. 185. This reasoning is similar to that of Augustine, who claimed that the reason Christ did not come sooner was that God knew the heathen living before the incarnation would not have accepted him. See his letter to Deogratias in *Nicene and Post-Nicene Fathers*, series 1, vol. 1, ed. Philip Schaff (1886; reprint, Grand Rapids: William B. Eerdmans, 1974), p. 418.

## Evaluation

All three views examined in this chapter manage to avoid the extreme assertions of restrictivism on the one hand and universalism on the other. They affirm God's universal salvific will and the universal accessibility of salvation without asserting that all will be saved. In particular, the final-option theory and views of salvation based on middle knowledge propound universal evangelization based solely on God's initiative. In a broad sense they make human evangelization less critical, asserting either that all people are directly evangelized or that God judges them as if they were evangelized. The "God will send the message" view affirms universal evangelization in quite a different sense, inasmuch as it asserts that human involvement is generally necessary for the transmission of the gospel message.

### God Will Send the Message

The theory that God will send the gospel message to those unevangelized people who respond to the conviction of the Holy Spirit is definitely a move away from restrictivism. Proponents of this view believe that God does in fact desire the salvation of all people. Furthermore, the view does have some support from Scripture: it is clear that God wanted the Ethiopian eunuch and Cornelius to hear about Christ. And yet, although I am quite sympathetic to this theory, I find some problems with it. In my opinion, it does not adequately take into account the radical nature of Christ's love for all people and his desire that all should come to a knowledge of him. It tends to lay too much stress on a human responsibility to respond to the light one has in order to receive a miraculous revelation from God (whether by human missionary or angel). Most proponents of the view grant that a miraculous sending of the message occurs only very rarely. Consequently, the theory implicitly consigns the vast majority of unevangelized people throughout history to eternal damnation. When the theory was developed by scholars in the Middle Ages, this implication appeared less horrible than it does today, because the people of that era believed that the world had already been evangelized and that there were only a handful of unevangelized people in the entire world. Contemporary evangelicals who hold this view have to come to terms with its implications for our understanding of God's salvific will and love for all human beings.

Other problems arise in connection with the manner in which God sends the message. Within the biblical record, the message of Christ is never said to have been delivered by means other than human agents. It is true that Abimelech, Nebuchadnezzar, and others are said to have received messages from God through dreams, visions, or visits by angels, but the word of Christ is never said to have been delivered by such means. If God sends the gospel message only by human agents, as McQuilken contends, then the distinction between his position and classic restrictivism becomes less evident, especially in light of the fact that some restrictivists are willing to grant that God may in some rare cases evangelize individuals by extraordinary means. The assertion that God is not obligated to send the gospel message to the vast majority of the unevangelized because they do not seek him strikes me as incompatible with the assertion that God truly desires to save everyone.

## Universal Opportunity at Death

As already mentioned, the final-option theory offers truly universal evangelization, since it asserts that everyone will encounter Christ at the moment of death. But its effectiveness in resolving a number of problematic issues associated with the universal accessibility of salvation comes at something of a cost: the theory places an incredible amount of weight on what must transpire in a brief moment. We are asked to grant that at the moment of death the soul of every man, woman, child, and infant becomes fully mature and awake, in full possession of the truth, and that every awakened individual then makes the ultimate decision determining his or her destiny — the most momentous snap decision imaginable. Furthermore, the idea that all people, regardless of their competence during life, are instantaneously transformed at death into fully mature individuals goes against the grain of all our present experience of how God works with us. "Such a doctrine empties the present life of its religious significance," says John Hick. "Indeed, it even suggests that those who die in the womb are more fortunate than those who survive to face the trials and temptations of life. . . . We cannot be content with a theory which gives meaning to death by depriving this life of its meaning."[41]

And although the final-option theory accommodates many of the traditional teachings of the Roman Catholic Church, it also conflicts with some. For instance, it is official Catholic dogma that all infants who die after baptism go to heaven, but the final-option theory suggests that some baptized infants could reject Christ at the moment of death and thus be damned. Proponents of the final-option theory respond that they view infants who die after baptism as belonging in the same category as baptized adults, who may also renounce Christ. There are no logical problems with this position per se, but the fact remains that it departs from the official teaching that *no* baptized infant who dies is lost.[42]

## Middle Knowledge

The first of the two schools of thought utilizing the theory of middle knowledge — that propounded by Goodman and Lake — holds that God knows who among the unevangelized would

41. Hick, *Death and Eternal Life* (New York: Harper & Row, 1976), p. 238.
42. For other objections, see *The New Catholic Encyclopedia*, 4: 693-94.

have accepted Christ had they been evangelized, and on the basis of this knowledge, he saves all such individuals. This view allows for a genuinely universal opportunity of salvation but in a manner quite different from the other views surveyed in this chapter, inasmuch as it attributes the decision to God rather than the human being. It would appear that proponents of this position deny that an act of faith is necessary for salvation. In essence, they separate the decision for salvation from any consideration of what a person actually did in this life in the way of responding or not responding to God.

Since Goodman and Lake do not elaborate on their position, several important questions remain unanswered. Do they in fact mean to assert that people can be saved without any sort of act of faith toward God? Can people be saved without any actual faith of their own? Can people be saved apart from any knowledge of Christ? Or would Goodman and Lake say that the unevangelized whom God saves in this fashion must learn about and accept Christ after death? They do not provide any answers to this last question, but it is perhaps worth noting that their position is not inherently incompatible with the idea of people being evangelized after death. Indeed, it could be argued that for those who endorse this position and also believe that both knowledge of Christ and an act of faith are essential for salvation, some sort of evangelization after death is a logical necessity.

Regarding the second version of middle knowledge, propounded by William Craig, we might legitimately ask whether it actually supports universally accessible salvation or not. Craig says he believes that God supplies sufficient grace for the salvation of every individual, but he also says he believes that one cannot be saved without hearing about Christ from human agents, and for all practical purposes this entails a belief that all the unevangelized are damned. In other words, Craig gives every evidence of being a restrictivist attempting to relieve God of blame for not giving all people an opportunity to hear of Jesus the Savior. His assertion that it does not matter whether the damned had an opportunity to hear about Christ since they would not have accepted him anyway sounds rather hollow. It does not seem to reflect the biblical emphases on the love God has for his creatures or the pain he experiences when impenitent sinners refuse to return his love. On the other hand, Craig may not be welcomed into the restrictivist fold because of his claim that none of those who die unevangelized would have loved Jesus had they heard of him. This claim will be seen as unsatisfactory by many missions advocates because it goes against one of the most commonly held beliefs in the Christian community — that there are indeed people who would not have been saved and would have gone to hell had they never heard of Christ.

Finally, it remains a question whether God's omniscience entails middle knowledge at all.[43] It is true that Matthew 11:21-23 speaks of what certain cities would have done had circumstances been different, but other Scriptures present a different view. Jeremiah 3:7, for example, suggests that although God had thought some Israelites would repent when he sent them hard times, they failed to do so. If in fact this passage and others like it are suggesting that God chose certain paths of action based on his anticipation of his people's behavior, and yet they did not in fact behave in this fashion, then we have a strong argument against the existence of middle knowledge.

43. For some philosophical difficulties with middle knowledge, see William Hasker, "A Refutation of Middle Knowledge," *Nous* 20 (1986): 545-57; and chaps. 2 and 10 of his book *God, Time, and Knowledge* (Ithaca, N.Y.: Cornell University Press, 1989).

# CHAPTER 6

# *Eschatological Evangelization*

The idea that people will receive an opportunity after death to hear about Christ and to accept or reject him is not a new one on the theological scene. It became well known through the Alexandrian theologians Clement of Alexandria and Origen but fell out of favor after the time of Augustine. It was revitalized in the nineteenth century and is now finding increasing favor particularly among Lutheran theologians and even some noteworthy evangelicals. The view has been referred to as "future probation" and "probation after death" and even "postmortem evangelism."

The key element of this view is well summarized by John Lange: "Jesus, as a spirit, appeared to fallen spirits, to some, as conqueror and judge, to others, who still stretched out to him the hand of faith, as a Savior. . . . The preaching of Christ begun in the realms of departed spirits is continued there . . . so that those who here on earth did not hear at all or not in the right way, the good news of salvation through Jesus Christ, shall hear it there."[1] The principal reasoning used in support of this perspective is that God loves everyone and would not

---

1. Lange, *The First Epistle General of Peter* (New York: Charles Scribner, 1868), pp. 66-67.

allow any to be condemned to hell without knowing what response they would make to the grace of Jesus Christ.

On the current theological scene eschatological evangelization is primarily a Protestant position. It is not a real option among Roman Catholics because of the reigning belief in that community that the final destiny of an individual is fixed at death and cannot be changed. Nor is this contradicted by the concept of purgatory. Roman Catholic theology dictates that purgatory is a place where those who have already been saved are purified prior to their attainment of heaven. Inasmuch as purgatory is presumed to contain only those who are already destined for heaven, there is no need for evangelization there.

It should also be noted that the evangelization-after-death position is in no way a variety of universalism. None of the proponents of the position surveyed in this chapter endorses universalism. In fact, Lange asserts that "if this truth [evangelism after death] had always been sufficiently recognized, the anti-scriptural opinion of universal recovery would hardly have found such extensive circulation."[2] This is not to say that there are no points of contact between the evangelization-after-death position and universalism, however. Both affirm the universal salvific will of God and contend that death cannot halt God's will to save, for example. On the other hand, proponents of evangelization after death also agree with restrictivists that explicit knowledge of Jesus Christ is necessary for salvation, that general revelation is insufficient for salvation, and that not everyone will be saved.

## Key Biblical Texts

There are three categories of texts typically used in support of eschatological evangelization. The first set supports the restrictivist view that a person must possess explicit knowledge of

---

2. Lange, *First Epistle General of Peter*, p. 67.

Jesus Christ in order to be saved (see Chap. 2 herein for a discussion of this material). In commenting on John 1:9, Lange says that "Christ gives sufficient light to every man to leave him without excuse, but not sufficient to save."[3] Contemporary evangelical writer Donald Bloesch agrees: "outside of Christ and faith in His atonement there is no salvation either in this life or in the life to come."[4]

The second group of texts cited supports the idea that the only reason anyone is condemned to hell is for explicit rejection of the grace found in Jesus Christ. From this it is deduced that everyone must have an encounter with Jesus Christ in order to make a final decision about him. It is not ignorance of Jesus Christ that sends one to hell, but refusing Jesus Christ. Several passages of Scripture are used to support this idea. Proponents of the position interpret Mark 16:15-16 ("Go into all the world and preach the gospel to all creation. He who has believed and has been baptized shall be saved; but he who has disbelieved shall be condemned") as meaning that only the person who explicitly disbelieves in Jesus Christ will be condemned. Those who have never heard of Jesus Christ, they say, are not condemned. Jesus declared that he would confess before the Father anyone who confesses him and that he would deny before the Father all who deny him (Matt. 10:32-33). Perhaps those who obstinately to the end refuse to acknowledge the work of God in Jesus Christ are those who commit the unpardonable sin (Matt. 12:31-32; Heb.

3. Lange, *The Gospel according to John* (New York: Charles Scribner, 1871), p. 66.
4. Bloesch, *Essentials of Evangelical Theology*, 2 vols. (New York: Harper & Row, 1982), 2: 230. Bloesch would say that all people are saved *de jure* by the atoning work of Christ but not *de facto*, since personal faith in Christ is necessary for inclusion into the body of Christ. Bloesch adds that it is pernicious to believe that anyone can be saved apart from explicit faith in Jesus Christ, as though human searching and well-doing could effect salvation. His main concern is to guard against Pelagianism and semi-Pelagianism, though he does reject the restrictivist contention that all the unevangelized are automatically damned to hell (*Essentials of Evangelical Theology*, 1: 244-45).

6:4-6). All other sins may be forgiven but this one cannot be, because the person refuses the very ground of forgiveness.

Paul taught that the unrighteous would be condemned for their failure to obey the gospel of Christ (2 Thess. 1:8). Such ideas are especially prominent in the Gospel of John. "He who believes in Him is not judged; he who does not believe has been judged already, because he has not believed in the name of the only begotten Son of God" (John 3:18; cf. 3:36). Jesus informed his disciples that the Holy Spirit would convict the world of sin, righteousness, and judgment, and sin is explicitly defined as failure to believe in Jesus (John 16:8-9). Once one is confronted with the words and person of Jesus, one no longer has any excuse. Jesus said, "if I had not come and spoken to them, they would not have sin, but now they have no excuse for their sin" (John 15:22). According to John's Gospel, Jesus is the great watershed. The destiny of every person is decided on the basis of his or her response to him. But the warnings about judgment based on one's response to Christ are not applicable to the unevangelized. They are addressed only to those who know about Christ. Herbert Luckock asserts that Scripture "never speaks *of* persons when there is a physical impossibility of its speaking *to* them."[5]

If one holds (1) that salvation is universally accessible, (2) that explicit knowledge of Christ is necessary for salvation, and (3) that the only reason anyone is condemned to hell is for rejection of Jesus Christ, then it is not unreasonable to conclude that the unevangelized must receive some kind of opportunity after death to respond to Christ. Thomas Field goes so far as to assert that "if Christ died for every man, and faith in Christ is absolutely essential to salvation, then it follows, as a necessary inference, that the offer of this salvation will be made to very many before the final judgment. . . . It follows, as a necessary consequence from this view, either that all that do not hear of

5. Luckock, *The Intermediate State between Death and Judgment* (New York: Thomas Whittaker, 1890), p. 182.

Christ in this life will be lost, or that all will have an opportunity to hear of Christ that they may be saved."[6]

This leads to the third category of texts, about Christ's descent into hell and his preaching of the gospel there. Jesus anticipated his descent when he said that "just as Jonah was three days and three nights in the belly of the sea monster, so shall the Son of Man be three days and three nights in the heart of the earth" (Matt. 12:40). His prediction extended to the impact this descent would have on those who were dead: "truly, truly, I say to you, an hour is coming and now is, when the dead shall hear the voice of the Son of God; and those who hear shall live. For just as the Father has life in Himself, even so He gave to the Son also to have life in Himself; and He gave Him authority to execute judgment, because He is the Son of Man. Do not marvel at this; for an hour is coming, in which all who are in the tombs shall hear His voice, and shall come forth; those who did the good deeds to a resurrection of life, those who committed the evil deeds to a resurrection of judgment" (John 5:25-29). Many regard the prophet Hosea's statement that "I will ransom them from the power of Sheol; I will redeem them from death. O Death, where are your thorns? O Sheol, where is your sting?" (Hos. 13:14) as a prophecy concerning the release of souls from hell by Christ. The apostle Peter spoke of Christ in hades in his famous sermon in Acts 2. Peter declares that God did not abandon the Messiah to hell but raised him from the dead (Acts 2:24, 27, 31). The apostle Paul alludes to the descent into hell in Romans 10:7 and perhaps 1 Corinthians 15:54 but most emphatically in Ephesians 4:8-10: "therefore it says, 'When He ascended on high, He led captive a host of captives, and He gave gifts to men.' (Now this expression, 'He ascended,' what does it mean except that He also had descended into the lower parts of the earth? He who descended is Himself also He who ascended far

---

6. Field, "The 'Andover Theory' of Future Probation," *Andover Review* 7 (May 1887): 463.

above all the heavens, that He might fill all things.)."[7] Proponents of the evangelization-after-death position interpret this text as meaning that Christ descended into hell and led out of that captivity a great number of people.[8] Paul's point is that no part of the universe was to be unvisited by the Son of God. Other texts speak of those "under the earth" as confessing Jesus as Lord (Phil. 2:10; Rev. 5:13) and of Christ possessing "the keys of death and Hades" (Rev. 1:18).

The ideas of an intermediate state and the possible release from hell of sinners were common among both Jews and Gentiles of the New Testament era.[9] Of particular interest in this regard are Jewish prayers and sacrifices for the dead, including those who died in sin.[10] In 2 Maccabees 12:38-45 we read of a group of Jewish soldiers who died in battle. When their bodies were retrieved, their comrades found that they had been wearing idolatrous amulets for protection. One might think that this would automatically consign them to eternal damnation, but the leaders prayed and "made atonement for the dead that they might be delivered from their sin" (12:45). Some scholars contend that 2 Timothy 1:16-18 contains a reference to praying for the dead; they contend that the person for whom Paul prays, Onesiphorus, was dead.[11] Prayers for the dead entered the

7. For a study of these passages and several others in relation to the descent, see Edward Selwyn, *The First Epistle of St. Peter* (London: Macmillan, 1961), pp. 320-22, 346-51; and J. A. MacCulloch, *The Harrowing of Hell* (Edinburgh: T. & T. Clark, 1930), pp. 45-66.

8. Scholars of the time equated "the lower parts of the earth" with hell. See MacCulloch, *The Harrowing of Hell*, p. 46; and E. H. Plumptre, *The Spirits in Prison* (London: Isbister, 1898), pp. 108-9.

9. See Plumptre, *The Spirits in Prison*, pp. 102, 129-31; and Selwyn, *The First Epistle of St. Peter*, p. 346.

10. See MacCulloch, *The Harrowing of Hell*, pp. 32-42; and Plumptre, *The Spirits in Prison*, pp. 65, 128-29, 266-69.

11. Among those commentators who understand Paul to be praying for the dead here are the following: W. Robertson Nicoll, *The Expositor's Greek Testament*, vol. 4 (Grand Rapids: William B. Eerdmans, 1951), p. 159; Henry Alford, *The Greek Testament*, vol. 3 (Chicago: Moody Press, 1958), p. 376; William Barclay, *The Letters to Timothy, Titus and Philemon*, rev. ed.

Christian community at a very early date. Liturgies involving prayers for the dead were widespread throughout the entire geographic range of the early church.[12]

"From at least the second century there was no more well-known and popular belief, including the Descent to Hades, the overcoming of Death and Hades, the Preaching to the Dead, and the Release of Souls, and its popularity steadily increased."[13] That the doctrine was taken for granted by A.D. 150 is evident from the fact that the heretics Marcion and the Valentinians, who were criticized on most of their beliefs by the early Church Fathers, were not challenged at all on this point. Both the early Fathers and the heretics agreed that Christ descended into hell. Even the cautious Tertullian accepted the doctrine without squabble. In the Arian controversy again, both sides agreed on the descent into hell.[14] It can be concluded from this that the doctrine of Christ's descent into hell and the

_____

(Philadelphia: Westminster Press, 1975), pp. 155-57; J. E. Huther, *Critical and Exegetical Handbook to Timothy and Titus* (Edinburgh: T. & T. Clark, 1871), p. 263.

12. Plumptre, *The Spirits in Prison,* 269-86. He points out that even Augustine prayed for his dead parents (p. 283).

13. MacCulloch, *The Harrowing of Hell,* p. 45. For extensive reviews of the literature and further bibliographies, see MacCulloch; Plumptre, *The Spirits in Prison;* Loofs, "Descent to Hades (Christ's)," *Encyclopedia of Religion and Ethics,* 12 vols., ed. James Hastings (New York: Scribner's, 1908-26), 4: 653-63; Bo Reicke, *The Disobedient Spirits and Christian Baptism* (Copenhagen: Egnar Munksgaard, 1946); and William J. Dalton, *Christ's Proclamation to the Spirits: A Study of 1 Peter 3:18–4:6* (Rome: Pontifical Biblical Institute, 1965). Of particular worth are Ralph Turner, *"Descendit Ad Inferos:* Medieval Views on Christ's Descent into Hell and the Salvation of the Ancient Just," *Journal of the History of Ideas* 27 (1966): 173-94; Milton Gatch, "The Harrowing of Hell: A Liberation Motif in Medieval Theology and Devotional Literature," *Union Seminary Quarterly Review* 36 (1981): 75-88; and Dewey Wallace, "Puritan and Anglican: The Interpretation of Christ's Descent into Hell in Elizabethan Theology," *Archive for Reformation History* 62 (1978): 248-86.

14. See Plumptre, *The Spirits in Prison,* pp. 85-87; and Frederic Huidekoper, *The Belief of the First Three Centuries concerning Christ's Mission to the Underworld* (New York: Charles Francis, 1854), p. 137.

release of souls therefrom was well established by the end of the first century. The only question through this time involved *who* was released.

Two main schools of thought concerning this point developed in the early church. Both groups agreed that the purpose of the descent was to give salvation to the dead.[15] Early Christians such as Ignatius of Antioch, Irenaeus, and Tertullian limited "the dead" who benefited from Christ's redemptive work to the Old Testament patriarchs and prophets. The heretic Marcion claimed the reverse: he maintained that when Christ went to hell, he condemned all the Old Testament believers to hell and released all the Gentiles from Old Testament times. The second school of thought held that Christ released any who desired salvation from the realm of hell, including Gentiles who had no contact with the Jewish faith and had no conception of a Messiah whatsoever. This view was put forward as early as the second century by Melito and later by Hippolytus, Clement of Alexandria, Origen, Athanasius, Gregory of Nazianzus, Ephraem, and Ambrose, and perhaps by Jerome and Hilary, Cyril of Alexandria, Maximus the Confessor, and John of Damascus.[16] Clement of Alexandria established this line of

15. Several important early writings such as the *Shepherd of Hermas*, the *Gospel of Nicodemus*, and the *Gospel of Peter* refer to the preaching of Christ and the release of people, but it is difficult to determine whether or not they limit the benefits to Old Testament believers. These writings do provide further evidence that the communities that produced them viewed baptism as necessary for salvation, since they indicate that baptism was administered in the realm of hell to those who had not been baptized before they died. This definitely points to a widening of the hope of salvation beyond the grave. The *Shepherd of Hermas* says that the apostles continued preaching in hell when they died. This would seem to suggest that the author believed in the possibility of conversion after death (see MacCulloch, *The Harrowing of Hell*, pp. 244-46).

16. For discussion of these, see MacCulloch, *The Harrowing of Hell*; Plumptre, *The Spirits in Prison*; Dalton, *Christ's Proclamation to the Spirits*; and Reicke, *The Disobedient Spirits and Christian Baptism*. Regarding the inclusion of Hippolytus in this list, see Dalton, *Christ's Proclamation to the Spirits*, pp. 26-29.

thinking in the church when he claimed that Jesus preached to Jews on earth and then in hell, and the apostles after him preached to Gentiles on earth and then in hell. "If, then, He preached only to the Jews, who wanted the knowledge and faith of the Saviour, it is plain that, since God is no respecter of persons, the apostles also, as here, so there, preached the Gospel to those of the heathen who were ready for conversion."[17]

By far the most important and controversial texts used in support of postmortem evangelism are 1 Peter 3:18-20 and 4:6. Peter, addressing Christians who were being maligned by their unbelieving neighbors, invites them to imitate Christ:

> For Christ also died for sins once for all, the just for the unjust, in order that He might bring us to God, having been put to death in the flesh, but made alive in the spirit, in which also He went and made proclamation to the spirits now in prison, who once were disobedient, when the patience of God kept waiting in the days of Noah, during the construction of the ark, in which a few, that is, eight persons, were brought safely through the water. . . . For the gospel has for this purpose been preached even to those who are dead, that though they are judged in the flesh as men, they may live in the spirit according to the will of God.

Commentators have been divided over the interpretation of this difficult text ever since it was written. The different interpretations stem from the answers given to three key questions: (1) Who are the "spirits in prison"? (2) What did Jesus preach? and (3) When did Jesus preach? Four main positions have developed.[18] Perhaps the earliest view was that Christ

---

17. *Stromata*, 6.6, in the *Ante-Nicene Fathers*, vol. 2, ed. Alexander Roberts and James Donaldson (1893; reprint, Grand Rapids: William B. Eerdmans, 1975), p. 491.

18. For more views and discussions of commentators who held them, see Wayne Grudem, "Christ Preaching through Noah: 1 Peter 3:19-20 in the Light of Dominant Themes in Jewish Literature," *Trinity Journal* 7 (1986): 3-31. See also Dalton, *Christ's Proclamation to the Spirits*, pp. 15-41.

preached the gospel to the Old Testament believers in hell
during his descent and then released them. Augustine put forward the view that the text is simply suggesting that Christ
preached repentance through Noah while Noah was building
the ark, and hence the text says nothing about a descent into
hell. The view taken by most modern commentators is that
after Jesus died, he descended and proclaimed triumph over the
"fallen angels." A fourth view, held by many in the early church
and regaining popularity today, is that during his descent into
hell Jesus preached the gospel to all present and then led all
who accepted him as Savior out of that prison.[19] Each of the
four views has the support of widely respected exegetes. Consequently, John Feinberg says, "it should be clear that one could
hold to any number of positions and not be thought to be on
the fringe."[20]

The fourth view is of most interest for this study since it
corresponds well with the idea of postmortem evangelism.
G. R. Beasley-Murray well sums up this interpretation when
he says, "the primary lesson in the writer's mind is to exemplify
the universal reach of Christ's redeeming work and the divine
willingness that all should know it. The preaching of Christ
between his cross and his Easter is intended to prove that the
wickedest generation of history is not beyond the bounds of

19. For a listing of others who have taken this view, see Reicke, *The
Disobedient Spirits and Christian Baptism,* pp. 47-49; Dalton, *Christ's Proclamation to the Spirits,* p. 21n.34; and Grudem, "Christ Preaching through
Noah," p. 4n.2. This interpretation has always been present in the Eastern
church but has been viewed with disfavor in the West because of the influence
of Augustine. Clement of Alexandria used 1 Peter 3:19 in connection with
the descent perhaps as early as the second century (see Reicke, *The Disobedient
Spirits and Christian Baptism,* pp. 16-27). Reicke argues that it is not surprising
that Ignatius and Irenaeus fail to connect it to the descent, since it does not
agree with their view of what took place in the descent (*The Disobedient Spirits
and Christian Baptism,* pp. 12-16). They rejected the concept of conversion
after death and thus may have ignored this text.

20. Feinberg, "1 Peter 3:18-20, Ancient Mythology, and the Intermediate State," *Westminster Theological Journal* 48, no. 2 (Fall 1986): 312.

his pity and the scope of his redemption, hence there is hope for *this* generation, that has sinned even more greatly than the Flood generation in refusing the proclamation of a greater Messenger of God and that faces the *last* judgment."[21]

Some comments on the text are in order. First, it should be noted that Peter did believe Jesus descended into the realm of the dead (Acts 2:24, 27, 31). Second, the word "proclamation" *(ekēryxen)* used here is the usual New Testament word for preaching the gospel.[22] That the people Peter has in mind had an opportunity to repent is made clear by the fact that he speaks of the patience of God in verse 20 and that in 4:6 he uses the term gospel *(euēngelisthē)*. Third, the point about Christ preaching to unbelievers fits into the context, since Peter has just admonished his audience always to be ready to witness for Christ among their unbelieving neighbors (3:15). The Christians are encouraged to witness to the non-Christians around them even though they may suffer for it — after all, Christ never stopped preaching even though he suffered unjustly. The fact that he continued preaching beyond the grave should encourage them not to give up despite the fact that their unbelieving neighbors seem uninterested in the call of Christ.

An objection is often raised at this point: if Peter is suggesting that Jesus preached to *all* the people in hell, then why did he single out the generation of Noah's day? J. A. MacCulloch lists three possible responses: "They may be typical of a larger number to whom the good news was brought, or they may be mentioned in order to introduce a reference to the Flood as typical of baptismal grace. Or the reference to the men of Noah's time may be due to the fact that our Lord had referred to them along with the men of Sodom, and thus the writer's thoughts are turned to

21. Beasley-Murray, *Baptism in the New Testament* (Grand Rapids: William B. Eerdmans, 1962), pp. 258-59.
22. See, for example, Matt. 4:23; 9:35; 24:14; 26:13; Mark 1:14; 13:10; 14:9; 16:15; Acts 8:5; 9:20; 12:13; 1 Cor. 1:23; 15:12; Gal. 2:2; Phil. 1:15; Col. 1:23; 1 Thess. 2:9.

them."[23] Most commentators who espouse this view favor the last of MacCulloch's reasons. C. E. B. Cranfield, for example, says they were singled out "because they were generally regarded as the most abandoned of sinners: if those whom Jewish opinion excluded altogether from hope (cf. Sanh. 10.3: 'The generation of the Flood hath no share in the world to come, nor shall they stand in the judgment . . .') were not beyond the reach of Christ's saving work, then none could be."[24] Regarding the preaching to the dead in 4:6, Cranfield suggests that "the most natural interpretation is surely to connect it with 3:19, and to understand a reference to 'the spirits in prison.' . . . The meaning will be: 'in order that, though they have died, as all men must (death itself being regarded as God's judgment), they might nevertheless live by God's power in the spirit.' In the opinion of men the dead have had their judgment; but the Good News has been preached even among them, in order that those who respond to it might live eternally."[25] But most commentators who find postmortem evangelism in this text admit that the text is open to other interpretations. Many would agree with Cranfield's assertion that

> it is a hint within the Canon of Scripture, puzzling indeed and obscure yet at the same time reassuringly restrained, that the mysterious interval between Good Friday afternoon and Easter morning was not empty of significance, but that in it too Jesus Christ was active as the Savior of the world. . . . It is a hint, too, surely, that those who in subsequent ages have died without ever having had a real chance to believe in Christ are not outside the scope of His mercy and will not perish eternally without being given in some way that is beyond our knowledge an opportunity to hear the gospel and accept Him as their Savior.[26]

23. MacCulloch, *The Harrowing of Hell,* p. 60. For the significance of references to Noah in Judaism and the New Testament, see Selwyn, *The First Epistle of Peter,* pp. 328-33.
24. Cranfield, "The Interpretation of 1 Peter 3:19 and 4:6," *The Expository Times* 69 (Sept. 1958): 372.
25. Cranfield, *First Epistle of Peter* (London: SCM Press, 1954), p. 91.
26. Cranfield, "The Interpretation of 1 Peter 3:19 and 4:6," p. 372.

## Theological Considerations

The theological arguments for eschatological evangelization fall into four basic categories, all of which are set within the framework of God's universal salvific will.

### 1. The Insufficiency of General Revelation for Salvation

The advocates of postmortem evangelism are in general agreement with restrictivists that general revelation alone cannot lead to salvation. According to Donald Bloesch, "the universal awareness of God made possible by the light in nature and conscience is the basis for the *misunderstanding*, not the *understanding* of God. . . . Because of sin, our inward eyes are blinded to the objective glory of God reflected in nature, and yet we have enough intimation of this glory to render us inexcusable (Rom. 1:20; 2:1). The natural knowledge of God is sufficient neither for a valid understanding nor for salvation but only for condemnation."[27]

Lutheran theologians who uphold postmortem evangelism also emphasize the insufficiency of general revelation. Paul Althaus, for instance, says that "outside of Christ there is indeed a self-manifestation of God, and therefore knowledge of God, but it does not lead to salvation."[28] The contemporary Lutheran theologian Carl Braaten utilizes the traditional Lutheran emphases on the "bondage of the will," Christ alone, faith alone,

---

27. Bloesch, *The Future of Evangelical Christianity: A Call for Unity amid Diversity* (Garden City, N.Y.: Doubleday, 1983), p. 121. Bloesch also rejects the idea of "universal sending for those who desire God" on the grounds that it is "semi-Pelagian" (pp. 123-24). Furthermore, Bloesch characterizes the claim that anyone can be saved apart from knowledge of the gospel of Christ as "pernicious" for the Christian faith (see *Essentials of Evangelical Theology*, vol. 1 [San Francisco: Harper & Row, 1978], p. 244).

28. Althaus, cited by Carl Braaten in "Lutheran Theology and Religious Pluralism," *Lutheran World Federation* 23-24 (Jan. 1988): 118.

and faith coming by hearing to support his claim that saving faith comes *only* through hearing about the grace of Jesus Christ. He insists that only an encounter with Jesus Christ can break the bondage of the will and usher in salvation: "outside of Christ and apart from the preaching of the gospel, there are no known historical alternatives that may be theologically accepted as divinely authorized means of salvation. If, traditionally, Roman Catholic theology has taught that 'outside of church there is no salvation', Lutheran theology has taught that 'outside of Christ there is no salvation.'"[29] Since God desires that everyone be saved, and since no one can be saved without encountering Jesus Christ, it is argued that an opportunity after death is the best solution to the dilemma.

## 2. Our Destinies Are Not Necessarily Determined at Death

Proponents of the postmortem evangelization position argue that our final destinies are not sealed at death but rather at the "day of Christ." Though the New Testament suggests that *some* fates are determined at death, there is no rigid and explicit doctrine stating that the fates of *all* categories of people are settled at death. Hebrews 9:27 states that "it is appointed for men to die once, and after this comes judgment," and this has traditionally been understood to indicate that death and judgment are coterminous. "We have neglected the eschatology of Scripture," says Thomas Field, "and made death the judgment, and death the coming of Christ."[30] He contends that the judgment being spoken of in this text is not death but the final judgment, which will occur on the day of Christ.

John Lange argues along the same lines that "Holy Scripture nowhere teaches the eternal damnation of those who died as heathens or non-Christians; it rather intimates in many

29. Braaten, "Lutheran Theology and Religious Pluralism," p. 122.
30. Field, "The 'Andover Theory' of Future Probation," p. 469.

passages that forgiveness may be possible beyond the grave, and refers the final decision not to death, but to the day of Christ."[31] Several texts are customarily cited in defense of this assertion: "He has fixed a day in which He will judge the world in righteousness through a man whom He has appointed [Jesus]" (Acts 17:31); "I know whom I have believed and I am convinced that He is able to guard what I have entrusted to Him until that day" (2 Tim. 1:12); "in the future there is laid up for me the crown of righteousness, which the Lord, the righteous Judge, will award to me on that day; and not only to me, but also to all who have loved His appearing" (2 Tim. 4:8); and "we may have confidence in the day of judgment" (1 John 4:17; see also John 5:25-29). In addition, it is pointed out that Jesus said that "many shall come from east and west, and recline at table with Abraham, and Isaac, and Jacob, in the kingdom of heaven" (Matt. 8:11//Luke 13:29) and that the gates of the heavenly Jerusalem will never be closed (Rev. 21:25). These texts are taken to mean that God still invites sinners from all areas of the globe and all periods of history to repentance in the afterlife.[32]

### 3. Implications of the Belief That Infants Who Die Are Saved

In 1886 Egbert Smyth called attention to the change that occurred in Puritan New England regarding beliefs about the fate of infants who died:

> The same church, with the same Bible as its rule of faith, now as commonly encourages the hope that all infants will be saved,

---

31. Lange, *The First Epistle General of Peter,* p. 75.

32. Many evangelicals cite the parable of the rich man and Lazarus (Luke 16:23ff.) as evidence that our destinies are fixed at death. But so literalistic an interpretation is by no means generally accepted in the scholarly community, especially in light of the fact that the point of all three parables in Luke 16 is to instruct us about the use of wealth, not about eschatology.

as two centuries ago it discountenanced such an expectation. . . .
Now, our most rigorous adherents to the Augustinian and Reformed type of doctrine encourage the belief that all infants are
"elect," and will be saved. . . . No new text has been discovered
in the Bible. No explicit, decisive Scriptural testimony is
claimed. The change has come about through . . . a clearer
perception of the true character of God as revealed in Christ,
of the scope of the atonement, of the "philanthropy of God our
savior," of the nature of moral agency and the meaning of
personality. . . . A similar change of opinion has been going on
in respect to the salvation of the heathen. Once, nearly the
entire pagan world was regarded as doomed. Comparatively few
maintain this today.[33]

Smyth proceeds to argue for an extension of this view of God
and atonement to the unevangelized. If all infants who die are
saved, he argues, then nearly one-half the human race is saved
without any earthly moral probation. But since acceptance of
Christ as Savior is a requisite for salvation, it follows that such
infants must "grow up" and accept Christ as Savior in the next
life. If we grant the reality of postmortem evangelism for infants
who die, and if they are part of the category of unevangelized
persons, then why not extend the idea to include all the unevangelized? He argues that both infant and adult unevangelized are evangelized after death on the grounds that "no man
is condemned to eternal punishment by Christ who has not
had an opportunity to be saved by Christ."[34]


### 4. The Broad Implications of Universally Accessible Salvation

The final theological argument is actually a summary of the
others. It is argued that postmortem evangelism provides the


33. Smyth, "Probation after Death," *The Homiletic Review* 11 (April
1886): 286-87.
34. Smyth, "Probation after Death," p. 289.

best answer as to *how* God makes salvation universally accessible. It has tremendous "theological fit" when accompanied by the control beliefs of God's universal salvific will, the necessity of faith in Christ for salvation, the necessity that one hear about Christ in order to have faith, and the fact that God is loving, just, and fair. Furthermore, it makes use of the long-standing belief in Christ's descent into hell and the release of certain souls there. It provides a means to hold up Jesus Christ as the universal Savior without succumbing to universalism.[35]

\* \* \*

Before proceeding, I think some qualifications may be helpful in preventing certain misunderstandings. First, eschatological evangelization and the descent of Christ into hell "is not," says Bloesch, "to be confounded with the doctrine of a second chance. What the descent doctrine affirms is the universality of a first chance, an opportunity for salvation for those who have never heard the gospel in its fullness."[36] Herbert Luckock concurs; for the unevangelized, he writes, "the time of probation is nowhere fixed . . . but for all those whose circumstances are such that the offer of salvation has been fully and adequately presented in this life, it is limited; and there is nothing in Holy Scripture to induce even a hope that it can ever be extended beyond the grave."[37]

But this raises the difficult question of who has heard the gospel "fully and adequately" and what would qualify a person

35. For a discussion of how this position comports with the doctrines of the Church of England, see Alan Fairhurst, "Death and Destiny," *The Churchman* 95 (1981): 317-18. For a discussion of how it comports with the Thirty-Nine Articles and Presbyterian Confessions, see Field, "The 'Andover Theory' of Future Probation," p. 465.

36. Bloesch, "Descent into Hell," *Evangelical Dictionary of Theology*, ed. Walter Elwell (Grand Rapids: Baker Book House, 1984), p. 314.

37. Luckock, *The Intermediate State between Death and Judgment* (New York: Thomas Whittaker, 1890), p. 198.

for postmortem evangelization. Have people actually heard the "gospel" if they are given a tract or watch a television evangelist or even if friends attempt to make it as clear as possible to them? Luckock sought to answer this question when he wrote that "no human being can tell exactly what constitutes an adequate presentment of the truth to any man; God alone will be the Judge of that. . . . There are a thousand reasons which may obstruct the admission of the truth into a man's heart. . . . Every one of these will be considered by the Infallible Judge before He passes sentence."[38] Stephen Davis asserts that it is possible that people who have "heard" the gospel but have not responded positively to it before death will respond positively after death. "Some who hear the gospel," he says, "hear it in such a way that they are psychologically unable to respond positively. Perhaps they heard the gospel for the first and only time from a fool or a bigot or a scoundrel. Or perhaps they were caused to be prejudiced against Christianity by skeptical parents or teachers. Whatever the reason, I believe it would be unjust of God to condemn those who did indeed hear the good news but were unable to respond positively."[39] Thus he contends that we are not in a position to judge whether someone has "heard the gospel" fully and adequately; only God knows who will receive an opportunity after death to receive Christ.

Finally, some proponents of this view uphold the *possibility* that people may be rescued even from hell. Donald Bloesch describes the argument that God *can* deliver from hell but argues that Christians should acknowledge that it is beyond their powers to know whether he actually does so or not:

> We do not wish to build fences around God's grace, however, and we do not preclude the possibility that some in hell might

38. Luckock, *The Intermediate State between Death and Judgment,* pp. 190, 208.

39. Davis, "Universalism, Hell, and the Fate of the Ignorant," *Modern Theology* 6 (Jan. 1990): 183-84. See also John Lawson, *Introduction to Christian Doctrine* (Wilmore, Ky.: Francis Asbury Press, 1980), pp. 262-64.

finally be translated into heaven. The gates of the holy city are depicted as being open day and night (Isa. 60:11; Rev. 21:25), and this means that access to the throne of grace is possible continuously. The gates of hell are locked, but they are locked only from within. . . . Hell is not outside the compass of God's mercy nor the spheres of his kingdom, and in this sense we call it the last refuge of the sinner. Edward Pusey voices our own sentiments: "We know absolutely nothing of the proportion of the saved to the lost or who will be lost; but this we *do* know, that none will be lost, who do not obstinately to the end and in the end refuse God."[40]

## Leading Defenders

### *Joseph Leckie*

Interest in the intermediate state and an opportunity for evangelization after death was widespread among both conservative and liberal Protestants of the nineteenth and early twentieth centuries. Joseph Leckie drew on this interest in his Kerr Lectures and outlined his belief in postmortem evangelism. He gives both biblical and theological evidence in support of his position. As biblical evidence, he appeals to Ephesians 4:8-10 and 1 Peter 3:19 and 4:6. "St. Peter almost certainly meant to teach that Jesus in the interval between death and resurrection went down into the lower world and there proclaimed good tidings."[41] He then points out that the early church favored the idea that Christ descended into hell and even that he released people there. He

40. Bloesch, *Essentials of Evangelical Theology*, 2: 226-28. Though Bloesch believes that although God's Yes is stronger than the sinner's No, he does not force the sinner to accept his grace, and consequently universalism does not follow. See also Davis, "Universalism, Hell, and the Fate of the Ignorant," p. 184.

41. Leckie, *The World to Come and Final Destiny*, 2d ed. (Edinburgh: T. & T. Clark, 1922), p. 91.

also argues that the New Testament nowhere rules out such an interpretation but rather seems to agree with common Jewish notions of the day regarding the intermediate state.[42]

On the theological side, he asserts that a person must have explicit knowledge of Christ in order to be saved and hence that all must be given an opportunity of hearing about Christ. His defense of this affirmation is centered in the doctrine of judgment. Leckie claims that Jesus' teaching that all will have to give an account of their actions and the chastening of un-dutiful servants in his kingdom is evidence that "the world to come will contain something besides the perdition of the lost and the perfect glory of the saints, namely, an experience of discipline and trial . . . an intermediate state."[43] The idea of an intermediate state was well known in Judaism and became commonplace in the early church. It is still affirmed by the Eastern churches but was modified into the doctrine of purga-tory in Roman Catholicism. Leckie gives three further reasons why Protestants should accept this doctrine.

1. "It cannot be said that the brief span of mortal existence affords equal opportunity or fair probation for every one that is born of woman."[44] Many die in infancy, some are born with mental incapacities, and others are born into conditions in which thoughts of the spiritual realm are not encouraged.

One can imagine an arm of the sea stretching between two shores, of which it might be said — "This strait seems perfectly designed to afford a test of the sea-going qualities of ships. It has in it all kind of perils — rocks, shoals, currents: also all sorts of weather — squalls, storms, calms, heat and cold." . . . But suppose we found on inquiry that of all the vessels launched on that sea the greater number sank before they cleared the harbor bar; that of those which survived to reach the open waters some experienced favoring winds and peaceful skies, while others had

42. Leckie, *The World to Come and Final Destiny*, pp. 92-93.
43. Leckie, *The World to Come and Final Destiny*, p. 93.
44. Leckie, *The World to Come and Final Destiny*, p. 96.

test of continual storms and buffetings and varied perils; that finally, only a few of the craft which attempted this voyage ever made the opposite shore, we should surely be disposed to doubt whether this stretch of sea was really designed after all to afford a fair test. . . . This mortal life is such a sea.[45]

2. Leckie argues that since so many of the human race die in infancy, these must be afforded an opportunity after death to receive Christ. Rejecting the Roman Catholic notion of limbo, the early Reformed idea that only elect infants are saved, and the "liberal" belief that all infants that die are saved, Leckie opts for the idea that all infants who die are allowed to mature and develop in the next life and are then given an opportunity to accept Christ. He argues that the other three views all allow infants to be saved apart from any time of probation or reception of the Lord Jesus. "If the battle is the only path to victory, how can those who have never fought be counted among the conquerors?"[46]

3. Leckie appeals to the widespread and long-standing practice of praying for the dead. Although it cannot be proven that such prayers are efficacious, he argues, it cannot be proven that they are not. Moreover, the New Testament does not rule out such a practice, and the great majority of Christians throughout the ages have engaged in it. If prayers for the departed are to be effective, then some sort of transformations must be possible after death.

Leckie maintains that, taken together, these arguments constitute a cumulative case for postmortem evangelism for both those who die in infancy and those who die unevangelized.

### Gabriel Fackre

Gabriel Fackre, a professor at Andover Newton Theological School, has developed a theological formulation of postmortem

45. Leckie, *The World to Come and Final Destiny*, p. 96.
46. Leckie, *The World to Come and Final Destiny*, p. 97.

evangelism based on the guiding themes found in the Scriptures. His discussion is centered not on the fate of the unevangelized but on the relationship between Christ and the world religions. His main concern is to formulate a position that does justice to both God's universal salvific will and the particularity of salvation only in Jesus Christ. He calls his view "universal particularity."[47]

Fackre's belief in postmortem evangelism is grounded in three central themes of Scripture. First, the deed of reconciliation by God in Jesus Christ is for everyone. The work of grace by Jesus is designed for every human being. Second, the disclosure of God's revelation is twofold. General revelation is true revelation but is insufficient for salvation. Only the particular revelation of Jesus Christ can bring the fullness of salvation. All truth is God's truth and is therefore part of the revelation of Jesus Christ, but general revelation is not the "fullness" of revelation. According to Fackre,

> wherever truth illumines the inquiring mind, the alert conscience, the sensitive spirit, the passionate and devoted heart, a gift is given by the presence and power of Jesus Christ. . . . What he did in Galilee, Calvary, and on Easter morning is carried by the Savior wherever justice is understood, love is envisioned, peace is perceived, beauty is grasped, wisdom granted. Universal revelation so conceived is not the fullness of truth nor the ultimacy of disclosure, but it is truth and it is disclosure.[48]

The third scriptural theme that Fackre highlights is the nature of the deliverance of redemption, and again he points to both universal and particular aspects. "Life in its most basic sense is the breath of life, and the sustenance of that breath which is the healthy and *good* life of self and society. Redemp-

47. See Fackre, *The Christian Story: A Narrative Interpretation of Basic Christian Doctrine*, rev. ed. (Grand Rapids: William B. Eerdmans, 1984), pp. 219-21, 229-41; and "The Scandals of Particularity and Universality," *Midstream* 22 (Jan. 1983): 32-52.

48. Fackre, "The Scandals of Particularity and Universality," p. 46.

tion, therefore, includes deliverance from all that makes for death and the release of the grace that makes for life. Here is redemption in its universality."[49] This is the "bread" by which human life is sustained. Universal redemption comprises the bread and breath of life and is experienced in deliverance by grace through love. But we do not live by bread alone; we need the particular redemption from sin by grace through faith in the Lord Jesus. Faith in Jesus brings deliverance from sin and death. It brings the fullness of life — eternal life — through selfless love. These two aspects of redemption relate to God's universal grace outside the church and the particular grace of Jesus manifested in the Christian life. Universal particularity is exhibited "by seeing and celebrating *basic life* as a saving grace, the gift of Jesus Christ's work accessible through love to multitudes outside the church and the faith. But we have . . . reserved the decision of faith and the fullness of life to explicit Christian belief and commitment."[50]

Fackre proceeds to apply these themes to the issue of the unevangelized. Jesus is reaching out and showing grace to all people via general revelation. But since there is no fullness of redemption outside of personal knowledge of Jesus, and since it is God's will that all have this knowledge, there must be an eschatological opportunity to encounter Christ. "Because Christ really is Life, death has no hold on him. His ministry cannot be constrained by our 'No trespassing' signs."[51] "The God whose 'will it is that all men should find salvation and come to know the truth' (1 Tim. 2:4) has the power of the Holy Spirit to keep that promise and accomplish that Dream."[52] Fackre cites 1 Peter 3:19–4:6 as well as all the related texts surveyed above in support of this thesis.[53] He maintains that

---

49. Fackre, "The Scandals of Particularity and Universality," p. 47.
50. Fackre, "The Scandals of Particularity and Universality," p. 51.
51. Fackre, "The Scandals of Particularity and Universality," p. 51.
52. Fackre, *The Christian Story*, p. 240.
53. Fackre's most detailed explanation of postmortem evangelism is found in *The Christian Story*, pp. 232-37.

the concept of evangelization after death best holds together
the universal and particular themes of revelation and salvation
found in the Scriptures and also helps explain certain enigmatic
passages in Scripture such as Christ's statement that he has
"other sheep, not of this fold" (John 10:16) and Paul's great
claim that "all Israel will be saved" (Rom. 11:26).[54] But Fackre
also insists that the offer of Christ beyond the grave must not
be confused with an automatic universalism, since the offer is
not made indefinitely and it "is made by the same vulnerable
Love that does not force its will and way upon anyone, and
thus in the eschatological encounter grants the right to respond
with a No as well as a Yes."[55]

### George Lindbeck

George Lindbeck, a professor at Yale University, affirms postmortem evangelization but defends it in ways quite distinct from
those examined thus far. Like Fackre, Lindbeck sets his treatment
of the unevangelized in the context of a discussion of the relationship between Christ and other religions.[56] He asserts that
today it is psychologically and sociologically untenable to assign
all the unevangelized to damnation, that only sectarian groups
and conservative evangelicals persist in supporting such inhuman
and un-Christian beliefs. Consequently, what he calls "quasiuniversalist" views have become quite popular. Proponents of
these views do not say that all will be saved, but they do typically
argue that the traditional "exclusivist" New Testament texts must

---

54. Fackre, *The Christian Story*, pp. 234-35.
55. Fackre, *The Christian Story*, p. 234.
56. See Lindbeck, "*Fides ex auditu* and the Salvation of Non-Christians:
Contemporary Catholic and Protestant Positions," in *The Gospel and the
Ambiguity of the Church*, ed. Vilmos Vajta (Minneapolis: Fortress, 1974), pp.
92-123; "Unbelievers and the Sola Christi," *Dialog* 12 (1973): 182-89; and
*The Nature of Doctrine: Religion and Theology in a Postliberal Age* (Philadelphia:
Westminster Press, 1984), pp. 46-72.

be interpreted in light of the "universalistic" texts: the statements about hell are directed against Israel and the church, not primarily against those in other religions. Lindbeck holds out hope for the salvation of the unevangelized, but he insists on adherence to a belief in salvation by Christ alone. What is needed, he says, is a theological formulation that imaginatively reconciles the *sola Christi* doctrine with the salvation of non-Christians. Failure to develop such a formulation, he claims, constitutes a "recipe for disaster."

Lindbeck sees only two real options for developing this needed formulation: either the inclusivism of Karl Rahner or the eschatological evangelization of the human race. We cannot turn to tradition for help in deciding between these alternatives, he says, because the Roman Catholics have a varied tradition on this issue, and Protestants can hardly be said to possess any tradition at all on this point. And appeals to Scripture present other problems. Lindbeck argues that all interpreters deal with Scripture within particular systematic and historical frameworks. We all grow up within particular cultural-linguistic frameworks through which we interpret all of our experiences and make sense of life. Native Americans view the battle of Little Bighorn differently from most white Americans, and management and labor traditionally differ in their interpretation of the same set of circumstances. In the same way, concepts of such things as sin and salvation vary from one cultural-linguistic context to another. And so, argues Lindbeck, simplistic appeals to Scripture cannot settle the debate, since "interpretation is dependent on one's preunderstanding."[57]

57. Lindbeck, "*Fides ex auditu* and the Salvation of Non-Christians," p. 111. One of Lindbeck's criticisms of what I call inclusivism is that it does not sufficiently take this point into account. He contends that it is not possible for someone outside the Christian cultural-linguistic setting to experience sin and guilt with respect to a personal God in the same way that someone inside this setting does. This may be so, but even if it is, I am still not certain that it is fatal to inclusivism. After all, would this state of affairs not constitute just as serious a problem in the afterlife? Lindbeck must either postulate an instantaneous cultural-linguistic shift for the unevangelized in the afterlife or

A better approach, says Lindbeck, is to construct a theological formulation based on three essential criteria: (1) the attitude of the early church toward unbelievers, (2) the assertion that faith comes solely through hearing the gospel of Jesus Christ, and (3) specific pastoral concerns.

Regarding the first criterion, Lindbeck writes that

> Christians in the first centuries appear to have had an extraordinary combination of relaxation and urgency in their attitude toward those outside the church. On the one hand, they do not seem to have worried about the ultimate fate of the overwhelming majority of non-Christians among whom they lived. We hear of no crisis of conscience resulting from the necessity they were often under to conceal the fact that they were believers even from close friends or kindred. Christians did not seem to have viewed themselves as watchmen who would be held guilty of the blood of the pagans they failed to warn . . . (Ez. 3:18). Yet, on the other hand, missionary proclamation was urgent and faith and baptism were life from death: the passage from the old into the new. . . . It is therefore at least plausible to suppose that the early Christians had certain unrecorded convictions that would relieve the tensions about how God saves unbelievers. . . . Perhaps reflected in the reference to Christ preaching to the souls in prison (1 Peter 3:19), and others are suggested in universalist-sounding biblical texts (e.g., Col. 1:20; Eph. 1:9f.; Phil. 2:10f.; 1 Cor. 15:28; 1 John 2:2; Acts 3:21).[58]

Lindbeck expresses the second criterion as follows: "saving faith cannot be wholly anonymous, wholly implicit, but must be in some measure explicit: it comes, as Paul puts it, *ex auditu*,

---

else allow for a long period of development during which they might change their worldviews to the extent that their encounter with Christ would make sense. If God can enable people to overcome cultural-linguistic problems in the next life, why can he not do it in this one? I appreciate much of Lindbeck's cultural-linguistic analysis, but I am not convinced that he escapes fideism or even relativism. For more on this, see Tom Morris, "Philosophers and Theologians at Odds," *Asbury Theological Journal* 44 (Fall 1989): 31-41.

58. Lindbeck, *The Nature of Doctrine*, p. 58.

from hearing (Rom 10:17)."[59] "It is only through explicit faith in Christ that men and women are redeemed; and if this does not happen during life, then the beginning of salvation must be thought of as occurring through an encounter with the risen Lord in or after death."[60] Since no person can be saved apart from hearing about Jesus Christ, he reasons, it must be the case that all will eventually hear about him even though some will have to wait until after death. Lindbeck believes that Protestants ought to find eschatological evangelization more to their liking than Roman Catholics because it comports better with their general affirmation of "faith by hearing."[61]

Moving to the third criterion, Lindbeck holds that there are four pastoral concerns that Christians writing about Christ and other religions seek to implement, all of which are best met by postulating postmortem evangelism.

1. *Christians ought not to boast about their relationship to God.* "One can say that the situation of the Christian is in some respects more, not less, perilous than that of the non-Christian. Judgment begins in the house of the Lord (1 Peter 4:17), and many of the first shall be last, and the last first (Matt. 19:30)."[62]

59. Lindbeck, *The Nature of Doctrine,* p. 57. Lindbeck is here specifically rejecting Karl Rahner's "anonymous Christianity." He is critical of both Protestant and Catholic forms of inclusivism. Although he contends that both models can be harmonized with Scripture, he claims that *fides ex auditu* best fits with his "cultural-linguistic" model of doctrine. His most specific criticisms of inclusivism are found in "Unbelievers and the Sola Christi."

60. Lindbeck, "Unbelievers and the Sola Christi," p. 184. He notes that this was the view of an "older group of Lutheran dogmaticians."

61. Lindbeck suggests that the major reason Protestants fail to take an interest in postmortem evangelization — or indeed in individual salvation at all — is that the subject has become disreputable. Salvation is discussed only in its social, secular, and cosmic aspects. The subject of individual salvation is associated with a dangerous objectivizing of the text or a literalizing the mythical (see "Unbelievers and the Sola Christi," p. 184).

62. Lindbeck, *The Nature of Doctrine,* p. 59. Lindbeck adds that "a refusal to accept the church's invitation to believe is not to be equated with a refusal to accept God's invitation" (see *"Fides ex auditu* and the Salvation of Non-Christians," p. 115).

2. *Christians should remain trustful regarding the salvation of unbelievers.* Non-Christians are heading toward neither heaven nor hell at the present time because they have not yet been confronted with the salvation of Jesus Christ. Jesus Christ can be denied only where he is known.[63] "On this view, there is no damnation — just as there is no salvation — outside the church."[64] We can be trustful about the salvation of unbelievers since "dying itself is the point at which every human being is ultimately and expressly confronted by the gospel, i.e., by the crucified and risen Lord. It is only then that the final decision is made for or against Christ, and this is true, not only of unbelievers but also of believers. All previous decisions whether of faith or unfaith are preliminary."[65]

3. *Christians should seek genuine dialogue with other religions, avoiding purely defensive and critical attitudes and instead remaining open to learning some truths from them.* If we believe in a postmortem encounter with Christ in which all adherents of other religions will have to face the Son of God in truth, then we should feel free to talk with them confidently and at the same time learn from them. "To hold that the Christian language is the only one which has the words and concepts which can authentically speak of the ground of being, goal of history, and true humanity (for one cannot genuinely speak of these apart from telling and retelling the story of Jesus Christ), is not at all the same as denying that other religions have resources for speaking truths and realities . . . of which Christianity as yet knows nothing and by which it could be greatly enriched."[66]

63. See Lindbeck, *The Nature of Doctrine*, pp. 58-59, 68. Lindbeck asserts that one cannot deny or accept Jesus unless he is within a particular cultural-linguistic model.

64. Lindbeck, *The Nature of Doctrine*, p. 59.

65. Lindbeck, *"Fides ex auditu* and the Salvation of Non-Christians," p. 115.

66. Lindbeck, *"Fides ex auditu* and the Salvation of Non-Christians," p. 117. He makes a similar assertion in *The Nature of Doctrine*, p. 61, but there his argument is set within a discussion of compatibility with his cul-

When we live this out we are, says Lindbeck, following the early church, which learned some truths from the philosophies and pagan religions then present.

4. *Christians must persevere in preaching the gospel.* If faith comes only by hearing, then our sharing the language of Christ allows others the opportunity of becoming new creatures in him. "Evangelism is . . . the offer to teach one's own beloved language, the language which speaks of Jesus Christ, to all those who are interested, and then leave it to them and to God as to whether they choose the new language over the old."[67]

If we combine belief in eschatological evangelization with Lindbeck's cultural-linguistic model, he believes that we arrive at the best possible framework for evangelism and dialogue with other religions. We can remain hopeful of their salvation without being arrogant about ours. We can recapture the same attitude of urgency and relaxation that the early Christians manifested toward their unbelieving neighbors. We can imitate the patience of God which is profitable for salvation.

## Evaluation

The proponents of eschatological evangelization have developed a position with a number of special strengths. For one thing, they offer what is perhaps the strongest affirmation of

---

tural-linguistic model and not primarily postmortem evangelism. He does maintain that such a stand allows us to uphold the unsurpassibility of grace in Jesus Christ. See *The Nature of Doctrine*, pp. 46-52.

67. Lindbeck, *"Fides ex auditu* and the Salvation of Non-Christians," p. 118. Lindbeck modifies the end of this sentence in his later work to read as follows: ". . . with all those who are interested, in the full awareness that God does not call all to be part of the witnessing people" (*The Nature of Doctrine*, p. 61). I am not sure what to make of this change. Does he mean that God does not actually desire all people to follow Christ or simply that not all people choose to follow Christ?

universally accessible salvation of any of the positions we have surveyed thus far, inasmuch as they contend not only that all people have an opportunity to be saved but that all people will eventually come face to face with the risen Lord. Their position allows them to affirm that Jesus Christ will personally invite every individual who ever lived into his love. Although not all will accept this invitation (the mystery of iniquity!), the presentation of the gospel is absolutely universal. They also affirm the necessity of an act of faith for salvation. No person will be saved who has not responded to God's grace, they say — including those who die as infants. This, in my opinion, represents an improvement over both the exclusivist view that only baptized or elect infants are saved and the quasiuniversalist view that all infants who die are automatically saved. The concept of evangelization after death offers support for the proposition that no one is saved without an act of faith — including those who die unevangelized. And beyond this, the position is also compatible with the assertion that explicit knowledge of Christ and a personal relationship with Christ are necessary for salvation.

The concept of postmortem evangelism also makes use of a point of faith affirmed by millions of Christians every Sunday: the descent of Christ into hell. Few doctrines are as familiar but as little discussed as this one. Connecting the descent of Christ with evangelization after death gives the position a tremendous foothold in church tradition as well as biblical warrant.

Finally, Fackre's presentation of eschatological evangelization and his distinction between the dual aspects of revelation and redemption appear to bolster the position in a significant way. According to Fackre, revelation and redemption are particularized and experienced most fully in the person of Jesus, but God has a universal outreach through general revelation that contains an element of redemptive grace. By presenting his case in this way, Fackre avoids a criticism of other presentations of postmortem evangelism — namely, that they inadequately affirm the principle that God's grace is active *now* in seeking all people.

On the other hand, the concept of postmortem evangelism has been subject to criticism from both the restrictivist and inclusivist camps. The restrictivist complaints fall into four basic categories.

1. Restrictivists question whether 1 Peter 3:19–4:6 in fact contains a reference to Christ's descent into hell and his preaching to sinners there.[68] The basic issue is whether this interpretation best fits with the context of Peter's exhorting his readers to persevere in their witness to Christ even if they must suffer for doing so. If their unbelieving neighbors are going to be given an opportunity after death to be converted then, "what need would there be to endure suffering for the sake of witnessing if those who fail now can repent later, after they die? And what point is there in enduring suffering as a Christian now if one will have another chance to be saved after death?"[69] Such questions would seem to reflect the belief that the only value of salvation in Christ is the reward of heaven. If people will have an opportunity of receiving heaven after death, then why bother to tell them about Christ now? Why suffer as a Christian if I can sin profligately now and still be saved after I die? Such questions imply a very low valuation of the abundant life, the experience of the comfort and fruits of the Holy Spirit, the joy and peace that Christ brings, the experience of the love of God in this present life. A more mature sensibility acknowledges that there are many good reasons for living the Christian life even if suffering

68. See Dalton, *Christ's Proclamation to the Spirits;* Grudem, "Christ Preaching through Noah"; and Feinberg, "1 Peter 3:18-20, Ancient Mythology, and the Intermediate State."

69. Grudem, "Christ Preaching through Noah," 23. Such questions go as far back as Augustine in his letter to Evodius. Augustine also had problems with this interpretation on the grounds that it implies that baptism is not necessary for salvation and it weakens the call to a holy life (see MacCulloch, *The Harrowing of Hell,* p. 258).

should arise and even if the people we witness to turn a deaf ear to our efforts. Eternal life is a new kind of life that begins now, not simply a ticket to heaven.

2. Restrictivists also oppose the contention that the only reason anyone will be condemned to hell is for explicitly rejecting Jesus Christ. "Man is lost by nature," writes Louis Berkhof, "and even original sin, as well as all actual sins, makes him worthy of condemnation. The rejection of Christ is undoubtedly a great sin, but is never represented as the only sin that leads to destruction."[70] John Frame agrees: "John 3:18 and similar passages teach that Jesus is the only way to salvation, but not that disbelief in him is the only ground for condemnation; we are condemned for all our sin, including our corporate sin in Adam."[71] Those who believe in evangelization after death could, however, respond in at least two ways. They could argue that God does indeed judge us for our sin but that this judgment occurs in this life and not at the final judgment, that at the final judgment the issue will be our response to Christ. Or they could argue that the judgment referred to in Romans 3 was dealt with at the cross of Christ, that no one is now under that judgment because Christ has removed it, that there remains only the final judgment, and our destiny there will be decided by our relationship to Jesus. Whether all the texts which speak of a judgment for the evil done while in the body can be explained in this way is a legitimate question.[72] If it can be demonstrated that Mark 16:15-16; Matthew 10:32-33; John 3:18, 36; 15:22; 16:8-9;

70. Berkhof, *Systematic Theology* (Grand Rapids: William B. Eerdmans, 1946), p. 693.

71. Frame, "Second Chance," in *Evangelical Dictionary of Theology*, ed. Walter Elwell (Grand Rapids: Baker Book House, 1984), p. 992.

72. Murray Harris does not think they can be. He claims that the basis of the final judgment is twofold: people will be judged for works of evil done in the body and for their rejection of Jesus Christ. Failure on either count will provide warrant for eternal punishment. See *From Grave to Glory* (Grand Rapids: Academie Books, 1990), pp. 234, 241.

and 2 Thessalonians 1:8 do, in fact, teach that the only reason anyone will be condemned to hell is for conscious rejection of the grace of Jesus Christ, then the theory of eschatological evangelization is on very firm ground.

3. Far and away the most debated claim made by proponents of postmortem evangelism is that human destiny is not fixed at death. The Western church, after Augustine, made this a dogma that was seldom questioned until the nineteenth century.[73] John Frame takes a particularly hard line: "God owes man nothing; he has already given to us a fair probation (in Adam); that any of us has opportunity to hear the gospel is an extraordinary divine kindness."[74] Though it is true that God owes us nothing, that is not the point in question. The issue is rather which view best makes sense of God's universal salvific will and the other guiding themes of Scripture. The verses typically cited in support of the belief that human destinies are sealed at death are easily dealt with by advocates of eschatological evangelization, as we have seen. At the very least, proponents of postmortem evangelization can argue that the biblical witness is not clear-cut on this matter.

4. Restrictivists also complain that the theory of postmortem evangelism takes the wind out of the sails of missions. If people will have an opportunity after death to accept Christ then, asks Louis Berkhof, "Why not leave them in ignorance as long as possible?"[75] Such an attitude again reflects an extremely narrow view of salvation. Proponents of postmortem evangelization would argue that we ought not leave anyone in

73. On this, see Alan Fairhurst, "Death and Destiny," *The Churchman* 95 (1981): 313-14. Also see Aquinas, *Summa Theologica*, Part 3, q.52, a.7; Jonathan Edwards, *The Works of Jonathan Edwards*, vol. 2 (Carlisle, Pa.: Banner of Truth, 1984), pp. 515-25; chap. 17 of the Scottish Confession of Faith (1560); chap. 26 of the Second Helvetic Confession (1566); the Westminster Confession (1646), 32.1; and question 86 of the Westminster Larger Catechism (1647).

74. Frame, "Second Chance," p. 992.

75. Berkhof, *Systematic Theology*, p. 693.

ignorance, because Christ has indicated that he wants to bring eternal life into their lives now. Some restrictivists counterargue that if it were in fact the case that all the unevangelized would hear the gospel in the clearest manner possible after death, and if the character and habits they develop during this life will influence their choice on that day, then evangelism now only constitutes a threat, since if it is imperfectly executed, it may only serve to harden them in their disbelief. The answer is that we must continue evangelizing because our Lord commanded us to do so, and we must take care to distinguish hardness against our presentation of the gospel from hardness against Jesus himself. It remains a possibility that those who have received the gospel message in this life and rejected it may still decide to accept it when they are confronted by the risen Lord himself. This is not to downplay the influence our character and habits will have on us in that day of decision, however. Proponents of postmortem evangelization concede that people can harden themselves against Christ and refuse him even after death. Most also grant that those who are confronted by the risen Lord will not necessarily find it any easier to accept him for that reason.[76]

Inclusivists also criticize the concept of eschatological evangelization on several counts. They challenge the assertion that general revelation is insufficient for salvation and that explicit knowledge of Jesus is necessary for salvation. Since I have already outlined these criticisms as they have been applied to restrictivists, I will not repeat them here. As we will see in Chapter 7, inclusivists reject these ideas in order to formulate a different model encompassing universally accessible salvation.

76. Herbert Luckock is one of the few proponents of evangelization after death who does argue that it will be easier to accept Christ after death. Even so, he contends that we must preach the gospel and leave such problems to God (*The Intermediate State between Death and Judgment*, pp. 192-93).

## Historical Bibliography

### 1. Early Church through the Eighteenth Century

Many of the early Church Fathers taught the release of souls in hell via the descent of Christ. Some of those mentioned in the following list held that Christ delivered all prisoners from hell, while others maintained that not all chose to follow him from hell. Although not all of these figures mention whether or not evangelization after death continues to the present time, all may be included as defending the wider hope. The list includes some of the greatest names in the history of the church: Melito, Hippolytus, Clement of Alexandria, Origen (the last two developed this position in a universalistic direction), Athanasius, Gregory of Nazianzus, Ephraem, perhaps Jerome and Hilary, Cyril of Alexandria, Maximus the Confessor, John of Damascus, the seventh-century Irish missionary Clement, and the ninth-century monk Probus. For documentation see J. A. MacCulloch, *The Harrowing of Hell* (Edinburgh: T. & T. Clark, 1930); E. H. Plumptre, *The Spirits in Prison* (London: Isbister, 1898); Bo Reicke, *The Disobedient Spirits and Christian Baptism* (Copenhagen: Egnar Munsksgaard, 1946); and William Dalton, *Christ's Proclamation to the Spirits: A Study of 1 Peter 3:18–4:6* (Rome: Pontifical Biblical Institute, 1965).

Though Dante did not advocate the theory of postmortem evangelism, he does give voice to a similar concept in his narrative of Trajan's reincarnation from limbo and conversion (see *Paradiso,* 20.43-48). Luther's colleague Melanchthon did not believe in postmortem evangelism, but he said that it was plausible that in his descent into hell, Christ may have saved "the most distinguished men from all nations, as, for example, Scipio, Fabius, and others" (see George Williams, "Erasmus and the Reformers on Non-Christian Religions and *Salus Extra Ecclesiam,*" in *Action and Conviction in Early Modern Europe,* ed. Theodore Rabb and Jerrold Seigel [Princeton: Princeton University Press, 1969], p. 353). It has been argued that Andreas Carlstadt held so strong a view of the teaching function of purgatory as to have advocated a form of evangelization after death (see Williams, "Erasmus and the Reformers," pp. 364-65).

## 2. Nineteenth Century

Once the acrimony over the doctrine of purgatory died down after the Reformation, Protestants were able to reopen the discussion of Christ's descent into hell and the possibility of postmortem evangelization. See John Lange, *The First Epistle General of Peter* (New York: Charles Scribner, 1868), pp. 66-75; I. A. Dorner, *A System of Christian Doctrine* (Edinburgh: T. & T. Clark, 1890), pp. 130-35; Herbert Luckock, *The Intermediate State between Death and Judgment* (New York: Thomas Whittaker, 1890), pp. 183-208; Frederic Huidekoper, *The Belief of the First Three Centuries concerning Christ's Mission to the Underworld* (Boston: Crosby, Nichols, 1854); Egbert Smyth, "Probation after Death," *The Homiletic Review* 11 (April 1886): 281-91. Franz Delitzsch says, "so long as there is Time, conversion must be possible" (*A System of Biblical Psychology*, 2d ed. [Edinburgh: T. & T. Clark, 1879], pp. 483-84, 553). Herman Cremer says, "no one now can be lost or blessed except as this is determined by his attitude towards Christ and the redemption. . . . In the realm of death, there is still a preaching of the gospel . . . for the purpose of winning even the dead for the Lord's kingdom of heaven" (*Beyond the Grave* [New York: Harper, 1886], p. 107). And for the views of Julius Müller, F. Godet, H. Meyer, Van Oosterzee, Martenson, and T. Field, see Thomas Field, "The Andover Theory of Future Probation," *The Andover Review* 7 (May 1887): 461-75.

Some writers have mistakenly thought that E. H. Plumptre believed in postmortem evangelism, but he only went so far as to say that all those living before the incarnation had an opportunity to accept Christ when he descended into hell (*The General Epistles of Peter and Jude* [Cambridge: Cambridge

University Press, 1903], pp. 131-42). He believed that those born after the incarnation can be saved apart from knowledge of Christ. In other words, he held an inclusivist position concerning postincarnation humanity (see *The Acts of the Apostles* [New York: Cassell, n.d.], pp. 72, 178-79).

### 3. Twentieth Century

The twentieth century has witnessed a tremendous proliferation of belief in eschatological evangelization among theologians and biblical commentators from diverse traditions. Commentators such as Charles Bigg, F. W. Farrar, J. L. König, Beyschlag, E. Huther, and Ernest Best have interpreted 1 Peter 3:19 as teaching evangelization after death (see Bo Reicke, *The Disobedient Spirits and Christian Baptism*, pp. 47-49; Dalton, *Christ's Proclamation to the Spirits*, 21n.34; and Wayne Grudem, "Christ Preaching through Noah: 1 Peter 3:19-20 in the Light of Dominant Themes in Jewish Literature," *Trinity Journal* 7 [1986]: 4n.2).

　　For additional affirmations of this position, see the following: C. E. B. Cranfield, "The Interpretation of 1 Peter 3:19 and 4:6," *The Expository Times* 69 (Sept. 1958): 369-72; and *The First Epistle of Peter* (London: SCM Press, 1954), pp. 80-91; G. R. Beasley-Murray, *Baptism in the New Testament* (Grand Rapids: William B. Eerdmans, 1962), pp. 258-59; Bo Reicke, *The Epistles of Peter and Jude* (Garden City, N.Y.: Doubleday, 1964), pp. 108-19; and *The Disobedient Spirits and Christian Baptism*, pp. 52-131; Joseph Leckie, *The World to Come and Final Destiny* (Edinburgh: T. & T. Clark, 1922), pp. 88-102; J. A. MacCulloch, *The Harrowing of Hell*, pp. 324-25; Donald Bloesch, *Essentials of Evangelical Theology*, 2 vols. (San Francisco: Harper and Row, 1978), 1: 242-47, 2: 224-30; and "Descent into Hell," *Evangelical Dictionary of Theology*, ed. Walter Elwell (Grand Rapids: Baker Book House, 1984), pp. 313-14; John Lawson, *Introduction to Christian Doctrine* (Wilmore, Ky.:

Francis Asbury Press, 1980), pp. 216-17, 262-63; Wolfhart Pannenberg, *The Apostles' Creed* (Philadelphia: Westminster Press, 1972), pp. 90-95; and *Jesus — God and Man,* 2d ed. (Philadelphia: Westminster Press, 1977), pp. 269-74; Richard Swinburne, *Faith and Reason* (New York: Oxford University Press, 1981), p. 169; Richard Creel, *Divine Impassibility* (Cambridge: Cambridge University Press, 1986), p. 147; Brian Hebblethwaite, *The Christian Hope* (Grand Rapids: William B. Eerdmans, 1984), pp. 218-19; Carl Braaten, "Lutheran Theology and Religious Pluralism," *Lutheran World Federation* 23-24 (Jan. 1988): 105-28; and *The Flaming Center: A Theology of the Christian Mission* (Philadelphia: Fortress Press, 1977), p. 117; Stephen T. Davis, "Universalism, Hell, and the Fate of the Ignorant," *Modern Theology* 6 (Jan. 1990): 173-86; Gabriel Fackre, *The Christian Story,* rev. ed. (Grand Rapids: William B. Eerdmans, 1984), pp. 219-21, 229-41; and "The Scandals of Particularity and Universality," *Midstream* 22 (Jan. 1983): 32-52; George Lindbeck, *The Nature of Doctrine: Religion and Theology in a Postliberal Age* (Philadelphia: Westminster Press, 1984), pp. 46-72; "Unbelievers and the Sola Christi," *Dialog* 12 (1973): 182-89; and *"Fides ex auditu* and the Salvation of Non-Christians: Contemporary Catholic and Protestant Positions," in *The Gospel and the Ambiguity of the Church,* ed. Vilmos Vajta (Minneapolis: Fortress Press, 1974), pp. 92-123.

On Paul Althaus's advocacy of the position, see George Lindbeck, *"Fides ex auditu* and the Salvation of Non-Christians," p. 114; on P. T. Forsyth, see Donald Bloesch, *Essentials of Evangelical Theology,* 1: 246.

# CHAPTER 7

## *Inclusivism: Universally Accessible Salvation apart from Evangelization*

Some advocates of the wider hope maintain that some of those who never hear the gospel of Christ may nevertheless attain salvation before they die if they respond in faith to the revelation they do have. Proponents of this position — which I will be referring to as *inclusivism* — contend that the unevangelized are saved or lost on the basis of their commitment, or lack thereof, to the God who saves through the work of Jesus. They believe that appropriation of salvific grace is mediated through general revelation and God's providential workings in human history. Briefly, inclusivists affirm the particularity and finality of salvation only in Christ but deny that knowledge of his work is necessary for salvation. That is to say, they hold that the work of Jesus is ontologically necessary for salvation (no one would be saved without it) but not epistemologically necessary (one need not be aware of the work in order to benefit from it). Or in other words, people can receive the gift of salvation without knowing the giver or the precise nature of the gift.

Inclusivism clearly stands apart from most of the other views we have surveyed in its insistence that explicit knowledge of the historical work of Christ is not necessary for salvation. This is not to say that there are not points of contact, however. Inclusivists agree with restrictivists that there will be no opportunity after death for obtaining salvation, for example. They also agree with both restrictivists and proponents of eschatological evangelization that an act of faith (trusting God) is essential for obtaining salvation. But inclusivism also departs from both views in its assertion that God is working toward the salvation of all people at the present time and makes salvation universally accessible even though not all hear about Jesus before death. If the redemption procured by Jesus objectively provides for the salvation of every human being, and if God intends this salvation to be genuinely universal, then it must be possible for every individual who has ever lived personally to receive that salvation regardless of the historical era, geographic region, or cultural setting in which these people have lived. Inclusivists argue that the salvation God so magnanimously gives is, and has been, available in every age and culture and spot on the globe apart from any specific knowledge of God's historical activity in Israel and in his son Jesus.

Inclusivism has its roots in the early church, and since the time of the Reformation it has steadily increased in popularity. Today it is the dominant view among Roman Catholic theologians, and it is beginning to challenge restrictivism for supremacy within evangelical circles.[1]

1. A survey conducted at the 1975 Urbana missions conference indicated the 37 percent of the five thousand evangelicals who responded could be classified as restrictivists, while 25 percent could be classified as inclusivists (see Arthur Johnston, "Focus Comment," *Trinity World Forum* 1 [Fall 1975]: 3). I believe the percentage of inclusivists would be much higher today. Moreover, inclusivism has always been an option within even conservative evangelicalism — a fact Paul Knitter fails to take into account in his discussion of evangelicalism in *No Other Name?* (Maryknoll, N.Y.: Orbis Books, 1985), pp. 79-80. As we shall see, inclusivism is well represented among conservative evangelicals as well as neo-evangelicals.

## Key Biblical Texts

In making their case, inclusivists typically cite not only those texts affirming universally accessible salvation but also a variety of texts dealing with the character and will of God and his dealings with Gentiles.

The first set of texts dealing with God's character and will focuses on God's extension of grace to all who believe in him. For example, 1 Timothy 4:10 ("we have fixed our hope on the living God, who is the Savior of all men, especially of believers") is interpreted as meaning that the living God saves all who believe in him and that the specific content of saving faith may vary so long as it is grounded in an essential trust in God. Texts referring to the fact that Jesus came into the world to save sinners rather than condemn them (e.g., 1 Tim. 1:15, John 3:16-17) are cited as evidence of God's universal salvific will. Jesus is the light that came into the world and enlightens every person (John 1:9). Not all respond positively to this light — it is not irresistible — but every person experiences the illumination of the Logos to one degree or another.

Inclusivists maintain that through the power of his resurrection, the light of the world is seeking to draw all people to himself (John 12:32). This same Jesus was successful in drawing to himself those specifically considered outcasts in Jewish society — publicans and sinners (Luke 15). The term *sinner* in the synoptic Gospels denotes a Jew who willfully refused to follow God's instructions as laid out in the Mosaic covenant. Such people were considered worse than Gentiles by Jewish religious leaders. Luke 15 contains three parables illustrating God's compassion for and willingness to save them. The parables of the lost sheep and lost coin speak of God's perseverance in searching for these people — whom he considers to belong to him but who are, at the moment, lost. The parable of the prodigal son teaches about the patience God has in waiting for repentance and the joy he has when it is forthcoming. If God is indeed not willing that any should perish but wishes all to come to repentance (2 Pet. 3:9), and if he does seek the lone lost publican and sinner in this way, is it credible that he would create billions of people without any hope for salvation? The one who prayed, "Father, forgive them; for they do not know what they are doing" (Luke 23:34) would not leave the unevangelized without hope, say the inclusivists. They reject as inconceivable the assertion that the Son of God who forgave those who hated him and persecuted him to death would simply condemn with the wave of a hand all the unevangelized. They maintain that when all people stand before Christ in the eschaton, the question will not be "Do you know Jesus?" (as restrictivists believe) but rather "Does Jesus know you?" (Matt. 7:23).

The second group of texts focuses on God's attitude toward and relationship with the Gentiles outside the covenant with Israel. The Old Testament contains specific declarations that God's benevolent activity is not restricted to the Hebrew people. Deuteronomy mentions several nations for whom God provided land by driving out the previous inhabitants (Deut. 2:5, 9, 19, 21-22; cf. 2 Kings 5:1). The prophet Amos declared that God had performed events similar to the exodus of Israel for other nations (9:7). Inclusivists see in these texts an indication that God did not cut off his gracious activity among the nations just because he elected Israel for a special task. God's salvific will is universal, and that is clearly manifested in the universal covenants of Genesis, which were neither revoked nor replaced by later covenants.[2]

The first covenant mentioned in the Bible is one made between God and the human race, not God and Israel. God created human beings in his own image and gave them responsibilities (Gen. 1:26-28). After the fall, God promised Eve

2. The following information is drawn from Richard Drummond's *Toward a New Age in Christian Theology* (Maryknoll, N.Y.: Orbis Books, 1985), pp. 5-6. The idea that God made such covenants with the Gentiles existed in Judaism at the time the New Testament was being written. Sirach 17:12 says that God made an "eternal covenant" with them.

a "seed" who would provide deliverance from the curse (Gen. 3:15). This promise, which is fulfilled in the work of Christ, is destined for the benefit of all people. Noah's sons are considered the fathers of the nations, and the Noachic covenant is made with "all flesh" (Gen. 9:8-19). When God selected Abraham for a special work, he still had the blessing of "all the families of the earth" in mind (Gen. 12:3). We can get a sense of the considerable importance of this universal blessing from the fact that it is mentioned four more times in the book of Genesis (18:18; 22:18; 26:4; 28:14). All the covenants that God made after these were intended not to abrogate but rather to bring to fruition his universal blessing. The universal is made manifest through the particular: first through the Israelites and then specifically through the incarnation of the Son of God.

These universal covenants are not the only source of information in the Old Testament concerning God's dealings with the Gentiles. The Bible contains numerous indications that God showed favor to Gentiles and other individuals who lived before the establishment of the covenant with Abraham.[3] Not a few of these individuals occupy prominent places in the biblical narrative — Abel, Enoch, Lot, Job, Balaam, the Queen of Sheba, and Ruth, for example. Of particular significance are such Gentiles as Melchizedek, Jethro, Rahab, and Naaman. Melchizedek is elevated above Abraham in the Genesis narrative and becomes in later biblical history the model of the ideal priesthood (Ps. 110:4; Heb. 7:17). Remarkably, Scripture ascribes the establishment of Israel's judiciary system to Moses' father-in-law, the pagan priest Jethro (Exod. 18:17-23). Moreover, this Gentile priest was allowed to offer sacrifices to the God of Israel, presumably at the tent of meeting (Exod. 18:12). Rahab is singled out as an example of faith for all people to emulate (Heb. 11:31), despite the fact that her faith was clearly not theologically well informed.

3. For a discussion, see Drummond, *Toward a New Age in Christian Theology*, pp. 11-13; and Part 1 of Walbert Bühlmann's *God's Chosen Peoples* (Maryknoll, N.Y.: Orbis Books, 1982).

The case of the Syrian military officer Naaman is quite interesting. The Bible affirms his faith as genuine, despite the fact that he came to it reluctantly. When Elisha told him to dip himself in the Jordan River seven times to rid himself of his leprosy, he initially refused, skeptical that such a ritual would bring a response from any god (2 Kings 5:11-12). In the end, however, he did as he was told and was healed. In response he confessed his faith in the God of Israel and asked forgiveness for when he would have to go into the temple of the god Rimmon in Syria. Elisha gave his blessing upon this. The interesting point here is not only that Naaman came to faith in God reluctantly but that he also labored under a serious theological misconception. Even after his confession of faith he seems to have persisted in a geographic god concept (different gods for different lands), and the fact that he took dirt from the land of Israel back with him to Syria for sacrificial purposes (5:17) seems to suggest a touch of animism in his beliefs as well. Inclusivists view God's acceptance of Naaman despite his errors in belief and his persistence in entering a pagan temple as evidence that God is more inclined to grant salvation to those who exhibit faith than to those who are simply adhering to a detailed set of doctrines or liturgical practices.

Elsewhere we learn that God worked through Cyrus the king of Persia and desired Cyrus to acknowledge this fact (Isa. 45:1-7). Daniel expected Nebuchadnezzar to know who the God of heaven was and acknowledge him. In the story of Jonah, the faith of the pagan sailors who "feared the Lord greatly" and who "offered a sacrifice to the Lord and made vows" (1:16) is hailed as exemplary, whereas the theologically well-informed faith of Jonah is called into question. God announced through the prophet Amos that though he had chosen Israel for a special work, he did not show favoritism (9:7): his gracious activities were present in other peoples as well. And while it is true that God did sometimes call the Gentile nations to account, the judgments he leveled against them were primarily for moral failures rather than religious failures as such (Amos 1:1–2:8;

Obad. 15; Nah. 1:2; Zech. 9:1). Furthermore, the fact that God did hold them accountable is testimony that they did have genuine knowledge of God and obligations to him even though their religion did not line up exactly with that revealed to Israel. Inclusivists contend that the Old Testament clearly witnesses to the fact that God is concerned with those outside the special covenant with Israel.

They find much the same kind of evidence in the New Testament — for example, the apostle Paul's emphatic declaration that God is the God of the Gentiles and not of the Jews only (Rom. 3:29). Jesus addressed his harshest criticisms and talk of a narrow way to those who had the Old Testament revelation; he used a much softer tone in reference to the Gentiles. And, as in the Old Testament, so in the New, certain Gentiles are lifted up as examples of faith. Matthew appears to have considered the account of the magi quite important, inasmuch as he devotes a considerable amount of space to it. And he cites them as examples of faith despite the fact that they were pagan astrologers who had a very limited understanding concerning Jesus: they were seeking a king, not a savior. The Gospel of Matthew also notes that Jesus found "great faith" in such unexpected individuals as a Canaanite woman (15:21-28) and a Roman centurion. Regarding the centurion, Jesus said, "truly I say to you, I have not found such great faith with anyone in Israel" (Matt. 8:10). Yet, what was his faith? Did he acknowledge the divinity of Jesus? Did he formulate in his own way the essential beliefs expressed in the Apostles' Creed? No! He simply believed that Jesus had miraculous powers and a benevolent character. Although his understanding was not theologically developed, it was commended for its existential quality. Such positive appraisals of the faith and even salvation of certain Gentiles is also found among some Rabbis and Jewish literature of Jesus' day (e.g., 1 Enoch 108:11-14).[4]

4. See E. P. Sanders, *Paul and Palestinian Judaism* (Philadelphia: Fortress Press, 1977), pp. 207-12.

But the Gentile of most interest to inclusivists is Cornelius. Acts 10 gives the account of how a Roman centurion who feared God and prayed regularly became a convert to Christianity. This is a key story for Luke, since it recounts how God took the initiative in reaching out to the Gentiles and brought the church to the realization that the gospel is truly universal in its application. The primary point of the story is that the Jewish Christians believed that the message of Christ was directed solely to Israel, but God had other ideas. They had a very difficult time accepting the proposition that Jesus is the promised blessing for all the nations (Gen. 12:3).

Cornelius was a God-fearing uncircumcised Gentile who prayed continually. An angel informed him that his prayers and alms were a memorial offering of which God took note (Acts 10:4). As noted in Chapter 2, it is generally the understanding of the Christian community that Cornelius was a "saved" believer before Peter arrived and that he became a Christian after receiving Christ and being baptized. Both Luther and Calvin endorse this assessment.[5] Calvin's point is that Cornelius was not saved by works but that his works were a sign that he was already illumined by the Spirit, endowed with wisdom from above, and sanctified. Cornelius had already subjectively appropriated the merits of Christ's objective redemption through genuine faith in God. He was already worshiping the *God* who saves through Jesus Christ. What he received from Peter was the fullness of salvation that comes from a personal relationship with Christ. To argue that Cornelius could not have been saved until he heard about the work of Jesus is to exhibit precisely the sort of narrowness that God worked to overcome in the early Jewish church.

Peter learned that God's salvific vision transcended such narrowness: "I most certainly understand now that God is not

5. See Luther, *Lectures on Galatians,* vol. 26 of *Luther's Works,* ed. Jaroslav Pelikan (St Louis: Concordia Publishing, 1963), p. 210; and Calvin, *Institutes of the Christian Religion,* 3.17.4.

one to show partiality, but in every nation the man who fears Him and does what is right, is welcome to Him" (Acts 10:34-35). Such a change in theology did not come easily for Peter. He admitted that he did not understand at first the vision God had given him (10:10-17) and that he was ethnocentric to the point that he did not question the validity of his cultural norms (10:28). The impartiality of God and the universality of his grace finally got through to Peter. "So Peter says, 'but in *every* nation *anyone* who fears him and does what is right is acceptable to him' (10:35). Again, Peter calls Jesus the 'Lord of *all*' (10:36) and describes how he did good and healed *all* that were oppressed by the devil (10:38). This Jesus will be the judge of all, the living and the dead (10:42), and *every one* who believes will receive forgiveness of sins through his name (10:43). Although this universality seems so obvious today, it was not always apparent to the church."[6]

The incident with Cornelius led Peter to broaden the scope of his theology concerning those who fear God. He no longer included only those who kept the Old Testament covenant but opened his arms to embrace all those who trusted God and sought to follow him as best they knew. The righteousness Peter had in mind here was not the righteousness derived from being associated with the Mosaic covenant but the righteousness derived from being in a proper relationship with God regardless of how he has been revealed to the individual.

Inclusivists do not claim that people are saved by their righteousness; they contend that people like Cornelius are saved because they have the "habit of faith," which involves penitence. But inclusivists do claim that it is not necessary to understand the work of Christ in order to be saved. G. Campbell Morgan wrote, "no man is to be saved because he understands the doctrine of the Atonement. He is saved, not by understanding it, but because he fears God, and works righteousness. Oh, the glad and glorious surprise of those ultimate days when we find

---

6. Frank Matera, "Acts 10:34-43," *Interpretation* 41 (Jan. 1987): 64.

that there will be those who walked in the light they had, and wrought righteousness, and were acceptable to Him; not because of their morality, but by the infinite merit of the Cross, and by the fact that they yielded themselves to the light they possessed."[7]

Inclusivists use the story of Cornelius and the other biblical references about the Gentiles of faith mentioned above as evidence for their contention that God gave saving grace to the Gentiles long before the church arrived on the scene and that the unevangelized may be saved by Christ without knowing about Christ. E. H. Plumptre summed up the position well: "the truth which St. Peter thus set forth proclaims at once the equity and the love of the Father, and sweeps away the narrowing dreams which confine the hope of salvation to the circumcised, as did the theology of the Rabbis; or to those who have received the outward ordinance of baptism, as did the theology of Augustine and the medieval church; or, as do some forms of Protestant dogmatism, to those who have heard and believed the story of the Cross of Christ."[8]

## Theological Considerations

### 1. Believers vs. Christians

There are five basic theological arguments put forth in support of inclusivism. The first of these centers on a distinction between believers and Christians and is usually closely connected with the issue of faithful Gentiles. In this context, believers can be defined as all those who are saved because they have faith

---

7. Morgan, *The Acts of the Apostles* (New York: Fleming H. Revell, 1924), p. 281.
8. E. H. Plumptre, *The Acts of the Apostles with Commentary*, ed. Charles John Ellicott (New York: Cassell, Petter & Galpin, n.d.), p. 179.

in God. Inclusivists contend that all Christians are believers but that not all believers are Christians. They define a Christian as a believer who knows about and participates in the work of Jesus Christ.

Inclusivists grant that saving faith certainly involves knowledge, but they maintain that it is an open question how much knowledge is required and what its specific content is. Is cognitive information the most important element in saving faith, or is a person's attitude the decisive factor? On the basis of 1 Corinthians 15:3-4, restrictivists state flatly that "first, one must know the fact that the death of Christ was for sins according to the Scriptures; second, that He was buried; and, third, that He arose from the dead."[9] Inclusivists respond that in this passage Paul is not saying that an individual has to know these facts to be saved; he is simply stating that he had proclaimed these facts to the Corinthians. In response to the general assertion that one must have explicit knowledge of Christ to be saved, J. N. D. Anderson asks, "Does ignorance disqualify for grace? If so, where in Scripture do we have the exact amount of knowledge required set out? For *assurance*, no doubt, knowledge is required, but for grace it is not so much knowledge as a right attitude towards God that matters."[10] This raises the issue of the nature of saving faith, and on this point inclusivists appeal to the Old Testament believers for their definition.[11]

If knowledge of Christ is necessary for salvation, then how are we to explain the salvation of the Old Testament believers, whose knowledge was quite limited concerning the Messiah but who were justified by faith in God's word? The majority of Old Testament believers certainly had no conception of Christ's death

9. H. Phillip Hook, "A Biblical Definition of Saving Faith," *Bibliotheca Sacra*, April-June 1964, p. 136.

10. Anderson, *Christianity and Comparative Religion* (Downers Grove, Ill.: InterVarsity Press, 1977), p. 99.

11. For a discussion of the nature of salvation in the Old Testament as it relates to the unevangelized, see Russell Aldwinckle, *Jesus: A Savior or the Savior?* (Macon, Ga.: Mercer University Press, 1982), pp. 19ff.

and resurrection, and yet they experienced the saving hand of God. It is true that Paul says the gospel was preached to Abraham (Gal. 3:6), though it seems doubtful that Abraham could have understood the historical incarnation and the meaning of Christ's death and resurrection.[12] The Old Testament believers did not connect the coming of the messianic king with atonement for their salvation in the sense that they thought of the Messiah as the primary object of faith for forgiveness of sins. All that was required of them was to "call on the name of the Lord" (Gen. 4:26). Anderson asserts that the Old Testament believers' "knowledge was deficient, their assurance often fitful, but their forgiven status identical with ours."[13] Inclusivists concede that in an ontological sense their salvation ultimately depended on the atonement of Jesus, since no one is saved apart from the redemptive work of Christ. That is why Paul said that they drank from the rock of Christ (1 Cor. 10:4). But inclusivists hold that while the source of salvific water is the same for all people, it comes to various people through different channels.

Inclusivists contend not only that the Old Testament believers drew on the same source of salvation as Christians do today but also that they appropriated salvation in the same way — namely, by trust in God. God is pleased whenever and however a person manifests trust in him. But the specific occasions for and content of the trust of the Old Testament believers varied. Abraham trusted God to give him a son in old age, Gideon trusted that God would be with him in battle, and Samson trusted that God would help him destroy a temple. The specific content of faith varied from one person to the next throughout the Old Testament, but the common threads were trust in the object of their faith — God. The famed English poet John Milton applied this idea to the unevangelized: "the ultimate object of faith is not

12. There are those who do believe that Abraham knew these truths, however. See, for example, James M. Boice, *God the Redeemer* (Downers Grove, Ill.: InterVarsity Press, 1978), p. 116.

13. Anderson, *Christianity and Comparative Religion*, p. 99.

Christ, the Mediator, but God the Father. . . . So it does not seem surprising that there are a lot of Jews, and Gentiles too, who are saved although they believed or believe in God alone, either because they lived before Christ or because, even though they have lived after him, he has not been revealed to them. In spite of this they are saved by means of Christ."[14]

Paul brings out these very points in his discussion of the salvation of Old Testament saints in Romans 4. He claims that the justification by faith he is preaching was taught in the Old Testament as well. To substantiate this, he points to Abraham, who was justified because he believed that God would fulfill his promise to grant him a son (Gen. 15:6). This is an astonishing action by God: giving someone salvation because he believes he will have a son in old age! Paul applies this same principle to his contemporaries when he says that the benefits of justification by faith were not just for Abraham but "for our sakes too, to whom it will be reckoned [i.e., faith reckoned as righteousness], as those who believe in Him who raised Jesus our Lord from the dead" (Rom. 4:24). Our faith is not reckoned as righteousness because it has the same content as Abraham's but because the object of our faith (God) and the action of our faith (trust) are identical. We believe in the same God even though Abraham identified him as the God who kept his word and we identify him as the God who raised Jesus from the dead.

Many commentators interpret Romans 4:24 as specifying that we must believe in the resurrection of Jesus in order to be saved, but, as Godet correctly pointed out, Paul did not say "when we believe in the resurrection of Jesus" but "when we believe in *God who raised Jesus.*"[15] Paul definitely says we must believe in the same God as Abraham for salvation, but he does not say we must know about the resurrection in order to be saved. All those who

14. Milton, *Christian Doctrine,* trans. John Carey, in *The Complete Prose Works of John Milton,* vol. 6 (New Haven: Yale University Press, 1973), p. 475.
15. F. Godet, *Commentary on St. Paul's Epistle to the Romans* (New York: Funk & Wagnalls, 1883), pp. 183-84.

are saved are saved by believing in the same God even though he may be known to various people through various identifying characteristics — to Abraham as the God who gives a son in old age, to the evangelized as the God who raised Jesus from the dead, to the unevangelized as the God who created and providentially cares for them (Acts 14:17). "It is the Name," says Dale Moody, "the personal reality of God known in personal relation, that saves, not knowledge *about* the historical Jesus."[16]

Hebrews 11:6 also brings out this idea: "without faith it is impossible to please Him, for He who comes to God must believe that He is, and that He is a rewarder of those who seek Him." Anyone who believes that God will respond benevolently to those who seek him thereby gives evidence of trusting God and thus possesses saving faith. According to E. H. Plumptre, being saved through the sort of faith described in Hebrews 11:6 "is compatible with ignorance of any historical revelation through Moses or through Christ."[17] Inclusivists contend that saving faith involves the process of moving from some truths about God's character to a degree of trust in the person of God that results in obedience to his will.[18]

There are two points we should note in connection with this definition of faith. First, most inclusivists maintain that an "act of faith" or a conscious decision for God is necessary for salvation.[19] Without a positive response to God, a person cannot be saved.[20] One essential aspect of this act of faith is

16. Moody, *The Word of Truth* (Grand Rapids: William B. Eerdmans, 1981), p. 61.

17. Plumptre, *The Spirits in Prison* (London: Isbister, 1898), p. 163.

18. No merely formal act (religious ritual) or profession of belief will save a person. What is required is heartfelt trust and willingness to do God's will (Matt. 7:21-22; 25:31-46; 3 John 11).

19. Aldwinckle disagrees with Karl Rahner on this point; see *Jesus: A Savior or the Savior?* pp. 179-81, 189.

20. Neal Punt disagrees. He asserts that all are saved except those who pointedly reject God. In a sense, then, he contends that an act of unfaith is required to lose the salvation that one otherwise has. See *Unconditional Good News* (Grand Rapids: William B. Eerdmans, 1980), pp. 30, 89-90.

penitent humility. According to E. J. Carnell, "God only asks humility, and humility is within the reach of one who feels even the faintest stirring of guilt in his heart."[21] God is looking for the kind of confession found in the Babylonian text "Prayer to Any God," in which the supplicant says, "the sin I have sinned — turn thou to good; the transgression I have committed — may the wind carry away! My iniquities (which are) many — like a garment strip off. My god — the transgressions seven times seven, my transgressions, forgive."[22] God desires such a heart, and lack of it constitutes sufficient cause for damnation. E. B. Pusey asserted that "we *do* know, that none will be lost, who do not obstinately to the end and in the end refuse God."[23]

The second point worthy of note in connection with the inclusivist definition of faith is that it does affirm that some degree of cognitive information is essential for saving faith but that the Scriptures do not set out the precise amount of information that is required. J. Gresham Machen said, "no one knows how little a person can believe and still be saved."[24] It is not a perfectly developed theology that saves but the gracious Lord and Creator of all. The Baptist theologian A. H. Strong wrote that "the patriarchs, though they had not knowledge of a personal Christ, were saved by believing in God so far as God had revealed himself to them; and whoever among the heathen are saved, must in like manner be saved by casting themselves as helpless sinners upon God's plan of mercy, dimly shadowed forth in nature and providence. But such faith, even among the patriarchs and heathen, is implicitly a faith in Christ, and would become explicit and conscious

21. Carnell, *Christian Commitment: An Apologetic* (New York: Macmillan, 1957), p. 238.
22. "Prayer to Any God," in *Documents from Old Testament Times,* ed. D. Winton Thomas (New York: Harper & Row, 1961), p. 114.
23. Pusey, *What Is of Faith as to Everlasting Punishment?* (London: Rivington, 1880), p. 23.
24. Machen, cited in *Eternity,* Dec. 1976, p. 15.

trust and submission, whenever Christ were made known to them."[25]

These general inclusivist principles entail a distinction between believers and Christians: both groups are saved by the name of Jesus, but only the latter are informed about that name.[26] Both believers and Christians are saved in that they are accepted by God and have experienced some aspects of redemptive grace. But believers have not experienced salvation in its fullness since they are ignorant of the work of Christ.[27] Although believers may make intellectual errors, this does not prevent them from trusting the living God as authentically as Christians do. Stuart Hackett asserts that "it is not unthinkable for even the most orthodox Christian believer to suppose plausibly that there are certain unidentified persons, involved in very different religious traditions than our own and having their minds clouded in varying degrees by errors quite different from our own — but who are, in spite of these conceptual shortcomings, nevertheless trusting in the true God as genuinely as ourselves."[28] Missiologist Charles Kraft makes a similar point when he suggests that there is a significant sense in which it is impossible to distinguish Christians from non-

25. Strong, *Systematic Theology* (Philadelphia: Judson Press, 1947), p. 842.

26. The distinction between believers and Christians goes back at least to the eighteenth century, when William Paley distinguished the "dispensation" of Christianity from the "revelation" of Christianity. The dispensation, he said, is the gracious way God has always dealt with the human race, whereas the revelation is the knowledge of that grace as revealed in Jesus. See George Fisk, *Paley's View of the Evidences of Christianity* (Cambridge: J. Hall, 1890), pp. 219-20; and Edward Grinfield, *Salvability of the Heathen* (London: Rivington, 1827), pp. 8-9, 392.

27. On the use of the word *saved* in this way, see pp. 64-67 herein. Most inclusivists would say that were believers to hear the word of Christ, they would accept it and experience salvation in its fullness as many believers did in Acts 2:41. See, e.g., Anderson, *Christianity and Comparative Religion*, p. 105.

28. Hackett, *The Reconstruction of the Christian Revelation Claim* (Grand Rapids: Baker Book House, 1984), p. 246.

Christians on the basis of their behavior or professed beliefs. "The basis on which God interacts with (and reveals himself to) human beings is . . . a *directional* basis rather than a *positional* one," says Kraft.[29] By this he means that God accepts or rejects people not primarily on the specific knowledge they possess or the concrete behavior they display — the position they are at — but the *direction* in which they are heading. People are either heading toward God or away from him. There are, after all, people who speak and act in what appears to be a Christian manner who are in fact not Christians; Kraft maintains that there are also people without knowledge of Christ who nevertheless are accepted by God since they are believers moving in the proper direction.[30] He contends that there is a tremendous range of acceptable starting points from which God begins his transforming work.

Restrictivists and proponents of eschatological evangelization object strongly to the believer/Christian distinction on the grounds that it opens to the door to salvation apart from knowledge of Christ. They maintain that there are no believers who are not Christians. Inclusivists respond by pointing out that virtually all orthodox Christian groups allow for the salvation of some human beings without knowledge of Christ — namely, infants who die. Lutheran, Reformed, Roman Catholic, and evangelical communions have all affirmed that such infants are saved without evangelization and without explicit knowledge of the person and work of Christ. If these human beings are saved without knowledge of Christ, say inclusivists, why is it impossible that the unevangelized

29. Kraft, *Christianity in Culture* (Maryknoll, N.Y.: Orbis Books, 1979), p. 240.
30. See Kraft, *Christianity in Culture*, pp. 240-44. C. S. Lewis makes a similar point when he says, "there are people . . . who are slowly ceasing to be Christian but who still call themselves by that name. . . . There are other people who are slowly becoming Christians though they do not yet call themselves so." He includes peoples in other religions in this last category (*Mere Christianity* [New York: Macmillan, 1960], pp. 176-77).

might be saved? The Quaker Robert Barclay put this argument
to his contemporaries in 1676: "if there were such an absolute
necessity for this outward knowledge, that it were even of the
essentials of salvation, then none could be saved without it;
whereas our adversaries deny not, but readily confess, that
many infants and deaf persons are saved without it: so that
here they break that general rule, and make salvation possible
without it."[31]

By arguing that believers are saved without knowledge of
Christ, inclusivists imply that the unevangelized "may receive
a gift without knowing from whom it comes, or how much it
has cost."[32] Children who believe they are receiving gifts from
Santa Claus can enjoy them even though ignorant of the true
giver. And, just as we hope they grow up to know the real giver,
inclusivists express the hope that believers will come to know
the source of their salvation — Jesus Christ. It is true that if
believers are saved, their understanding of the nature of salvation must nevertheless remain quite limited and their assurance
of salvation be virtually nonexistent. But inclusivists contend
that assurance and fullness of understanding regarding salvation
are not required for salvation. They would be like motorists
driving in a fog, heading in the right direction but unable to
read the road signs in order to know where they are. Or, as
Charles Kraft notes, an electric light can be lit "whether or not
the person turning it on knows how the electricity got from its
source to the light bulb. Even so, God's requirement for salvation is now and ever has been the turning on of the switch of
faith commitment to him. He does not require us to know how
that faith activates the relationship between God and
humankind."[33]

31. Barclay, *An Apology for True Christian Divinity* (Philadelphia:
Friends Bookstore, 1908), p. 181. He goes on to say, "neither can they allege,
that it is because such are free from sin; seeing they also affirm, that all infants,
because of Adam's sin, deserve eternal damnation."
32. Strong, *Systematic Theology*, p. 843.
33. Kraft, *Christianity in Culture*, p. 255.

## 2. *The Role of General Revelation*

A second theological argument put forth in support of inclusivism is that God uses general revelation to mediate his salvific grace. Inclusivists argue that general revelation is salvific because its source is the saving God. God's mercy is communicated through even a fallen creation because he continues his redemptive work in it. Since all revelation is from God, "all revelation is *saving* revelation. The knowledge of God is always saving knowledge."[34] This does not mean that it is revelation which does the saving. Neither special nor general revelation save or condemn: it is *God* who saves or condemns. But can God save through general revelation? According to Dale Moody, "it is possible to say that this general revelation of God has only a negative function that leaves man without excuse. . . . But what kind of God is he who gives man enough knowledge to damn him but not enough to save him? The perception of God in creation has both negative and positive possibilities."[35] People can be saved or lost depending on their response to the general revelation. All truth, morals, and virtues find their source in the Creator. The sense of obligation to do the right and follow the truth is from God. Yet humans do not have to follow the truth or adhere to the right. Those who form a trusting relationship with God are saved, while those who turn their backs on the truths found in general revelation are heading for damnation.

Scripture speaks of God giving a "witness" of himself through the created order by providing "rains from heaven and fruitful seasons, satisfying your hearts with food and gladness" (Acts 14:17). General revelation also bears witness to God's divinity (Rom. 1:20) and glory (Ps. 19:1). The apostle Paul

34. Alan Richardson, *Christian Apologetics* (London: SCM Press, 1947), p. 127.
35. Moody, *The Word of Truth*, p. 59. For a study of some leading thinkers of the last two centuries on general revelation in relation to the unevangelized, see chap. 2 of R. Rubin Widmer's *Jesus, the Light of the World* (Nashville: Southern Publishing Association, 1967).

quoted from Psalm 19 in order to confirm the universal extent of God's redemptive grace: "But I say, surely they have never heard, have they? Indeed they have: 'Their voice has gone out into all the earth and their words to the ends of the world'" (Rom. 10:18).[36] Commenting on this verse, Millard Erickson says that "Paul appears to say that men have heard through this means. If that be the case, then perhaps the essential nature of saving faith can be arrived at without the special revelation."[37]

In their discussion of general revelation it is common for inclusivists to make four types of qualifications. The first is that they are in no way seeking to demean the value of the biblical revelation.[38] Their point is that God's activity in seeking people through the witness of general revelation should not be ignored. Moreover, the particular claims of the Christian message can be understood only within the universal framework provided by general revelation. "That, for example, Jesus Christ is God Incarnate, is perhaps the central thrust of the Christian truth-claim; but this thrust is fully intelligible only within a general theistic perspective in which God is antecedently recognized as the central reality. . . . There must, after all, be a recognition *that* God *is* real if there is to be a personal relationship *to* God *as* real."[39]

Second, inclusivists assert that the knowledge of God gleaned from general revelation is not attained simply by human reasoning but through the instruction of God (Rom. 1:19).

36. Restrictivists typically ignore this quote of Psalm 19 by halting their reading of the text at verse 17. See Dale Moody, *Word of Truth*, p. 61.

37. Erickson, "Hope for Those Who Haven't Heard? Yes, But . . . ," *Evangelical Missions Quarterly* 11 (Aug. 1975): 124.

38. Inclusivists view special revelation as more than merely a concrete illustration of the truths of general revelation. They grant that it brings far more understanding of God and life than we could ever gain from general revelation — and also that it brings judgment on our hopes, beliefs, and values.

39. Stuart Hackett, *The Reconstruction of the Christian Revelation Claim*, p. 80.

They deny that there is a purely natural or unaided knowledge of God.

Third, inclusivists contend that none are saved by their own moral efforts. Just as no Jews ever "lived up to" the light they had without failing, neither did any Gentiles. Bruce Lockerbie sees three types of peoples categorized in the first two chapters of Romans: Gentiles who know God but refuse to worship him (1:21), Jews who acknowledge God but in fact rebel against him (2:23), and Gentiles who acknowledge God and do his will (2:14-16).[40] On the day of judgment, people in this last category will be saved, Lockerbie says, "not because they have lived sinless lives; on the contrary, they too will have missed the mark that moral law sets for every man. But these will be devout pagans who, in the presence of sin, have been ashamed, have cried out in spiritual anguish, and confessed to whatever representation of the Holy Spirit they acknowledge."[41] All revelation is directed toward salvation; our response to it determines whether we have faith or not.

Fourth, inclusivists point out that in affirming salvation through general revelation they are not denying the universal sinfulness of humanity. They affirm Paul's assertion that all have sinned and fallen short of giving God the glory he deserves (Rom. 3:23) — for example, that none seek God (3:11), and that all people have been brought under God's judgment (3:9). They acknowledge that Paul paints a very bleak picture in the first three chapters of Romans but insist that judgment is not God's final word. Stuart Hackett explains: "All this [Rom. 1–3] would be quite unintelligible if it did not imply that, through a proper response to this universally accessible revelation, individual human beings of whatever circumstances could so re-

40. Lockerbie, *The Cosmic Center: The Supremacy of Christ in a Secular Wasteland* (Portland: Multnomah Press, 1986), pp. 175-76.
41. Lockerbie, *The Cosmic Center*, p. 178. The same point is made by William Shedd, *Dogmatic Theology*, 3 vols. (New York: Scribner's, 1888-94), 2: 709; and J. N. D. Anderson, *Christianity and Comparative Religion*, pp. 100-101.

nounce their moral guilt and corruption and could so commit themselves to God and his claim upon them, as to become the beneficiaries of divine grace and forgiveness."[42]

While it is true that none seek God apart from divine grace, say inclusivists, the Scriptures are replete with calls to seek God and promises that we shall find him when we seek him with all our heart and that he is good to those who seek him (Deut. 4:29; 2 Chron. 15:2; Prov. 8:17; Isa. 55:6; Jer. 29:13; Lam. 3:25; Amos 5:6; Luke 11:9-10; Acts 17:27; and Heb. 11:6). And they find hope in these Scripture passages regarding God's work among and concern for the Gentiles. But they maintain that the greatest cause for hope for the unevangelized despite the bleak picture of Romans 1–3 can be found in the book of Romans itself. Paul emphatically declares that Jesus died for all the sinners who were under the judgment spoken of in chapter 3 (Rom. 5). All people were together undone by sin, and all people are together offered salvation by grace through faith. "For God has shut up all in disobedience that He might show mercy to all" (Rom. 11:32). With these qualifications in mind, we can proceed to the third theological argument for inclusivism.

### 3. The Work of God in Effecting Salvation

Inclusivists emphasize the work of the triune God in salvation. God the Father loves all and desires the salvation of all, God the Son made this salvation possible through his redemptive work, and God the Holy Spirit has a universal outreach in seeking lost and sinful humanity. Though all people have sinned and turned away from God, the Holy Spirit is working to convict all people of their sin and turn them back to God (John 16:8). The convicting activity of the Spirit is a work of love;

---

42. Hackett, *The Reconstruction of the Christian Revelation Claim*, p. 245.

God showers his love upon us even before we repent. Edward Pusey upheld the universal convicting presence of the Spirit when he wrote that "God the Holy Ghost (it is a matter of faith) visits and has visited every soul of man whom God has made, and those who heard His voice and obeyed it, as far as they knew, belonged to Christ, and were saved for His merits, Whom, had they known, they would have obeyed and loved."[43] The convicting activity of the Holy Spirit is and has been universal in all ages and locations, say the inclusivists. The Spirit opens the door for humans to respond to whatever revelation God has given them. "If a person's ability to respond to revelation is not by means of reason or through any faculty possessed by that person, but by this initiative of God . . . is not this basic orientation towards God a gift of grace?"[44]

Inclusivists do not balk at the idea of God manifesting grace outside the church. Though the church is the recipient of the Spirit and salvation, they say, it does not and cannot contain the Spirit and salvation. The Spirit blows where it wishes (John 3:8). Belief in God's providence and sovereignty allows for his work of grace outside the confines of the visible church. The unevangelized are indeed "unreached" by human messengers with the word of Christ, but they are not unreached by the Holy Spirit's ministry of grace.[45] There is no salvation outside of Jesus Christ, but there is salvation outside the church. Inclusivists contend that salvation must not be identified with any culturally bound structure because the triune God is not limited to such structures. God is free to work universally in various cultural, temporal, geographical, and religious contexts.

43. Pusey, *What Is of Faith as to Everlasting Punishment?* (London: Rivington, 1880), p. 8. James O. Buswell makes the same point in his *Systematic Theology of the Christian Religion*, vol. 2 (Grand Rapids: Zondervan, 1963), p. 160.

44. Gavin D'Costa, *Theology and Religious Pluralism* (Oxford: Basil Blackwell, 1986), p. 69.

45. Moreover, inclusivists contend that refusal to accept the church's invitation should not be equated with refusal to accept God's invitation.

The Holy Spirit is the "breath of life" from which all life springs, the source of all truth, love, hope, and freedom.[46] The Spirit who was in Jesus Christ is the same Spirit who has brought a ministry of grace throughout human history, both before and after the historical incarnation of Christ.[47] Again, this does not diminish the importance of the Christian message of Jesus. We need the message of Christ (salvation in its fullness) to help free us from the ambiguities and futilities of this present life. Also, the revelation of Christ serves as the criterion for judging the spiritual presence outside the church. The work of the Spirit must not be confined to the church but neither can it be asserted that the Spirit does nothing new through the Christian message. "If we perceive the Spirit as being active only in the church, we fall prey to a Manichean dualism that surrenders the world to antigodly powers. If we perceive the Spirit as being active unipurposely in world and church, we rob the incarnation of God of its decisive significance."[48]

### 4. The Cosmic Work of Jesus Christ

Although inclusivists give the incarnation of the Son of God its rightful significance, they point out that the Son of God existed and was actively enlightening people prior to the incarnation (John 1:9). This cosmic work of the second person of the Trinity provides the heart of the fourth theological argu-

46. Inclusivists affirm that all people thus have a relationship with the Holy Spirit, but this is not to say that all people have a saving relationship with God. Their belief in the universal ministry of the Spirit is not the same as the neo-Platonic idea that all people are always in touch with divinity in their inner nature.

47. On the continuity of the work of the Holy Spirit and regeneration between the Old and New Testaments, see Art Lewis, "The New Birth under the Old Covenant," *Evangelical Quarterly* 56 (Jan. 1984): 35-44.

48. Hans Schwarz, "Reflections on the Work of the Spirit outside the Church," *Neue Zeitschrift für Systematische Theologie und Religionsphilosophie* 23 (1981): 211.

ment in defense of inclusivism. "A high view of the pre-existent and post-existent Son of God avoids the problems of a low missionary theology that confines all the revelation of the Son of God to the days of his flesh. The *supreme* revelation was in the days of his flesh, but it is not the sole revelation of the Son of God."[49] Historically this idea finds its root in the "logos christology" of several early Church Fathers.

Logos christology is, in many ways, the forerunner of inclusivism.[50] The attitude of the early church toward pagan learning and belief was mixed. While some rejected all of paganism, most Christians viewed what was "best" and "true" in paganism as having been revealed by God.[51] Many early Christians thought that the Son of God was actively involved in revealing truth and goodness outside the covenant with Israel and that any could be saved if they availed themselves of that revelation. Clement of Rome, for instance, said, "let us look steadfastly to the blood of Christ . . . which, having been shed for our salvation, has set the grace of repentance before the whole world. Let us turn to every age that has passed, and learn that, from generation to generation, the Lord has granted a place of repentance to all such as would be converted unto Him."[52]

Justin Martyr took this approach most clearly when he wrote that Christ "is the Word of whom every race of men were partakers; and those who lived reasonably *(meta logou)* are Christians, even though they have been thought atheists; as, among the Greeks, Socrates and Heraclitus, and men like

49. Moody, *The Word of Truth*, p. 62.
50. The following discussion is indebted to Robert Wilken, "Religious Pluralism and Early Christian Theology," *Interpretation* 4 (Oct. 1986): 379-91; and J. Dupuis, "The Cosmic Christ in the Early Fathers," *Indian Journal of Theology* (1966): 106-20.
51. See chap. 3 of Richard Drummond's *Toward a New Age in Christian Theology*. For a discussion of why the church strayed from this initial openness, see chap. 4.
52. *The First Epistle of Clement*, chap. 6, in *The Ante-Nicene Fathers*, vol. 1, ed. Alexander Roberts and James Donaldson (1885; reprint, Grand Rapids: William B. Eerdmans, 1975), p. 7.

them."[53] As Justin understood it, the seed *(sperma)* of the universal logos is present in all races, so all people have some degree of divine revelation from God, although in Jesus Christ the logos in his *fullness* is revealed to the human race.[54]

Irenaeus followed Justin in this regard and developed a full-fledged theology of history. He argued that God the Father has never been unknown to any race of people, since Christ, the universal Word, is inherent in the minds of all.[55] He asserted that all manifestations of divinity are personal manifestations of the logos, so any knowledge of God assumes a personal encounter with him — including the creation revelation, the Old Testament, and unique revelation in the historical incarnation of Christ. The continuity of divine revelation is ensured since all revelation finds its source in the Son of God. Consequently, there is "one salvation for all those who believe in him." The salvation Jesus provided was truly universal in its intent.

> For it was not merely for those who believed on Him in the time of Tiberius Caesar that Christ came, nor did the Father exercise His providence for the men only who are now alive, but for all men altogether, who from the beginning, according to their capacity, in their generation have both feared and loved God, and practiced justice and piety towards their neighbors, and have earnestly desired to see Christ, and to hear His voice. Wherefore He shall, at His second coming . . . give them a place in His kingdom.[56]

These early Church Fathers were aware of the plurality of religions surrounding them, and yet they did not shy away from claiming that the god of the pagan was the *same* God the

53. Justin Martyr, *The First Apology,* chap. 46, in *Ante-Nicene Fathers,* 1: 178. See also his *Second Apology,* chaps. 8 and 10.

54. See Justin Martyr, *Second Apology,* chaps. 8, 10, 13.

55. Irenaeus, *Against Heresies,* 4.6.5-7; 4.20.6-7; 2.6.1. Yet he also maintained that the incarnation was a unique revelation, 4.34.1.

56. Irenaeus, *Against Heresies,* 4.22.2, in *Ante-Nicene Fathers,* 1: 494.

Christians worshiped.[57] They did criticize many of the worship practices of the pagans, however; not all ways of worshiping God were considered edifying, holy, and legitimate. These early Christians rejected many of the *ways* the pagans worshiped but not *who* they worshiped. Contemporary inclusivists make the same claims in order to argue that any unevangelized individuals who worship the true God are saved even if some of their worship practices need correcting. This ties in closely with the final theological consideration.

### 5. The Implications of the Presence of Other Religions

The final theological argument in support of inclusivism draws on the previous arguments and applies them to the real-life situations in which the unevangelized find themselves — participants in religions other than Christianity. No one supposes that the unevangelized are devoid of religious practice or worship; the question is whether God is at work redemptively with such people. Inclusivists argue both theologically and anthropologically that God is at work redemptively in the lives of all people. Let us first consider three of their basic theological assertions.

a. *Although God is best defined by the historical revelation in Jesus Christ, he is not confined to it.* Inclusivists maintain that the revelation in Christ is the norm for evaluating the truths found in other religions, just as the revelation of Yahweh in the Exodus served as the norm for the Israelites in evaluating other gods. The song of Moses asks, "who is like thee among the gods, O LORD?" (Exod. 15:11). At that time in the Old Testament revelation the existence of other gods was acknowledged, but the work of Yahweh among the Hebrew people was seen as the highest revelation of the nature of divinity. Not only were other

---

57. Even Augustine stated that "their God is also our God" (*City of God*, 19.22).

gods acknowledged but various characteristics and activities of these gods were attributed to the Lord (Yahweh). "That these appropriations had a basis in principle and not only in merely co-incidental similarity is clear from the fact that the LORD took over names and attributes not only of El [a god of the Canaanites] (in relation to whom there is little mention of antithesis or polemics), but also of Baal and other gods, against whom there were strong antithetical (hostile) attitudes."[58]

The Old Testament writers learned certain things about the true God from other religions without falling prey to syncretism. Many biblical writers were able to appreciate the revelation of God outside Israel.

> In the great Hymn to God the Creator in Psalm 104 there are many parallels to the Egyptian "Hymn to Aton" which dates from the time of Akhenaton (1380-1362 B.C.). The Psalmist seems to accept this monotheism as revelation of *Yahweh* under the name of *Aton*, just as *Yahweh* was identified with *El Elyon*, a Canaanite concept, in the story of Melchizedek. . . . The most obvious conclusion is that the true God revealed himself indirectly in the monotheism of Akhenaton. Why not, if his mighty deeds were done outside Israel in Cyrus the Great? (Isa. 44:28; 45:1-25)[59]

Even the name of God was taken from other religions. The Hebrews appropriated the Semitic name *El* for God, while the New Testament made use of the Greek term *theos*.

If no point of comparison between the God of Israel and the other gods were possible, then the Israelites would have found it impossible to explain the distinctives of their God to the pagans. Those outside Israel thought of a divine being when they heard the word *El*, and this afforded Israel a basis on which to talk to other peoples about what God had done for them.

---

58. Adrio König, *Here Am I* (Grand Rapids: William B. Eerdmans, 1982), p. 17.

59. Moody, *The Word of Truth*, p. 58.

This idea is expressed by the Jewish author of the "Letter of Aristeas," written around A.D. 30. In writing to a Gentile king he says, "the (same) God who appointed them [Jews] their Law prospers your kingdom, as I have been at pains to show. These people worship God the overseer and creator of all, whom all men worship including ourselves, O King, except that we have a different name. Their name for him is Zeus or Jove (v 15)."[60] Modern translators of the Bible are faced with the same issue today. Lesslie Newbigin explains:

> In almost all cases where the Bible has been translated into the languages of the non-Christian peoples of the world, the New Testament word *Theos* has been rendered by the name given by the non-Christian peoples to the one whom they worship as the Supreme Being. It is under this name, therefore, that the Christians who now use these languages worship the God and Father of Jesus Christ. The very few exceptions, where translators have sought to evade the issue by simply transliterating the Greek or Hebrew word, only serve to prove the point; for the converts have simply explained the foreign word in the text of their Bibles by using the indigenous name for God. . . . The name of the God revealed in Jesus Christ can only be known by using those names for God which have been developed within the non-Christian systems of belief and worship.[61]

Hans Küng makes a similar point in describing the Roman Catholic missions in China from 1538 to 1742 regarding which names for God were permissible.[62] In the beginning the Jesuits decided that the ancient Confucian names for God should be used, but later the Vatican ruled that the traditional Latin names for God had to be used. The use of the Latin

---

60. From *The Old Testament Pseudepigrapha*, vol. 2, ed. James H. Charlesworth (Garden City, N.Y.: Doubleday, 1985), p. 13.

61. Newbigin, *The Open Secret* (Grand Rapids: William B. Eerdmans, 1978), p. 192.

62. Küng, *Does God Exist? An Answer for Today*, trans. Edward Quinn (New York: Vintage Books, 1981), pp. 588-94.

names made the Christian God seem like a foreign deity to the
Chinese, and this led to a great reversal of earlier successes in
Chinese missions. China became extremely closed to Christian
witness. Küng does not claim that the ancient Confucian religion had all the information about God it needed or that all
the information it had was correct. He simply argues that it
contained some fundamental truths about the true God. He
maintains that the major world religions contain both truths
and falsehoods about the true God and that the falsehoods do
not necessarily preclude salvation.[63] After all, if complete truth
were a prerequistite for salvation, then no human being could
be saved.

   b. *The biblical writers used indigenous names for God and
made use of ideas, values, and practices compatible with the worship
of the true God.* Modern translators and missionaries do the
same, and God makes use of their work. This is not all that
provocative a concept: most Christians affirm that all truth and
goodness find their source in God. Inclusivists do not contend
that all or even any beliefs about God in any particular non-
Christian religion are true, but they do advocate looking for
signs of God's presence among them.[64]

   For biblical support of this idea, inclusivists typically appeal to Paul's address to the Athenians in Acts 17. This speech
plays a crucial role in Acts as the second of Paul's three major
missionary speeches.[65] The first of the speeches (13:6-41) was
presented to a Jewish audience and the third (20:18-35) to a

63. Küng, *Does God Exist?* pp. 626-27. He says the question of salvation
must be distinguished from the question of truth.
   64. Some of the biblical writers expressed criticisms of beliefs and
practices of other religions and held Yahweh to be far superior to other gods
(see König, *Here Am I,* pp. 20-52), and yet their most trenchant criticisms
are always directed at Israel and the church. God judges people for failing to
be faithful to what they know (see Drummond, *Toward a New Age in Christian
Theology,* pp. 9-11).
   65. The following discussion is heavily indebted to L. Legrand, "The
Unknown God of Athens: Acts 17 and the Religion of the Gentiles," *Indian
Journal of Theology* 30 (July-Dec. 1981): 158-67.

Christian audience; the second was addressed to Gentiles, specifically Athenians. Thus, Luke gives a taste of the full spectrum of Paul's ministry.

In his speech to the Athenians, Paul brings out the fact that his audience has experienced to some degree God's revelation and grace. Most of those listening to him were interested in the religious philosophies of Stoicism and Epicureanism (17:18). It is customary for commentators to observe that Paul quotes a Greek poet in verse 28. It is less frequently noted that the whole body of his message reflects the teaching of the Stoics. Paul apparently had fewer points of contact with the Epicureans (they did not believe in providence) than with the Stoics, but he establishes several points of agreement with Stoicism in verses 24-29. Paul describes God as the Creator and Lord of heaven and earth who does not dwell in human temples. This would not necessarily have aroused any disagreement with the pantheism of the Stoics. In verse 25 he says that God is the one who gives life to all things, an idea with which they could readily agree. Then, in verses 26-29, he presents two beliefs that were especially prominent in Stoicism: (1) that the entire human race is one offspring from God[66] and (2) that God exercises a providential care for his creation.[67] This use of Stoic thought by Paul was not an innovation in his preaching here: he also stressed God's providential dealings with the Gentiles while he was at Lystra (Acts 14:17).[68]

Although Paul brought out several similarities between his faith and the views of the religious philosophers with whom he was speaking, some commentators doubt that Paul had a positive attitude toward their beliefs. They contend that his use of the Greek term *deisidaimonesterous* (religious) to describe the Athenians in verse 22 is derogatory. Some writers believe Paul

66. See the *Discourses of Epictetus*, 1.1; 1.3; 2.8; and the *Hymn to Zeus* by Cleanthes.
67. See the *Discourses of Epictetus*, 1.1; 4.1; and his *Manual*, 17, 53.
68. Cf. *Discourses of Epictetus*, 1.22.

is accusing them of demon worship, since the root word here is *daimon*. But there is a larger quantity of evidence suggesting that Paul had a positive meaning in mind.

For one thing, the term *daimon* was very common in both Greek philosophy and dramatic literature.[69] It was primarily used to refer to that aspect of divinity in all human beings commonly known in our culture as "soul" or "god." In Greek thought a "demon" was any sort of divine being — hence the Stoic references to the "demon present in all of us." In any event, the term as they used it was clearly not equivalent to the term used in the Gospels to refer to malevolent beings working against God. In recording Paul's message, Luke had no qualms about using the same term to describe the Christian faith. The Athenians said Paul was proclaiming strange "demons" (Acts 17:18), and Festus described both the Jewish religion and Paul's religion as "demon worship" (Acts 25:19). Consequently, Paul was paying the Athenians no disrespect when he said they worshiped the gods (demons).

c. *In some clearly imperfect but nonetheless genuine sense, the Athenians did worship the true God.* Regarding the altar to the "unknown god," Paul says, "what therefore you worship in ignorance, this I proclaim to you" (Acts 17:23). He also said the Athenians could find God, since he is not far off from any individual (17:27). In certain respects they did acknowledge the true God, and Paul makes use of this point of contact to further instruct them about this God.[70] God had overlooked their

69. See William Arndt and Wilbur Gingrich, *A Greek-English Lexicon of the New Testament* (Chicago: University of Chicago Press, 1979), p. 173; *New International Dictionary of the New Testament*, vol. 1, ed. Colin Brown (Grand Rapids: Zondervan, 1975), pp. 450-53; and Harry Wolfson, *Philo*, vol. 1 (Cambridge: Harvard University Press, 1947), pp. 367, 374-77.

70. It is true, however, that Paul did make some negative remarks about worship in Athens (17:24-25, 29). For more details on this, see Legrand, "The Unknown God of Athens," pp. 165-66. Paul also had some warnings for the Corinthian church when he said that the pagans in Corinth made their offerings to gods (demons) and not to God (1 Cor. 10:19-21). But his point was that the Christians knew the true God, and the old gods, having

ignorance and was now bringing them the fuller revelation of the gospel with an invitation to become followers of Christ (17:30). Paul then spoke of the eschatological judgment and the historical resurrection of Jesus. At this some in the audience scoffed, some expressed a desire to hear more, and some accepted the invitation and became Christians (17:32-34). These three types of responses were the same as those Paul received elsewhere. His preaching was a success in that those who were believers became Christians.[71]

In addition to offering these theological arguments, inclusivists also marshal certain anthropological observations in support of the claim that God has been at work in the lives of all people groups. Such observations focus on the similarities between the biblical revelation and beliefs, values, and practices

---

been superseded, should not be brought into Christian worship. Paul also describes his mission to the Gentiles as one of delivering them from the domain of Satan (Acts 26:17-18). But this does not contradict his otherwise positive attitude toward Gentiles in Acts. Rather, this statement emphasizes the lostness of humanity which is the other side of the coin: the Gentiles required both positive and negative assessments. Legrand observes that Paul is more negative in Romans 1 than in his speech in Acts 17 because in Romans 1–3 Israel and the Gentiles stand in *eschatological* judgment, their only hope being the grace of Christ. In contrast, Luke's viewpoint in Acts is *historical,* demonstrating that the grace of God is at work in human history and culture (see "The Unknown God of Athens," pp. 166-67).

71. Many Christians have dismissed the Athenian discourse as an example of what should not be done — mixing biblical and general revelation. They argue that Paul changed his style when he went to Corinth, where he preached only Jesus Christ crucified (1 Cor. 2:2). This interpretation is dubious for several reasons. First, there were Christians in Corinth before Paul arrived (1 Cor. 16:15; Acts 18:10), so Paul did not have to lay the same groundwork there that he did in Athens. Second, Paul's assertion that he preached only Christ crucified in Corinth does not constitute adequate evidence that his preaching there differed from that in Athens. Third, as we have seen, Acts 17 serves as a model for missionary preaching, and it seems unlikely that Luke would spend this much time on a story if it merely illustrated what ought not to be done. Fourth, Paul enjoyed the same success in Athens as he did elsewhere. For more on this, see Legrand, "The Unknown God of Athens," pp. 161-62.

found in other religions. The oral tradition of the Yoruba people of Nigeria, for instance, speaks of a supreme deity who is the creator, lord over space and time, the king of heaven, the one who discerns the hearts of people, the only one who "can speak and accomplish his words," the one who executes judgment, and the one who can be approached as Father.[72] Since beliefs such as these reveal a striking similarity to the biblical revelation, inclusivists argue that God is at work redemptively with these people.

Missionary anthropologist Don Richardson has documented a striking number of parallels between Christian and non-Christian beliefs. He calls them "redemptive analogies" and argues that they are present in every culture, making the gospel accessible to the people.[73] He views these analogies as evidences of God's gracious activity among the unevangelized. He argues that Melchizedek was not the only Gentile in history with whom God worked salvifically. Richardson documents instances in which God has worked through general revelation, dreams, and reasoning to bring people to conviction and commitment. He categorizes these redemptive analogies into three groups: (1) "peoples of the vague God," who know something of the true God and desire to serve him but are hampered by lack of knowledge (e.g., the Athenian, Inca, Santal, and Gedeo peoples); (2) "peoples of the lost book," who are looking for special revelation that has been lost to them (e.g., the Karen, Kachin, Lahu, and Maga peoples); and (3) peoples with strange

72. See E. Dada Adelowo, "A Repository of Theological and Ethical Values in Yoruba Oral Traditions, the Qur'an, the Hadith, and the Bible," *African Theological Journal* 15 (1986): 128-32, 136.

73. See Richardson, *Eternity in Their Hearts* (Ventura, Cal.: Regal Books, 1981). Richardson's position is not immediately evident. There is the suggestion of restrictivism in his assertion that the analogies are "redemptive" in that they help contribute to God's redemptive work but they are not "redeeming," since that would imply that people could find a relationship with God apart from the gospel (p. 61). In any event, this sort of anthropological information is commonly enough cited by those who are unambiguously inclusivists; see, for example, Strong, *Systematic Theology*, pp. 843-44.

customs that graphically portray redemption and forgiveness (e.g., the Sawi, Dyak, and Asmat peoples).

In general, African, Asian, and older South American religions emphasize a supreme creator deity, human sin (in some cases even a fall), and a personal God who cares for the individual.[74] The chief structural difference between these religions and Christianity is that they tend to be merely historical, whereas Christianity is both historical and eschatological. Moreover, they tend to be sociocentric (concerned with community) where Christianity is theocentric. Nevertheless, inclusivists view the points of contact as evidence that God has not been sitting idly by waiting for human missionaries to bring the gospel to these peoples. Although God desires that the gospel of Christ be brought to them, he does not hesitate to begin working redemptively with them before missionary contact.

## Leading Defenders

### John Wesley

The eighteenth-century English evangelist John Wesley proclaimed that he did not "conceive that any man living has a right to sentence all the heathen and Mahometan world to damnation." He added, "it is far better to leave them to Him

---

74. See chap. 3 of Walbert Bühlmann, *God's Chosen Peoples*, trans. Robert Barr (Maryknoll, N.Y.: Orbis Books, 1982). Unfortunately, Bühlmann glosses over significant differences between Christianity and other religions and at times even shortchanges the inspiration of the biblical writers. For other surveys of this sort that better uphold the distinctives of the biblical message, see Drummond, *Toward a New Age in Christian Theology;* and Aldwinckle, *Jesus: A Savior or the Savior?* Colin Turnbull has produced varying assessments in his studies of "primitive" peoples. In *The Forest People* (New York: Simon & Schuster, 1962), he speaks of signs of common grace among the pygmies, whereas in *The Mountain People* (New York: Simon & Schuster, 1972) he portrays the Ik as a deceitful, cruel, and selfish people.

that made them, and who is 'the Father of the spirits of all flesh'; who is the God of the Heathens as well as the Christians, and who hateth nothing that he hath made."[75] Though he never gave the subject of the unevangelized any systematic treatment, on several occasions Wesley clearly showed himself to be an advocate of universally accessible salvation. Regarding the means by which the unevangelized could be saved, he held that God had given them general revelation and that some peoples had retained traditions handed down from the time of Noah. "God never, in any age or nation, 'left himself' quite 'without a witness' in the hearts of men; but while he 'gave them rain and fruitful seasons,' imparted some imperfect knowledge of the Giver. 'He is the true Light that' still, in some degree, 'enlightens every man that cometh into the world.'"[76] Though he considers these lights dim compared to the brightness of the revelation of the Son of God in Jesus, he nonetheless maintains that they enable God to reach the unevangelized. At one point Wesley spoke of God sending the gospel message to the unevangelized by miraculous means as he did in Acts 8, but his preferred solution to the problem was along inclusivist lines.[77]

In a sermon entitled "On Faith," Wesley argues that the unevangelized cannot be blamed for failing to accept Christ, since they have never heard of him. "Inasmuch as to them little is given, of them little will be required. . . . No more therefore will be expected of them, than the living up to the light they had. But many of them . . . we have great reason to hope, although they lived among the Heathens, yet were quite of another spirit; being taught of God, by his inward voice, all the essentials of true religion."[78]

75. Wesley, "On Living without God," in *The Works of John Wesley*, 3rd ed., 14 vols. (Peabody, Mass.: Hendrickson, 1986), 7: 353.
76. Wesley, "Walking by Sight and by Faith," in *The Works of John Wesley*, 7: 258.
77. See Wesley, "The General Spread of the Gospel," in *The Works of John Wesley*, 6: 286.
78. Wesley, "On Faith," in *The Works of John Wesley*, 7: 197.

Compared to his contemporaries, Wesley was quite generous in his views regarding those groups among which salvation was present. He believed the faith of the Protestants *and* the Roman Catholics to contain all that is necessary for salvation. For his part, he wished not to rule out the salvation of modern Jews but to leave them in the hands of the Master.[79] He was quite adamant, however, that a merely intellectual faith would save no one. The requirement for saving faith is "such a divine conviction of God, and the things of God, as, even in its infant state, enables every one that possesses it to 'fear God and work righteousness.' And whosoever, in every nation, believes thus far, the Apostle declares, is 'accepted of him.'"[80] Any who exercise such faith are accepted by God and are received into the kingdom, said Wesley. But he characterized those saved outside the Christian community in this fashion as *servants* of God but not yet *sons*. Even so, he held that they are saved and the wrath of God does not abide on them. In other words, the unevangelized who come to a saving faith are believers. If they continue in their faith, they will be adopted as sons, but they will not have assurance of their salvation; according to Wesley, only Christians can have such assurance.[81]

## C. S. Lewis

C. S. Lewis has influenced a tremendous number of people with his views on the unevangelized through his very popular writings. Though he was not a theologian, he presented carefully thought out theological ideas. His position on the unevangelized can be organized into five theses.

1. Lewis affirms both the finality of salvation only in Jesus Christ and the universality of salvation wrought by Christ.

79. Wesley, "On Faith," 7: 197-98.
80. Wesley, "On Faith," 7: 199.
81. Wesley, "On Faith," 7: 199. See also *John Wesley,* ed. Albert Outler (New York: Oxford University Press, 1964), p. 137 (questions 5 and 6).

Commenting on the Church of England's eighteenth article of faith, which asserts that salvation comes only through the name of Jesus Christ, Lewis writes, "of course it should be pointed out that, though all salvation is through Jesus, we need not conclude that He cannot save those who have not explicitly accepted Him in this life."[82] Elsewhere, Lewis explicitly interprets Jesus as having said that "no man can reach absolute reality, except through Me."[83] Yet he refuses to draw from this the conclusion that all those who have never heard of Christ are damned. "Is it not frightfully unfair that this new life should be confined to people who have heard of Christ and been able to believe in Him? . . . We do know that no man can be saved except through Christ; we do not know that only those who know Him can be saved through Him."[84]

2. Lewis affirms that people from all lands are saved by faith in God because God is seeking all those who worship him in spirit and truth. Those who commit themselves in trust to that which lies behind all truth and goodness will be saved even though they are ignorant of the Savior. "There are people in other religions who are being led by God's secret influence to concentrate on those parts of their religion which are in agreement with Christianity, and who thus belong to Christ without knowing it."[85] Moreover, "I think that every prayer which is sincerely made even to a false god . . . is accepted by the true God and that Christ saves many who do not think they know him. For he is (dimly) present in the *good* side of the inferior teachers they follow."[86] Lewis contends that it is impossible to know whether individuals are saved merely by looking at their

82. Lewis, *God in the Dock,* ed. Walter Hooper (Grand Rapids: William B. Eerdmans, 1970), p. 102.

83. Lewis, *God in the Dock,* p. 160.

84. C. S. Lewis, *Mere Christianity* (New York: Macmillan, 1967), p. 65.

85. Lewis, *Mere Christianity,* p. 176.

86. *Letters of C. S. Lewis,* ed. W. H. Lewis (New York: Harcourt Brace Jovanovich, 1966), p. 247.

behavior — and he finds corroboration for this view in the passage about the sheep and goats (Matt. 25:31-46), both of which express surprise when they are informed at the judgment about their true relationship with the Savior.[87]

3. Lewis affirms that God is at work redemptively in other cultures and religions, that he is "not pronouncing all other religions to be totally false, but rather saying that in Christ whatever is true in all religions is consummated and perfected."[88] God reaches people in other cultures and religions through various kinds of revelation, including "stories scattered all through the heathen religions about a god who dies and comes to life again and, by his death, has somehow given new life to men."[89]

Lewis also contends that there is an absolutely universal revelation that all great religions have in common.[90] This universal revelation contains three elements. (1) It includes the experience of the "numinous" — awe and dread of something beyond the natural world. On this point Lewis draws explicitly on Rudolf Otto's *The Idea of the Holy*. The experience of the numinous involves both a sense of fear and a sense of love and joy. (2) This universal revelation also involves an awareness of "oughtness," or moral law. All human beings have standards of right and wrong that we fail to live up to, and most cultures ground these standards in something beyond the natural realm. (3) The universal revelation assumes the existence of some sort of supernatural authority that holds all human beings accountable. Lewis maintains that all great religions make the numinous the guardian of the moral

87. See *Letters of C. S. Lewis*, p. 247; and *Mere Christianity*, p. 177.
88. Lewis, *God in the Dock*, p. 102.
89. Lewis, *Mere Christianity*, p. 54. In his Narnia stories Lewis expresses the same idea by explaining that the kingdom of the "Emperor beyond the sea" extends throughout all times and worlds and that his ambassador, Aslan (the Christ figure), is at work in all lands though he is known under different identifications in those lands. In Narnia Aslan is depicted as a lion, whereas in England he is known as a lamb. See *The Voyage of the Dawn Treader* (New York: Collier, 1971), pp. 214-15.
90. He explains this most fully in *The Problem of Pain* (New York: Macmillan, 1962), pp. 16-25.

law and that God uses this universal revelation to reach out toward those outside the church.

We should note that Lewis qualifies his third thesis in two ways. First, although he believes God to be at work in the great non-Christian religions, he is not uncritical of them. He does speak of the need for those who belong to these religions to find the fulfillment of what they seek in Christ. The moral law directs all of us toward moral goodness, but this is never enough. We need to become Christians in order to enter into the divine life and be made "real men."[91] But Lewis also made a second qualification in the opposite direction. Although he believed that all seekers of God will finally need to become Christians, he did allow that "honest rejection of Christ, however mistaken, will be forgiven and healed — 'Whosoever shall speak a word against the Son of man, it shall be forgiven him.' "[92] He had in mind the sort of person who truly seeks God but for one reason or another is unable to see Christ as the fulfillment that he or she seeks.

4. Lewis affirms that all those who have sought God in this life will have a postmortem encounter with Christ in order to meet the one who saved them. Just as Christ descended into hell in order to preach the gospel to those who lived before he came, says Lewis, so there will be an opportunity after death for present-day unevangelized persons. In *The Great Divorce* Lewis speculates that some may leave "hell" for heaven as a result of postmortem evangelism.[93] Though he follows George Macdonald in this regard, he expressly rejects Macdonald's universalism.[94] Our freedom allows us to say No to God in the

---

91. See *God in the Dock*, pp. 111-12.

92. Lewis, *God in the Dock*, 111.

93. Lewis, *The Great Divorce* (New York: Macmillan, 1946), pp. 69, 124. Lewis also believed in the effectiveness of prayers for the dead (see *Letters to Malcolm: Chiefly on Prayer* [New York: Harcourt Brace Jovanovich, 1963], p. 107).

94. See *The Great Divorce*, pp. 124-25; *The Problem of Pain*, pp. 122-24; *George Macdonald: An Anthology* (Garden City, N.Y.: Doubleday, 1947), p. 25; and *The Last Battle* (New York: Macmillan, 1970), pp. 143-48, 152-53.

end, and, says Lewis, some of us will. "There are only two kinds of people in the end: those who say to God, 'Thy will be done,' and those to whom God says, in the end, 'Thy will be done.'"[95]

5. Finally, Lewis affirms that the opportunity for post-mortem salvation will be extended *only* to those who have responded positively *in this life* to God's universal revelation.[96] The door of salvation provided by Christ is open to all who desire to go through, but that desire must have been present before death. In one of his letters, Lewis distinguishes the idea of a "second chance in the strict sense" from purgatory, which he defines as "a process by which the work of redemption continues, and first perhaps begins to be noticeable after death."[97] Lewis thus indicates that he did not believe that everyone would receive a second chance at redemption. Instead, he understood purgatory traditionally, as a place where those who began the process of redemption before death continue in their efforts. Yet, he cautions that there may be people in purgatory whom we would not anticipate being there when he says that the redemption in their lives may first begin to be noticeable only after death. Lewis is clear that *we* cannot distinguish the sheep from the goats on this side of the veil. God will see to it that all those who made some sort of positive response to his grace in this life are welcomed into the kingdom.

All five of these theses are wonderfully summed up in Lewis's story of the salvation of the pagan Emeth in *The Last Battle*. Emeth had been raised in a different country and followed a different religion (that of Tash). He describes Aslan as simultaneously beautiful and terrible. Having been

95. Lewis, *The Great Divorce*, p. 72.

96. Some Lewis scholars find it difficult to believe that he actually meant what he said about the salvation of the unevangelized. See, for instance, Clyde S. Kilby, *The Christian World of C. S. Lewis* (Grand Rapids: William B. Eerdmans, 1964), pp. 142-43.

97. *Letters of C. S. Lewis*, pp. 246-47.

welcomed by Aslan into the kingdom, he relates the dialogue that ensued:

> I fell at his feet and thought, Surely this is the hour of death, for the Lion (who is worthy of honour) will know that I have served Tash all my days and not him. . . . But the Glorious One bent down his golden head and touched my forehead with his tongue and said, Son, thou art welcome. But I said, Alas, Lord, I am no son of Thine but the servant of Tash. He answered, Child, all service thou hast done to Tash, I account as service done to me. . . . I take to me the services which thou hast done to him, for I and he are of such different kinds that no service which is vile can be done to me, and not which is not vile can be done to him. Therefore if any man swear by Tash and keep his oath for the oath's sake, it is by me that he has truly sworn, though he know it not, and it is I who reward him. And if any man do a cruelty in my name, then though he says the name Aslan, it is Tash whom he serves and by Tash his deed is accepted. . . . But I said also (for the truth constrained me), Yes I have been seeking Tash all my days. Beloved, said the Glorious One, unless thy desire had been for me thou wouldst not have sought so long and so truly. For all find what they truly seek.[98]

In this story all five of Lewis's theses are present. (1) Emeth experiences the numinous — both joy and terror at meeting Aslan (Christ). (2) He was saved by his faith though he was ignorant of the true nature of Aslan.[99] Moreover, just like the sheep in the parable, Emeth is unaware that he had served Aslan. (3) God is at work even among the adherents of other religions and accepts those who "honestly reject" Aslan, but he rejects those who dishonestly reject him (i.e., he rejects universalism). (4) There is a postmortem encounter with Christ. (5) This encounter informs those who sought God before death who it is

98. Lewis, *The Last Battle*, pp. 164-65.

99. Lewis's choice of Emeth for the character's name was calculated: *emeth* means "truth" in Hebrew (see Lewis's *Reflections on the Psalms* [New York: Harcourt, Brace & World, 1958], p. 61).

that saves them. There they discover the fulfillment of their longings. All find what they seek: those who seek the true, the good, and the beautiful will find God; those who seek falsehood, evil, and the ugly will find it in hell.

## Clark Pinnock

In the twentieth century, belief in inclusivism has increased in popularity among both Protestants and Roman Catholics. Clark Pinnock has emerged as one of the stronger evangelical proponents.[100] Referring to his position as "inclusive finality," Pinnock expressly works within the framework of two axioms: (1) salvation only in Christ and (2) God's universal will to save.[101] Any solution to this vexing problem must, he believes, be worked out in accordance with these two axioms; one must not be elevated at the expense of the other. Believing that God grants everyone an opportunity to accept his grace, Pinnock places great emphasis on texts such as Titus 2:11 ("the grace of God has appeared, bringing salvation to all men") and 1 Timothy 2:3b-4 ("God our Savior . . . desires all men to be saved and to come to the knowledge of the truth").[102] But he also emphatically main-

100. Pinnock's writings on the topic include "Why Is Jesus the Only Way?" *Eternity,* Dec. 1976, pp. 14-15, 34; "The Finality of Jesus Christ in a World of Religions," in *Christian Faith and Practice in the Modern World,* ed. Mark Noll and David Wells (Grand Rapids: William B. Eerdmans, 1988), pp. 152-68; "Inclusive Finality or Universally Accessible Salvation," paper presented at the 1989 annual meeting of the Evangelical Theological Society; "Toward an Evangelical Theology of Religions," *Journal of the Evangelical Theological Society* 33 (Sept. 1990): 359-68; and "Acts 4:12: No Other Name under Heaven," in *Through No Fault of Their Own,* ed. William Crockett and James Sigountos (Grand Rapids: Baker Book House, forthcoming).

101. See his "Toward an Evangelical Theology of Religions," pp. 360-64; and "Inclusive Finality or Universally Accessible Salvation," p. 155.

102. Space does not permit the listing of all the biblical passages Pinnock utilizes, but some of the more important are Rev. 9:7; 21:26; Luke 11:29; Matt. 12:41-42; 25:31-46.

tains that salvation is possible only through Jesus Christ. It is in
this light that he rejects what he considers two extreme views:
universalism and the "fewness doctrine" — that being the assertion that only the small minority of the human race that has
explicitly heard and accepted the gospel of Jesus Christ will be
saved. Against the fewness doctrine he writes, "I am offended by
the notion that the God who loves sinners and desires to save
them tantalizes them with truth about himself that can only result
in their greater condemnation. . . . The problem is that God
cannot save those he would like to save if indeed it is true that
there is salvation only where the gospel is preached and accepted."[103] Universalism is also unacceptable to him because, he
argues, there are too many texts that speak of final judgment and
the possibility of placing yourself outside the kingdom (e.g., Mark
3:28-30).

Pinnock contends that salvation is made accessible outside
the church through what he calls "the faith principle." Basically,
he argues that people are saved when they fulfill the conditions
of Hebrews 11:6 — when they believe that God exists and that
he rewards those who seek him. All people are saved by trust
in God rather than primarily by knowledge. "Faith is our response to information about God in the direction of trusting
and obeying him," says Pinnock.[104] "Surely God judges the
heathen in relation to the light they have, not according to the
light that did not reach them."[105] At this point Pinnock introduces an important distinction. He is not claiming that such
people are "anonymous Christians"; rather, he sees them as
"pre-Christian" believers in God who are already saved by grace
through faith.

103. Pinnock, "Inclusive Finality or Universally Accessible Salvation,"
pp. 160, 163.
104. Pinnock, *A Wideness in God's Mercy* (Grand Rapids: Zondervan,
forthcoming), p. 24. The cited material and page reference here are from a
manuscript made available to me by the author prior to publication. Subsequent citations of the work are also taken from the manuscript.
105. Pinnock, "Toward an Evangelical Theology of Religions," p. 367.

In support of the faith principle Pinnock utilizes both biblical and theological arguments. Biblically Pinnock draws upon four types of texts. The first category includes verses such as Hebrews 11:6 and related examples from the Old Testament: Abel, Enoch, Noah, Job, Melchizedek, Jethro, Abimelech, and Naaman. Such "holy pagans" are cited by the author of Hebrews as examples of faith we should emulate. These people sought after God, and Paul declares that all who do likewise will receive eternal life, because God shows no partiality (Rom. 2:6-8). These God-seekers were saved as part of God's universal covenant with humanity. Just as they were saved by faith without any knowledge of Christ, says Pinnock, so "in the same way today, people who are spiritually 'Before Christ' even though are chronologically 'Anno Domini' can trust in God on the basis of the light they have."[106]

The second biblical argument is drawn from the salvation of premessianic Jews. They were saved by faith in God even though they knew very little about what the Savior would do and how he would do it. Abraham was saved by faith (Gen. 15:6), and all who have faith are the children of Abraham and share the same blessing of salvation which he received (Gal. 3:7). "Without actually confessing Christ they were saved by his work of redemption."[107]

Third, Pinnock makes use of Jesus' teaching about the separation of the sheep from the goats (Matt. 25:31-40) to say that the believing unevangelized will be saved by Christ even though they are unaware of having served Christ. "Serving the poor embodies what the love which God himself is and is accepted as the equivalent of faith."[108]

106. Pinnock, "Inclusive Finality or Universally Accessible Salvation," p. 163.

107. Pinnock, *A Wideness in God's Mercy*, MS. p. 24.

108. Pinnock, *A Wideness in God's Mercy*, MS. 26. This statement signals a change in Pinnock's views about the applicability of this text to the unevangelized. Cf. "Inclusive Finality or Universally Accessible Salvation," p. 166.

Fourth, Pinnock is particularly attracted to what he sees as Luke's remarkable openness to people of other faiths in the book of Acts. "Luke seems to be able to balance exclusive loyalty to Christ with an inclusive appreciation of what God is doing outside Christianity."[109] Cornelius "is the pagan saint par excellence of the New Testament."[110] Luke reports that Cornelius's prayers and alms ascended as a memorial before God (Acts 10:4). Peter was commissioned to preach Christ to him, and this indeed brought "messianic" salvation to his household. Just as Abraham was already saved from eschatological wrath by faith but still had to enter into life with Christ, so Cornelius "was a believer already and not hell bound. True, he needed to become a Christian to receive messianic salvation, including assurance and the Holy Spirit, but not to be saved from hell."[111] Peter finally came to understand this and declared that "in every nation the man who fears Him and does what is right, is welcome to Him" (Acts 10:35). Moreover, Luke presents Paul as having preached that God is at work among the peoples, that "He did not leave Himself without witness" (Acts 14:17), and that God expected that people in other religions would seek him and find him, since he is not far from each of us (Acts 17:27).

After surveying the biblical literature, Pinnock turns to theological argumentation, marshaling two lines of defense. First, he maintains that God uses general revelation to reach the unevangelized. God's witness is present universally, and the Holy Spirit makes use of this witness to reach the unevangelized and bring them into a salvific relationship with God. "All people possess a sufficient knowledge of God on the basis of which they are justly condemned if they reject it," says Pinnock. "But the converse is also true — it is possible for them to renounce their sin and seek God, even if ignorant of Christ's

109. Pinnock, "Inclusive Finality or Universally Accessible Salvation," p. 153.

110. Pinnock, *A Wideness in God's Mercy*, MS. p. 26.

111. Pinnock, *A Wideness in God's Mercy*, MS. p. 29.

provision, so that on the day of judgment the evidence of their conscience may 'accuse or *perhaps excuse* them' (Rom. 2:15)."[112]

Pinnock's second theological argument centers on the question of the salvation of babies (baptized or not) and mentally incompetent people who die. Most Christians (including most of those who adhere to the fewness doctrine) believe that such people are saved. But how can this be if they remain unevangelized? "Why so great compassion for infants who cannot believe and so little for numbers of others perishing without God lifting a finger to help them?" asks Pinnock.[113] He contends that evangelicals are correct in seeking to apply Christ's atonement to such people, but he believes that they do not go far enough. He insists that they must apply God's universal salvific will to the entire range of the unevangelized instead of limiting it to infants who die.

What happens after death for those who sought God but were never evangelized? Pinnock endorses the idea of postmortem evangelism. This notion was present in his first writing on the subject, but his conviction about it and articulation of it have since deepened. He believes that all people will stand before Christ, but only those (excepting infants) who partook of the faith principle will worship Christ. His defense of this belief is threefold. First, the logic of God's universal salvific will implies that God "would not send anyone to hell without first ascertaining what their response would have been to his grace."[114] Second, he believes that the idea is suggested in 1 Peter 3:19–4:6. "It seems plausible to suppose that Peter means that the gospel comes to the dead so that they 'might live in the spirit with God' if they respond to the proclamation they hear. In this way the universality of Christ's redemption is vindicated and made effective."[115] Third, he argues that all

112. Pinnock, "Inclusive Finality or Universally Accessible Salvation," pp. 163-64.
113. Pinnock, *A Wideness in God's Mercy*, MS. p. 31.
114. Pinnock, *A Wideness in God's Mercy*, MS. p. 33.
115. Pinnock, "Inclusive Finality or Universally Accessible Salvation," p. 165. See also *A Wideness in God's Mercy*, MS. pp. 33-34.

humanity will stand before God after death to give an account
(Rom. 14:7-12), and God will not cease to be gracious to sinners
just because they have died. He will remain the God who loves
sinners enough to have sent his Son to die for them.

At this point Pinnock anticipates a question: "But will
such people respond any differently after death than before?"[116]
Pinnock believes that those who exercised the faith principle
in life will continue in faith and love Christ, while those who
rejected God's revelation and mercy in life will continue to resist
and hate God. In other words, people will tend to be confirmed
in the direction they were already heading. Pinnock does grant
the possibility that some of those who hate God in this life
may begin to love him in the next, but on the whole he believes
that few will change their mind in this way. People like Herod
or Hitler will "only hate God all the more on the last day
because they would see more grace in God to hate."[117] The
desire for heaven implies a love of goodness, and those who
lack such love will not desire the God of absolute goodness.

Who will have the opportunity to accept Christ after
death? Pinnock suggests that the fate of the evangelized may
be sealed at death, that those who have heard and rejected the
gospel of Christ may not be given an opportunity to change
their mind after death. But he asserts that those who have never
heard certainly will. This group includes all the infants and
mentally incompetent who die, all premessianic believers such
as the holy pagans and the saints of the Old Testament, and
all those who have heard the gospel of Christ only inadequately
or have had difficulty separating the name of Jesus from Zion-
ism (e.g., Muslims) or Auschwitz (i.e., Jews).

Finally, Pinnock is quite sensitive to his evangelical heritage
and its emphasis on missions. Does hope for the unevangelized
reduce the necessity for missions? Pinnock thinks not. First of all
he claims that some who press this objection are ill-disposed to

116. See *A Wideness in God's Mercy,* MS. pp. 35-43.
117. Pinnock, *A Wideness in God's Mercy,* MS. p. 36.

do so because of the negative implications of their own beliefs for missions. "Neither the Reformers nor the post-Reformation orthodox people are known for their missionary zeal. Apparently one can believe the heathen are perishing and still not lift a finger to help them."[118] Furthermore, he criticizes those who raise the objection for being inconsistent in their exclusivism. Why do those who endorse the fewness doctrine allow for the salvation of babies who die and people like Job since all such remain unevangelized? What is needed, says Pinnock, is a view of missions developed from within an inclusive finality perspective. He sketches what this would look like.

The motivation for missions is to announce the gospel of the kingdom of God (Mark 1:14-15). The primary element in this announcement is love. God loves all people and has manifested this in the work of his Son. Jesus came to save the world, not to condemn it (John 3:17). Pinnock does not omit the aspect of God's wrath; he simply claims that it should not be the primary motivation for missions, since wrath is ultimately a subordinate expression of the divine love.[119] The announcement of the kingdom involves several goals. "One goal of missions is quantitative, to baptize and form congregations; the other is qualitative, to change life's atmosphere, to infect people with hope, love and responsibility for the world."[120] If we keep these goals in mind, our motivation for missions remains high. All people need the gospel of Jesus. Those who are not seeking God need to be challenged and stimulated to do so. Those unevangelized who are seeking God need to experience messianic salvation in the dimension of Pentecost, to experience the power of Christ and assurance of salvation. Consequently, says Pinnock, "we do not need to think of the church as the ark of salvation, leaving everyone

118. Pinnock, "Inclusive Finality or Universally Accessible Salvation," p. 167. See also *A Wideness in God's Mercy*, MS. p. 46.
119. See Pinnock, *A Wideness in God's Mercy*, MS. p. 51.
120. Pinnock, *A Wideness in God's Mercy*, MS. p. 48.

else in hell; we can rather think of it as the chosen witness to
fullness of salvation which has come into the world through
Jesus."[121]

## Evaluation

Proponents of inclusivism maintain that it does the best job of
balancing the two theological axioms of salvation only through
Christ and God's universal salvific will. Moreover, it provides
an account by which salvation is universally accessible in this
life. Although inclusivists contend that all "believers" will encounter Jesus after death, they hold that this encounter will be
provided not into order to offer them salvation but rather to
bring them salvation in its fullness. The believer/Christian distinction enables inclusivists to uphold the significance of God's
work through the church without restricting God's work to the
church.

   Inclusivists also emphasize the universal outreach of the
three persons of the Trinity (particularly the Holy Spirit) more
than proponents of the other views we have considered. As a
result, they tend to place fewer constraints on God's ability to
save. Inclusivists tend to be more sensitive than proponents of the
other views to the historical-social settings in which God works
redemptively. The Bible presents God as the ultimate missionary,
exercising tremendous cultural sensitivity. God's style is that of
working in and through (and sometimes against) human cultures.
Inclusivists appreciate this and provide plausible inferences about
how God might be continuing to work in this fashion in contemporary societies. Inclusivists also provide a very coherent framework for understanding the continuity of salvation between the

   121. Pinnock, "Acts 4:12: No Other Name under Heaven," p. 9. The
cited material and page reference here are from a manuscript made available
to me by the author prior to publication.

Old and New Testaments and subsequently between believers and Christians.

Proponents of a number of other views have raised criticisms of inclusivism, but most have come from restrictivists. The principal criticism is that inclusivism denies that Jesus must be the object of saving faith. Donald Bloesch, a proponent of eschatological evangelization, charges that inclusivism is "pernicious, for it undermines the New Testament message that there is salvation only in a living communion with Jesus Christ (Acts 4:12)."[122] According to Bloesch the normative understanding of the word *pistis* (faith) in the New Testament is conscious faith in Jesus Christ. Inclusivists disagree. Bloesch's argument that the object of saving faith is always and only Jesus Christ works well for him since he believes in postmortem evangelism. But inclusivists (and many restrictivists) argue that Old Testament believers were truly saved *before* they died and that they did not have Jesus Christ as their object of faith. That the New Testament use of *pistis* does not always mean faith in Jesus is demonstrated by the fact that it is commonly used in describing the saving faith of the Old Testament believers. Using the language of medieval theology, inclusivists see Jesus as the "final cause" of salvation, while those who insist that knowledge of Christ is necessary for salvation view Jesus as the "efficient cause." If Jesus is the final cause, then no salvation is possible except through his work (i.e., his work is ontologically necessary). Inclusivists believe the efficient cause to be an act of faith in accord with the knowledge of God that the individual possesses. They contend that Jesus is not the sole object of faith necessary for salvation (i.e., that he is not epistemologically necessary).

Restrictivists criticize the use of Cornelius as an example of an unevangelized person being saved. Robert Gundry states

---

122. Bloesch, *Essentials of Evangelical Theology*, vol. 1 (San Francisco: Harper & Row, 1978), p. 244. Bloesch is specifically concerned that inclusivists fall prey to Pelagianism and semi-Pelagianism.

the point well: "Luke and Peter are not talking about heathen people deficient of special revelation, but about God-fearers, Gentiles who know and follow the special revelation of God in the Old Testament. . . . Furthermore, God sent Peter to preach the Gospel to these people. They do not support the possibility of salvation for the unevangelized."[123] I have already provided an evaluation of this charge in the context of the consideration of restrictivism in Chapter 2, but a couple of further points seem in order here.

Gundry seems to suggest that Cornelius was not saved until Peter told him about Christ. If the faith of such "God-fearers" was insufficient for salvation, then who from the Old Testament era could have been saved? Few indeed, it would seem. If, on the other hand, he believes that Cornelius was saved before Peter came, he pulls the rug out from under his basic argument, since that is the very point inclusivists wish to make. The biblical record would seem indisputably to be suggesting at least that Cornelius was an unevangelized person before Peter arrived and that he was nonetheless experiencing some sort of relationship with God. Inclusivists maintain that this relationship involved the experience of God's redemptive grace apart from knowledge of Christ. In any event, Peter's information about the Lord Jesus was significant to Cornelius, for it enabled him to become a Christian — and, inclusivists would say, thereby experience salvation more completely.

The final significant criticism of inclusivism is that it undermines the motivation for missions. If people can be saved apart from being evangelized, then why bother? Three points may be made in response. First, although many restrictivists today view their position as giving the only genuine motivation for missions, this has not always been the case. It is interesting to note that Erasmus was an inclusivist, and yet "while the orthodox Reformers refused to support missions to the heathen,

123. Gundry, "Salvation according to Scripture: No Middle Ground," *Christianity Today*, 9 Dec. 1977, p. 14.

the 'liberal' Erasmus had a genuine 'missionary concern.'"[124] Second, as we have already noted, such language betrays a shallow view of salvation. Even if it is the case that unevangelized God-fearers are saved, they still are not experiencing the fullness of salvation in Christ. Third, this argument betrays an incorrect conception of the motivation for missions. Missiologist Charles Kraft argues that people are lost because they lack the willingness to respond properly to God's revelation, not because they lack essential information. The principal problem is will, not ignorance. Consequently, the true purpose for missions is "stimulating the hearers to action," not just imparting new information. Evangelism is important because it challenges people to respond to the gospel. "Though this view does not in the least diminish the imperative to witness for Christ to the ends of the earth, it does change our understanding of the *aim* of Christian witness. It focuses our attention on the proper function of witnessing — stimulation to faith — rather than on the lesser end to which our western predilections would likely lead us — to inundate our hearers with new information."[125]

## Historical Bibliography

### 1. New Testament Era through the Middle Ages

The book of 1 Enoch contains one of the few references to the salvation of Gentiles before the Rabbinic period (108:11-14). It speaks of those "born in darkness" — Gentiles — who were faithful and so were given eternal life. (See also Sanders, *Paul and Palestinian Judaism* [Philadelphia: Fortress Press, 1977], pp.

---

124. E. C. Dewick, *The Christian Attitude to Other Religions* (London: Cambridge University Press, 1953), p. 125.
125. Kraft, *Christianity in Culture* (Maryknoll, N.Y.: Orbis Books, 1979), p. 255.

359-61). The question of salvation for Gentiles does not appear to have greatly interested the rabbis. Nevertheless, the "Hasideans" and the school of Hillel did maintain that the Gentiles could find salvation outside the covenant with Israel. Rabbi Joshua continued this tradition when he said that "there must be righteous men among the heathen who have a share in the world to come" (see E. P. Sanders, *Paul and Palestinian Judaism*, pp. 206-11, 147). It was surmised that the grace of God could be extended to Gentiles because God regarded their deeds of mercy as sacrifice. That some rabbis believed salvation was universally accessible is clear from the following statement: "to every human being that draws nigh unto me [God] in repentance I will come and heal him" (*Encyclopedia of Religion and Ethics*, 12 vols., ed. James Hastings [New York: Scribner's, 1908-26], 11: 147-48). Others believed the Messiah would save all the Gentiles who called on God (see *New International Dictionary of New Testament Theology*, vol. 2, ed. Colin Brown [Grand Rapids: Zondervan, 1976], p. 792).

Several of the Church Fathers arrived at inclusivism by way of logos christology (see Clement of Rome, *First Epistle*, chap. 6; Justin Martyr, *First Apology*, 46.1-4, and *Second Apology*, 6.3, 8.1, 10.1-3, 10.8, 13.2-6; and Irenaeus, *Against Heresies*, 2.6.1, 4.6.5-7, 4.20.6-7, 4.22.2, 4.34.1). Clement of Alexandria combined inclusivism with eschatological evangelization. He maintained that God gave the Greeks and other races divine revelation (he referred to it as a "covenant") peculiar to them for their salvation (see *Stromata*, 1.5, 15; 5.5, 13; 6.6-8, 17; 7.2; see also J. Dupuis, "The Cosmic Christ in the Early Fathers," *Indian Journal of Theology* [1966]: 106-20; and Robert Wilken, "Religious Pluralism and Early Christian Theology," *Interpretation* 4 [Oct. 1986]: 379-91).

During the Middle Ages inclusivism fell into disfavor. One notable exception was the twelfth-century theologian Abelard. His most extensive treatment is found in *Christian Theology*, trans. J. Ramsay McCallum (Oxford: Basil Blackwell, 1948). He believed the Trinity was revealed not only in the Old

Testament but also to pagan poets and philosophers — though, indeed, not in precise Christian terms (pp. 47-55). This was important, since medieval theologians held that belief in the Trinity is necessary for salvation. In reference to Paul's address to the Athenians, he asks, "How shall we dismiss these men to the realms of infidelity and damnation?" (p. 59). Abelard believed that God had given enough revelation for the salvation of the Gentiles and that even the unevangelized living in his day could be saved without sacrament by priests. He said of the noble pagans, "notable as they were in faith and life we cannot doubt that they obtained indulgence of God, or that their conduct and worship of the One God which they both held and made known by writing acquired for them the divine favour in the present existence and in the world to come, along with the things necessary for their salvation" (p. 66). Few inclusivists would agree with Abelard's assertion that the unevangelized believe in the Trinity, and many would also be troubled by certain passages in which his language might be construed as affirming salvation by merit (although he denied any such affirmation), but on the whole they would view him as a generous spirit in an ungenerous age.

## 2. From the Reformation through the Eighteenth Century

Zwingli said, "nothing hinders but that God may choose among the Heathen those who shall observe His laws and cleave to Him, for His election is free" (cited by E. H. Plumptre in *The Spirits in Prison* [London: Isbister, 1898], p. 168). Zwingli held (to Calvin's dismay!) that a great many unevangelized will be in heaven. He reasoned that the luminaries of antiquity could not have lived a life of goodness apart from God's influence, so it must have been the case that God elected them for salvation: "where there are works done worthy of God, there surely there has long since been a pious covenant with God" (see George Williams, "Erasmus and the Reformers on Non-Christian Religions and *Salus Extra Ecclesiam,*" in *Action and Conviction in Early Modern Europe,* ed. Theodore Rabb and Jerrold Seigel [Princeton: Princeton University Press, 1969], p. 358). He did not believe that God will condemn the unevangelized as he will those who have rejected Christ (see Edward Grinfield, *The Nature and Extent of the Christian Dispensation with Reference to the Salvability of the Heathen* [London: Rivington, 1827], p. 330). It is difficult to say for certain if Zwingli believed in universally accessible salvation, but he seems to have been more inclusivist than restrictivist, if we are to judge by his statement that "in short there has not lived a single good man, there has not been a single pious heart or believing soul from the beginning of the world to the end, which you will not see there in the presence of God" (*Zwingli and Bullinger,* Library of Christian Classics, vol. 24, ed. Geoffrey W. Bromiley [Philadelphia: Westminster Press, 1953], pp. 275-76).

Erasmus did not make as daring a pronouncement as Zwingli's, but he came to the same conclusion: "perhaps the spirit of Christ is more widespread than we understand, and the company of saints includes many not in our calendar." And shortly thereafter he went so far as to say, "Saint Socrates, pray for us!" (see *Ten Colloquies of Erasmus,* Library of Liberal Arts, vol. 48, trans. Craig Thompson [New York: Liberal Arts Press, 1957], pp. 155, 158). Erasmus vigorously affirmed both the concept of God's universal salvific will and the exclusive claims of salvation only in Christ. Following the lead of the medieval theologians, he combined the ideas of implicit faith, natural revelation (the logos Christ), and the invisible church to argue for an inclusivist position. He believed that through the death of Christ God invited "all the nations of the world unto salvation." Then, while discussing the "communion of saints," he claims that the church includes "all godly men from the beginning of the world even to the end of it" (see *Inquisitio de Fide: A Colloquy by Desiderius Erasmus Roterdamus,* 2nd ed., ed. Craig R. Thompson [Hamden, Conn.: Archon Books,

1975], pp. 63, 71). Basically Erasmus argues that the unevangelized are invincibly ignorant and need only to become members of the invisible church (by believing in God and a future judgment) in order to be saved, whereas the evangelized must become members of the visible church in order to be saved (see Thompson, *Inquisitio de Fide*, pp. 117-19). Erasmus seems to have downplayed the Scholastic idea that belief in a mediator is also necessary for salvation. Although he never systematized his ideas on the unevangelized, Erasmus definitely rejected the Augustinian predestinarian conception and was quite hopeful about God's salvific grace reaching the unevangelized. For two important studies of this subject in the writings of Erasmus, see Thompson, *Inquisitio de Fide*, pp. 106-21; and George Williams, "Erasmus and the Reformers on Non-Christian Religions and *Salus Extra Ecclesiam*," pp. 324-37.

Many significant writers of the seventeenth century advocated inclusivism: John Milton (*Christian Doctrine*, 1.17 and especially 1.20), the Quaker Robert Barclay (*An Apology for the True Christian Divinity* [Philadelphia: Friends Bookstore, 1908], pp. 180-81), Matthew Henry (*Exposition of the Old and New Testament*, 6 vols. [1828-29; reprint, New York: Fleming H. Revell, n.d.], 6: 133), and John Locke (*The Reasonableness of Christianity*, ed. I. T. Ramsey [Stanford: Stanford University Press, 1958], pp. 52-71). Locke argued that the unevangelized are saved by repentance and faith according to the information they have. He even took up the question of what advantage there is in knowing Jesus if one can be saved without knowledge of Jesus.

In the eighteenth century, Bishop Joseph Butler in his famous *Analogy of Religion* (Oxford: Clarendon, 1874), argued for inclusivism (pp. 214-15, 230-33), as did William Paley (see George Fisk, *Paley's View of the Evidences of Christianity* [Cambridge: J. Hall and Son, 1890], pp. 219-20; and Edward Grinfield, *The Nature and Extent of the Christian Dispensation with Reference to the Salvability of the Heathen*, pp. 391-92). William Cowper also espoused the view in one of his poems:

Ten thousand sages lost in endless woe
For ignorance of what they could not know?
The Speech betrays at once the bigot's tongue.
Charge not a God with such outrageous wrong!
Truly not I. — The little light men have,
My creed persuades me, well employed, may save . . .
That rule pursued with reverence and with awe,
Led them, however faltering, faint, and slow,
From what they knew to what they wished to know.

(Cited by Lucius Smith in "Is Salvation Possible without a Knowledge of the Gospel?" *Bibliotheca Sacra* 38 [Oct. 1881]: 622-23).

John Wesley is the most famous proponent of inclusivism in this century (see *The Works of John Wesley*, 3rd ed., 14 vols. [Peabody, Mass.: Hendrickson, 1986], 6: 286; 7: 196-99, 258, 353). Many other notable figures from the seventeenth and eighteenth centuries such as John Tillotson, Samuel Clarke, Richard Baxter, Dryden, Cardinal Manning, and Pope Pius IX are cited by Plumptre (*The Spirits in Prison*, pp. 171-83) and Grinfield (*The Nature and Extent of the Christian Dispensation*, pp. 383-413).

Within Roman Catholicism, some Jesuits as well as Christian humanists produced inclusivist arguments in response to the restrictivism of the Jansenist movement (see David Wetsel, "Histoire de la Chine: Pascal and the Challenge to Biblical Time," *Journal of Religion* 69 [April 1989]: 212-15).

### 3. The Nineteenth Century

Edward Grinfield's *The Nature and Extent of the Christian Dispensation with Reference to the Salvability of the Heathen* provided the most thoroughly argued case for inclusivism up to his time. The bulk of his book is an examination of biblical texts bearing on the subject, while the rest is a survey of the writings of other inclusivists. Better-known inclusivists include William G. T.

Shedd (*Dogmatic Theology*, 3 vols. [New York: Scribner's, 1888-94], 2: 704-12), William Booth, the founder of the Salvation Army ("The Atonement of Jesus Christ," in vol. 5 of *Twenty Centuries of Great Preaching*, ed. Clyde Fant and William Pinson [Waco, Tex.: Word Books, 1971], p. 224), John Watson ("The Mercy of Future Punishment," in vol. 7 of *Twenty Centuries of Great Preaching*, p. 13), George Knapp (*Christian Theology* [New York: Tibbals, 1868], p. 319), the great church historian Philip Schaff (*History of the Christian Church*, 8 vols. [Grand Rapids: William B. Eerdmans, 1950], 1: 74-75), and C. J. Ellicott (*Commentary on the Whole Bible*, vol. 7 [Grand Rapids: Zondervan, n.d.], pp. 22, 69).

Edward Pusey maintained that the opinion that the majority of souls will be damned was found only in the "rigid Calvinistic school" now gone from England (*What Is of Faith as to Everlasting Punishment?* [London: Rivington, 1880], pp. 6-26).

Lucius Smith pointed out that most conservative Christians allow for the salvation of some unevangelized — namely, infants who die — and he argued that this grace should be understood to have been extended to all the unevangelized. He asserted that those who seek God will experience a "holy surprise" after death. Smith also introduced an interesting caution into the debate when he said that there is an "apparent rejection of Christ" which is forgivable: he suggested that a person might accept Christ while rejecting the particular church from which he heard the gospel (see "Is Salvation Possible without a Knowledge of the Gospel?" pp. 622-45).

The list of well-known theologians who endorse inclusivism also includes Stewart Salmond (*The Christian Doctrine of Immortality* [Edinburgh: T. & T. Clark, 1913], pp. 530-33) and Augustus H. Strong (*Systematic Theology* [Philadelphia: Judson Press, 1947], pp. 842-45).

Søren Kierkegaard seems to have followed this line of thinking when he wrote, "If one who lives in the midst of Christianity goes up to the house of God, the house of the true God, with the true conception of God in his knowledge, and prays, but prays in a false spirit; and one who lives in an idolatrous community prays with the entire passion of the infinite, although his eyes rest upon the image of an idol: where is there most truth? The one prays in truth to God though he worships an idol; the other prays falsely to the true God, and hence worships in fact an idol" (*Concluding Unscientific Postscript*, trans. David Swenson [Princeton: Princeton University Press, 1944], pp. 179-80; see also his *Christian Discourses*, trans. Walter Lowrie [Princeton: Princeton University Press, 1971], pp. 248-49).

Toward the end of the century, E. H. Plumptre wrote a very comprehensive survey of arguments and defenders of the wider hope. He believed that all those who died before Christ were evangelized and given the opportunity to exercise faith in Christ during his descent into hell. He believed that all born after the incarnation can be saved by faith in God no matter what revelation they possess (see *Acts of the Apostles*, ed. Charles John Ellicott [New York: Cassell, Petter & Galpin, n.d.], pp. 178-79; and Plumptre, *The Spirits in Prison*, pp. 18-19, 163, 309).

## 4. The Twentieth Century

The twentieth century has witnessed a significant increase in the popularity of inclusivism. The list of advocates includes representatives from a wide array of denominations, including the mainline, evangelical, and even fundamentalist branches of the Protestant church. In fact, inclusivism has representatives from a broader cross-section of the church than any other wider-hope view, as is demonstrated by the following list: G. C. Morgan (*The Acts of the Apostles* [New York: Revell, 1924], pp. 280-81), Arnold J. Toynbee (*Civilization on Trial* [New York: Oxford University Press, 1948], pp. 249-52), Edward Selwyn (*The First Epistle of St. Peter* [London: Macmillan, 1961], p. 358), E. J. Carnell (*Christian Commitment: An Apologetic* [New York: Macmillan, 1957], pp. 237-40, 296-97), C. S.

Lewis (*Mere Christianity* [New York: Macmillan, 1960], pp. 54, 65, 176-77; *The Problem of Pain* [New York: Macmillan, 1962], pp. 16-25; and *The Last Battle* [New York: Collier, 1970], pp. 161-66), D. Elton Trueblood (*Philosophy of Religion* [New York: Harper, 1957], pp. 220-28), René Pache (*The Future Life*, trans. Helen Needham [Chicago: Moody Press, 1962], pp. 270-74), Alan Richardson (*Christian Apologetics* [London: SCM Press, 1947], pp. 116-31), E. C. Dewick (*The Christian Attitude to Other Religions* [London: Cambridge University Press, 1953], pp. 92-94), Bernard Ramm ("Will All Men Be Finally Saved?" *Eternity*, Aug. 1964, pp. 22-25, 33), Roger Forster and Paul Marston (*That's a Good Question* [Wheaton, Ill.: Tyndale Press, 1974], pp. 111-14), Charles Kraft (*Christianity in Culture* [Maryknoll, N.Y.: Orbis Books, 1979], pp. 240-45, 253-57), D. Bruce Lockerbie (*The Cosmic Center* [Portland: Multnomah Press, 1986], pp. 174-80), Peter Cotterell ("The Unevangelized: An Olive Branch from the Opposition," *International Review of Mission* 77 [Jan. 1988]: 131-35), Dale Moody (*The Word of Truth* [Grand Rapids: William B. Eerdmans, 1981], pp. 58-62), Stuart Hackett (*The Reconstruction of the Christian Revelation Claim* [Grand Rapids: Baker Book House, 1984], pp. 244-46), William Abraham (*The Logic of Evangelism* [Grand Rapids: William B. Eerdmans, 1989], pp. 217-23), sociologist Charles Garrison (*Two Different Worlds: Christian Absolutes and the Relativism of Social Science* [Newark: University of Delaware Press, 1988], pp. 95-125), Peter Kreeft (*Everything You Ever Wanted to Know about Heaven* [San Francisco: Harper & Row, 1982], chap. 10; and *Yes or No?* [Ann Arbor: Servant Publications, 1984], pp. 125-44), N. T. Wright ("Towards a Biblical View of Universalism," *Themelios* 4 [Jan. 1979]: 57), Evert Osburn ("Those Who Have Never Heard: Have They No Hope?" *Journal of the Evangelical Theological Society* 32 [Sept. 1989]: 367-72), Andrew O. Igenoza ("Universalism and New Testament Christianity," *Evangelical Review of Theology* 12 [July 1988]: 261-75), George E. Ladd (cited by J. O. Sanders in *How Lost Are the Heathen?* [Chicago: Moody Press, 1972], pp. 62-

63), William Dyrness (*Christian Apologetics in a World Community* [Downers Grove, Ill.: InterVarsity Press, 1983], pp. 108-10), Jerry Gill (*Faith in Dialogue* [Waco, Tex.: Word Books, 1985], chap. 6), Dick Cleary (*A Night Well Spent* [New York: Vantage Press, 1990], pp. 66-75), Stephen Travis ("The Problem of Judgment," *Themelios* 11 [Jan. 1986]: 56), Russell Aldwinckle (*Jesus: A Savior or the Savior?* [Macon, Ga.: Mercer University Press, 1982]), and Clark Pinnock ("Why Is Jesus the Only Way?" *Eternity*, Dec. 1976, pp. 14-15, 34; "The Finality of Jesus Christ in a World of Religions," in *Christian Faith and Practice in the Modern World*, ed. Mark Noll and David Wells [Grand Rapids: William B. Eerdmans, 1988], pp. 152-68; "Inclusive Finality or Universally Accessible Salvation," paper presented at the 1989 annual meeting of the Evangelical Theological Society; "Toward an Evangelical Theology of Religions," *Journal of the Evangelical Theological Society* 33 [Sept. 1989]: 359-68; "Acts 4:12: No Other Name under Heaven," in *Through No Fault of Their Own*, ed. William Crockett and James Sigountos [Grand Rapids: Baker Book House, forthcoming]; and *A Wideness in God's Mercy* [Grand Rapids: Zondervan, forthcoming]).

For a survey of some Baptist confessions and writers who allow for or affirm inclusivism, see Alan Neely, "Grace outside the Church," *Southwestern Journal of Theology* 28 (Spring 1986): 105-11.

M. J. Firey argues on the basis of Romans 5:18 that all people are saved in infancy and remain saved unless they grow up and reject it (*Infant Salvation* [New York: Funk & Wagnalls, 1902], pp. 345-47).

J. Herbert Kane allows for the possibility that some people will be saved without the full light of the gospel but contends that this occurs only very rarely (*Christian Missions in Biblical Perspective* [Grand Rapids: Baker Book House, 1976], pp. 160-64).

J. N. D. Anderson has written one of them most widely quoted works on the subject, *Christianity and Comparative Religion* (Downers Grove, Ill.: InterVarsity Press, 1977], chap. 5).

Richard Drummond generally endorses inclusivism and also points out that Eastern Orthodox theologians never followed Augustine's restrictivism and never lost sight of the cosmic Christ and so have an easy time accepting inclusivism (*Towards a New Age in Christian Theology* [Maryknoll, N.Y.: Orbis Books, 1985], pp. 83-85).

Diogenes Allen utilizes the writings of Simone Weil to argue for a version of inclusivism (*Christian Belief in a Postmodern World: The Full Wealth of Conviction* [Louisville: Westminster/John Knox, 1989], chaps. 10-11).

Hendrikus Berkhof gives some evidence of inclusivist beliefs (*Christian Faith*, trans. Sierd Woudstra [Grand Rapids: William B. Eerdmans, 1979], pp. 529-33).

J. I. Packer allows for inclusivism, although he says we cannot expect God to save in this way (see *God's Words: Studies in Key Biblical Themes* [Downers Grove, Ill.: InterVarsity Press, 1981], p. 210; and "Good Pagans and God's Kingdom," *Christianity Today*, 17 Jan. 1986, pp. 22-25).

Millard Erickson, an evangelical theologian, proclaims that salvation is possible apart from knowledge of Christ but then shies away from the consequences of this position. In one essay he follows A. H. Strong and says that saving faith is possible without knowledge of Christ ("Hope for Those Who Haven't Heard? Yes, but . . . ," *Evangelical Missions Quarterly* 11 [Aug. 1975]: 122-26), but elsewhere he says, "yet it is merely a theoretical possibility. It is highly questionable how many, if any, actually experience salvation without having special revelation. Paul suggests in Romans 3 that no one does" (*Christian Theology*, vol. 1 [Grand Rapids: Baker Book House, 1983], p. 173). Given Erickson's view on inerrancy, we can safely conclude that if he asserts that Paul says no one is saved in this way, then he believes that there is no possibility at all and that inclusivism must be false. At the very least he is uncomfortable with inclusivism, as demonstrated by his suggestion that universalistic thinking is creeping into evangelicalism through inclusivism ("Is Universalistic Thinking Now Appearing among

Evangelicals?" *United Evangelical Action* 48 [Sept. 1989]: 4-6).
Perhaps it would be best to conclude that Erickson is in fact a
restrictivist who merely uses the language of inclusivism.

Neal Punt, a Reformed pastor, presents a version of inclusivism different from that outlined in this chapter. He argues
from Romans 5:18 that all people are in Christ *except* those
who willfully and finally reject God. Thus, all the unevangelized
are saved in Christ except those who specifically turn their backs
on God. He does not deny the universality of sin, but he insists
that being worthy of eternal damnation is not the same as
receiving it. According to Punt, an "act of faith" is not necessary
for salvation; rather, an act of unfaith is necessary to forfeit it.
Does this imply, then, that most of the human race will be
saved? Although some of his Reformed colleagues interpret him
as giving a positive answer to this question, Punt himself refuses
to say. The logic of his argument could go either way: perhaps
in the end most people do willfully reject God. The crucial issue
is what exactly constitutes a willful and final rejection of God,
and unfortunately Punt does not spell out his views on this
point. See *Unconditional Good News* (Grand Rapids: William B.
Eerdmans, 1980) and *What's Good about the Good News?* (Chicago: Northland Press, 1988).

Roman Catholic theology in the twentieth century has
decisively embraced inclusivism. The voluminous literature produced by Roman Catholic writers on the subject of the unevangelized and the relationship between Christ and other religions
dwarfs that produced by Protestants. Although the move
toward inclusivism was well under way by the early part of the
century, it was at Vatican II that it came to prominence in
Catholic circles — and this in spite of the fact that the Council
claimed only that salvation is universally accessible and refused
to say exactly how God makes it so. Nevertheless, most Roman
Catholic writers on the subject have interpreted the Council's
statements in an inclusivist manner. The best-known statement
of the Council on the unevangelized is found in article 16 of
"The Constitution of the Church," which says, "those also can

attain to everlasting salvation who through no fault of their own do not know the gospel of Christ or His church, yet, sincerely seek God, and moved by grace, strive by their deeds to do His will as it is known to them through the dictates of conscience. Nor, does divine Providence deny the help necessary for salvation to those who, without blame on their part, have not arrived at an explicit knowledge of God, but who strive to live a good life, thanks to His grace" (*The Documents of Vatican II*, ed. Walter M. Abbott [New York: American Press, 1966], p. 35). This statement clearly suggests that God can save the unevangelized by *grace* if they respond positively to it (see *Commentary on the Documents of Vatican II*, ed. Herbert Vorgrimler [New York: Herder & Herder, 1967], pp. 182-84). For a helpful overview of the natural knowledge of God in the Roman Catholic tradition, see Gerald McCool, "God in the Catholic Tradition," in *God in Contemporary Thought*, ed. Sebastian Matczak (New York: Learned Publications, 1977), pp. 445-70.

Karl Rahner's "anonymous Christianity" is the most celebrated presentation of inclusivism in contemporary Roman Catholic thought. Rahner works out his idea within the framework of the two theological axioms of no salvation apart from Christ and God's universal salvific will. According to Rahner, an anonymous Christian is a pagan "who lives in the state of Christ's grace through faith, hope and love, yet who has no explicit knowledge of the fact that his life is orientated in grace-given salvation to Jesus Christ" (*Theological Investigations*, vol. 14 [New York: Seabury Press, 1966], p. 283). An anonymous Christian is one who has responded in faith to God's "supernatural existential" grace which is infused into ordinary human life. Because God's grace is available to all people, anyone can be an anonymous Christian, but this does not mean everyone actually is an anonymous Christian. Consequently, says Rahner, the Christian may believe that "God can be victorious by his secret grace even where the Church does not win the victory. . . . For it is a profound admission of the fact that

God is greater than man and the Church. The Church will go out to meet the non-Christian of tomorrow with the attitude expressed by St Paul when he said: What therefore you do not know and yet worship (and yet *worship!*) that I proclaim to you (Ac 17:23)" (*Theological Investigations,* 5: 134).

For further bibliographic information on Rahner's anonymous Christianity and inclusivism within Roman Catholicism, see the following: Gavin D'Costa, *Theology and Religious Pluralism* (New York: Basil Blackwell, 1986), pp. 80-116; and "Karl Rahner's Anonymous Christian — A Reappraisal," *Modern Theology* 1 (Jan. 1985): 131-48; Maurice Boutin, "Anonymous Christianity: A Paradigm for Interreligious Encounter?" *Journal of Ecumenical Studies* 20 (Fall 1983): 602-29, especially n. 1; and Paul F. Knitter, *No Other Name?* (Maryknoll, N.Y.: Orbis Books, 1985), pp. 120-35. Conservative Protestants interested in this issue would do well to consider Thomas F. Stransky, "Salvation of the Others?" *Southwestern Journal of Theology* 28 (Spring 1986): 112-16.

The Roman Catholic Hans Küng is sharply critical of Rahner's anonymous Christianity, but he does articulate an alternative version of inclusivism that is being taken seriously in both Catholic and Protestant circles. He affirms the particularity and finality of Jesus Christ while emphasizing his universal significance. Every human being can be saved because of the work of Christ, says Küng, and every human being can be saved by the grace of God mediated through the various religious structures in which they participate. See his *Freedom Today* (New York: Sheed & Ward, 1966), pp. 109-61; "The Challenge of World Religions," in *On Being a Christian,* trans. Edward Quinn (New York: Doubleday, 1976), pp. 89-116; "The God of the Non-Christian Religions," in *Does God Exist?* trans. Edward Quinn (New York: Vintage Books, 1981), pp. 587-627; and "A New Departure toward a Theology of the World Religions," in *Theology for the Third Millennium: An Ecumenical View,* trans. Peter Heinegg (New York: Doubleday, 1988), pp. 207-56.

# Conclusion

The survey of positions regarding the destiny of the unevangelized is now complete. I have given reasons why I prefer the wider-hope views to either restrictivism or universalism — chiefly because they do a better job of upholding my two preeminent theological axioms of salvation only in Christ and God's universal salvific will. I consider the wider-hope views superior to restrictivism especially because they better represent the loving, saving God we find in Scripture — the God who was crucified for all sinners. Universally accessible salvation theories flatly reject the notion that God created billions of people without any possibility of salvation. Consequently, they help in providing a theologically satisfying answer to this aspect of the problem of evil. I do not claim to have proved any of the wider-hope theories in any hard sense of the term, nor to have presented evidence that any of their proponents have provided incontrovertible arguments. I am merely suggesting that these positions have more biblical warrant and theological plausibility than either restrictivism or universalism and that the wider hope also has a venerable history in the church. I have attempted to assemble a sort of "cumulative case" for the wider-hope views. In the nature of it, such a case is not airtight;

my intent has simply been to suggest that we have more significant reasons to support universally accessible salvation and fewer reasons to oppose it than we do for either universalism or restrictivism.

Although the wider-hope theories all affirm that God makes salvation universally accessible, they differ regarding three crucial claims: (1) that a person must have explicit knowledge of Christ in order to be saved, (2) that it is necessary to learn about the work of Christ from human agents, and (3) that our final destiny is settled at death. One group affirms all three claims, asserting that God will send the message to any person who seeks him out. They maintain that only those who hear about and accept Christ from a human agent before death will be saved. Of all the wider-hope positions, this one is closest to restrictivism. A second group affirms the first and third claims but rejects the second; they maintain that all people have an encounter with Jesus at the moment of death. Others believe that God knows who would have followed Christ had they been evangelized and that he will save such people on the basis of this "middle knowledge"; they say that our destiny is decided at death but that evangelism is not necessary for salvation. Proponents of eschatological evangelism maintain that death is not final and that the unevangelized encounter Christ after death. This group also denies the necessity of the involvement of human agents for salvation but does maintain that no one can be saved apart from knowledge of Jesus Christ. Inclusivists take just the opposite route, affirming the finality of death but denying that explicit knowledge of Jesus is necessary for salvation. Inclusivists contend that a person can be ignorant of the work of Christ and still benefit from the redemption he provides.

All the views examined in Part 3 affirm universally accessible salvation but differ regarding the means God uses in order to provide it. Further variety in wider-hope views is generated by various views regarding the nature of faith and reason, general revelation, and the ministry of the Holy Spirit. I personally consider inclusivism to be the most attractive of the wider-hope views. Its assertion that God's universal salvific will is initiated now and consummated in the future is most compatible with the way I understand the biblical teaching about God's activity in the world. I believe that God is presently at work in the lives of all people through the ministry of the Holy Spirit, attempting to bring them to repentant faith. Those who are believers now will awaken in the next life to discover who it is that saved them and begin to experience the fullness of life in the Lord Jesus Christ. Nevertheless, I would suggest that any of the wider-hope views discussed in Part 3 is preferable to either universalism or restrictivism. I also see many strengths in the concept of eschatological evangelization, particularly theological plausibility of its account of universal evangelization.

Before concluding, I would like to say something about the need for missions if salvation is indeed universally accessible. The criticism most consistently brought against the wider-hope views is that they remove the need for evangelism and missions. Although I have spoken to this criticism at a number of points throughout the book, I would like to respond again here. The criticism is addressed primarily to two groups among the proponents of the wider hope: those who claim that all will encounter Jesus at the moment of death or after death and those who believe salvation is possible apart from knowledge of Christ (inclusivists and proponents of "middle knowledge"). If all people have an opportunity to be saved apart from the missionary enterprise, as these two groups contend, then why bother to evangelize? I would like first to respond briefly to this question and then give four reasons from a wider-hope perspective as to why we should be involved in missions.

I think it important to note that an argument from utility does not necessarily establish truth. In order to get my children to hurry up and get ready for church, I might tell them that it is 9:15 when it is actually only 9:00. If the strategy works, I don't take that as evidence that it really is 9:00. Similarly, even if it is true that a belief in restrictivism leads to stronger support from missions, this does not tell us anything about the truth of restrictivist beliefs. And, conversely, if belief in the wider hope were conclusively shown to reduce support for missions, this would not in itself indicate that the wider-hope view was false; the problem might well lie elsewhere — in an inadequate theory of missions, for instance. In any event, I believe there are a number of reasons why proponents of the wider hope are in fact strongly motivated to bring the gospel to the unevangelized.

1. The first and most obvious reason is that Jesus commanded us to go and preach the gospel to all people (Matt. 28:18-20; Mark 13:10, 16:15; Luke 24:47; Acts 1:8). This command is just as valid for those who accept the wider hope as for those who do not. We are to go for the glory of God. If the explicit instructions of our Lord are not motivation enough for evangelicals to engage in missions, then perhaps they are not as committed to the authority of Jesus as they claim (Luke 6:46).

2. Motivation for missions also arises from the desire to share what we cannot hold inside ourselves, to share with others the blessings we have received. Just as Mary and Peter were excited to tell the others about the risen Christ (John 20), so we, out of love and generosity, desire that others might share in the private and social blessings that come from a personal relationship with Jesus Christ.

3. The Bible indicates that God wants to bring the fullness of eternal life into the lives of all people *now*. Even if some of the unevangelized are already believers or all will encounter Christ at the moment of death or after, it is God's desire that people experience the joy, love, and hope that come from knowing Jesus and that they not put this experience off to some future time. To have a relationship with the risen Lord is much more satisfying spiritually than simply experiencing God's universal grace. God desires mature sons and daughters, the sort of maturity that can come only from a relationship with Christ, through whom the fullness of God's grace and power for the resurrection life is made manifest (Rom. 6). Peter Cotterell sums it well when he says that "Christian mission is valid not

only because it is commanded, and not only as a rescue from God's judgement. It is valid because only in Christ, in an overt knowledge of the good news, can we hope to live a truly human, meaningful life. . . . All peoples *deserve* to have the good news preached to them because it is good news, not only for the life beyond this one, but for the life we live now."[1] Just as Lydia, who was already worshiping God, came to a fuller experience of divine grace through Jesus Christ (Acts 16:14), the unevangelized whom God has already accepted will enjoy a richer spiritual life if they receive the gospel. By bringing the gospel to them, we will stimulate them in their walk with God and strengthen them in their spiritual commitment.

4. Finally, proponents of the wider-hope perspective are motivated to missions by the fact that the spiritual warfare that the prophets, apostles, and our Lord engaged in is not finished. The forces of evil still affect human affairs horribly. A great many people have turned their backs on God and seek to corrupt and destroy the lives of others. These people need the gospel; perhaps hearing the claim of Christ on their lives may lead them to respond in faith and turn from evil. Our motivation for evangelizing in this context is not merely to save people from the "second death" but from the "first death" — a life of rebellion against God (Luke 15:24).

Advocates of the wider hope are grateful that God is not willing that any should perish and that he desires all to be saved. Those who share that desire will seek to bring the good news of Jesus Christ to all the world. God is actively searching for those who will worship him in spirit and in truth. All such people will be invited to the marriage of the Lamb. It is God who makes the guest list for this event, and he is inviting people from every tongue and nation. Proponents of universally accessible salvation rejoice at the thought that God will save many. We have no right to consign anyone to hell. The church right-

---

1. Cotterell, "The Unevangelized: An Olive Branch from the Opposition," *International Review of Mission* 77 (Jan. 1988): 134.

fully has a long list of saints, but it has no right to publish a list of the damned. God may save whom he will, and I believe that he has made acceptance into the eternal city available to every person who has ever lived. With the apostle John, I look forward to seeing in that city a multitude that no human can number.

# Appendix: Infant Salvation and Damnation

Standing at the graveside funeral of a young child, one is most likely to hear strong words of conviction regarding the salvation of the child whether or not the child was baptized or even had Christian parents. But such was not always the case. In fact, throughout most of church history the prevailing view has been that such children are damned in hell.

The issue of the salvation or damnation of young children who die has a long and controversial history.[1] They constitute

1. Helpful bibliographical and historical surveys can be found in the following: Brian H. Butler, "Infant Salvation: An Ecumenical Problem," *Foundations* 14 (Oct. 1971): 344-60; G. G. Coulton, "Infant Perdition in the Middle Ages," *Medieval Studies* 16 (1922): 1-32; M. J. Firey, *Infant Salvation* (New York: Funk & Wagnalls, 1902); Benjamin B. Warfield, "The Development of the Doctrine of Infant Salvation," in *Studies in Theology* (New York: Oxford University Press, 1932), pp. 411-44; Jerry Frost, "As the Twig Is Bent: Quaker Ideas of Childhood," *Quaker History* 60 (Fall 1971): 67-87; M. J. Walker, "The Relation of Infants to Church, Baptism and Gospel in Seventeenth Century Baptist Theology," *Baptist Quarterly* 21 (April 1966): 242-62; and William Alger, *The Destiny of the Soul* (New York: Greenwood, 1968), pp. 954-57. Especially helpful on Roman Catholic views is Peter Gumpel, "Unbaptized Infants: May They Be Saved?" *Downside Review* 72 (1954): 342-458, and "Unbaptized Infants: A Further Report," *Downside Review* 73 (1955): 317-46.

a very large segment of the unevangelized; it has been estimated that about half the human race has died before being able to distinguish the right hand from the left. Moreover, although the discussion has centered on infants, this class of people also includes those who are mentally or emotionally incompetent to understand the gospel of Christ. Do people such as these have any opportunity of being saved? Four main answers have been proposed:

1. Only some are saved — only those who are baptized (according to some Roman Catholics, some Lutherans, and Anglicans) — or elect (according to some Calvinists).
2. No answer can be given concerning whether those dying unbaptized are saved or lost (a traditional Lutheran position).
3. Infants mature after death and are evangelized after a certain period of maturation. No guarantees are given, however, that all infants will grow up and accept Christ.
4. All who die in infancy or are incompetent are saved.

The fourth view is far and away the most widely held today in Protestant circles, conservative and liberal alike, and it is making headway among Roman Catholics. The majority of contemporary evangelicals of both Arminian and Calvinist persuasions agree that all young children who die will be saved.

Although proponents of the four views disagree about whether all or only some infants who die will be saved, most Christians agree that infants can be beneficiaries of salvific grace. Only those who envision a period of maturation after death deny that infants, as such, can be saved. All four views are based more on theological arguments than on Scripture. Informing doctrines such as original sin, baptism, justification, and election serve as guidelines for framing an answer to the question. Proponents of the various views make their assertions from within widely differing theological models.

Two passages from Scripture are cited most frequently in defense of infant salvation. The first is the story of the birth of

David's son by Bathsheba. The child was born unhealthy and lingered near death for several days. During this time David prayed and fasted. When he was informed of the child's death, he said that he would go to be with the child, but the child would not return to him (2 Sam 12:23). Many believe that "this incident verges very nigh to a dogmatic prooftext for the assertion *that all infants dying in infancy are finally saved.*"[2] Others argue that at best it only suggests that children of believing parents are saved. A more serious objection, however, is that modern interpreters are prone to read into David's words our own understanding of heaven, hell, and the afterlife and fail to understand the development of doctrines in the Bible. It is doubtful that David had anything as well articulated as the New Testament conception of the afterlife in mind. The text may mean no more than David would eventually join the boy in the realm of the dead. David may indeed have meant that the child would be in "heaven," but the text is far from clear that he intended this meaning.

The other passage frequently used in support of infant salvation is the story of Jesus rebuking his disciples for keeping the children away. "Permit the children to come to Me," he said; "do not hinder them; for the kingdom of God belongs to such as these. Truly I say to you, whoever does not receive the kingdom of God like a child shall not enter it at all" (Mark 10:14-15; cf. Matt. 19:14-15; Luke 18:16-17). Jesus then went on to bless them and lay his hands on them. Commenting on this text, Robert P. Lightner says, "since Christ was so interested in so many who could not believe and since he did much for them during his life, we have reason to believe he loves all such and grants them eternal life when they die."[3] That Jesus

2. R. A. Webb, *The Theology of Infant Salvation* (Harrisonburg, Va.: Sprinkle Publications, 1981), p. 21.
3. Lightner, *Heaven for Those Who Can't Believe* (Schaumburg, Ill.: Regular Baptist Press, 1977), p. 26.

healed *some* children and on at least two occasions talked with them is quite clear. Lightner's vision of Jesus' tremendous interest in and ministry to young children is less clear. Is such a conclusion validly derived from the biblical data? Furthermore, it is not clear what Jesus meant by "the kingdom of God belongs to such as these." Did he mean that heaven is filled with little children, or did he mean that all must become like little children to enter the kingdom? The context favors the latter.

Those who affirm the salvation of all infants who die are clearly bringing extrabiblical beliefs with them to these texts. Those who assert that only the baptized or children of Christian parents are saved if they die are on safer ground, since they point out that Jesus is reported to have blessed the children and laid hands on them. But a real problem for any who connect this passage with infant salvation is that the text is silent concerning the age of the children who were brought to Jesus. We do not know whether they were infants or ten-year-olds. In any event, given the ambiguity of the biblical record on this point, those seeking to develop a sensible theory for the salvation of infants who die have to appeal to theological doctrines and heartfelt beliefs.

In what follows I will take a closer look at the four basic views concerning the destiny of infants and the incompetent who die, paying special attention to the doctrines and beliefs that shape them.

## 1. Only Baptized or Elect Children Are Saved

Perhaps the oldest view on the issue is that some infants who die are saved while others are damned. Those holding to this view are divided concerning the reason why only some infants are saved. The sacramentalists consider baptism essential for salvation, while some Calvinists insist that only God's election is essential.

## Through Baptism

The early Church Fathers were largely silent concerning the destiny of unbaptized children and children of pagan parents. They did lean toward an endorsement of the concept of baptismal regeneration, however, and this led to grave fears for children who died without the sacrament. Some refused to rule out hope, but overall the tenor was that all unbaptized are damned to hell.

By the fourth century the belief had developed that original sin does not consign the unbaptized to the full pains of hell, but it does prevent entrance into heaven. Ambrose outlined this position: "no one ascends into the kingdom of heaven, except by means of the sacrament of baptism. . . . Moreover to this there is no exception, not the infant, nor he who is unavoidably prevented. They have however immunity from pains."[4] Here we have the seed of what would later become "limbo."

Augustine has the distinction of being the first theologian to teach positively the damnation of all unbaptized infants. He maintained that grace comes only through the sacraments and that all people deprived of grace are without hope and "the wrath of God abides on them."[5] This hard-line position led to terror among Christians in North Africa. Augustine relates the story of a child who died a catechumen before baptism. In despair at the prospect of his eternal damnation, his mother had his body taken to the shrine of St. Stephen, where he was raised from the dead so he could be baptized and then die again, thus permitting his entrance into heaven.[6] Augustine did allow, however, that unbaptized infants would not suffer as severe a

4. Ambrose, cited in *That Unknown Country* (Springfield, Mass.: C. A. Nichols, 1888), p. 45.
5. See Augustine, *On the Merits and Forgiveness of Sins and on the Baptism of Infants*, 1.28, 33, 34, 35.
6. See Peter Brown, *Augustine of Hippo* (New York: Dorset, 1967), p. 385.

punishment in hell as those who lived to adulthood and committed actual sins.[7]

Augustine's archrival Pelagius reacted against this harsh position, saying of unbaptized infants that "where they are not, I know; where they are, I know not." By this he meant to say that although he could not say for sure what their destiny is, he was at least certain that they were not in hell. Eventually he developed the idea of a middle place between heaven and hell where such infants might find "eternal life" but neither eternal bliss or torment. Augustine responded that this middle place was impossible since there are only heaven and hell. Pelagius's attempt to soften the harshness of Augustine's view would not take hold for several more centuries, however. Fulgentius of Ruspe, a devout follower of Augustine, insisted that all unbaptized children, even those who die in the womb, are damned and suffer eternal torment. This became the dominant view in the Western church throughout the Middle Ages.

Over time, however, there was increasing resistance to the concept of infant damnation, and the the notion of the infants' limbo grew in popularity.[8] In the twelfth century Peter Lombard made the distinction between *poena damni* and *poena sensus*, claiming that unbaptized children receive only damnation but do not actually experience the pain of hell. Aquinas adopted this line of thought, and though some such as Wycliffe rejected it, it became the most popular solution to the problem. Robert Bellarmine, a champion of the counter-Reformation, defended it against both Luther and Calvin. Limbo never became an official teaching of the Roman Catholic Church, but it is considered a "safe and widely held solution."

A second principal attempt to soften the harshness of the Augustinian formula went beyond hypothesizing a mitigation of the suffering of the infants in hell to actually affirming that

7. See Augustine, *On the Merits and Forgiveness of Sins . . .* , 1.21.
8. See *The New Catholic Encyclopedia*, s.v. "Limbo" (Washington: Catholic University of America Press, 1967), 8: 762-64.

they might have a place in heaven. The argument was put forth that some unbaptized children can be saved by means of the "baptism of desire" — that is, some might be saved if they desired baptism but were prevented from obtaining it before death. But how could infants "desire" baptism? It was variously argued that the desire of the parents or even the desire of the church could be effective on their behalf. This idea goes back at least to Hincmar of Rheims (A.D. 860).

One might initially suspect that, given its sacramentalism, the Roman Catholic Church would have difficulty with the concept of the baptism of desire. But in fact the concept of the damnation of unbaptized children poses even greater conflicts with key Roman Catholic control beliefs. One of them is the idea that all people who are condemned to hell are condemned by their own fault. "How can we maintain . . . that no one is damned except by his own fault while at the same time we say that a child innocent of any personal fault is excluded from heaven?"[9] Even limbo is problematic in this regard, since it is part of hell. The other conflicting control belief in Roman Catholicism is that all people are given sufficient grace for salvation so that none is left bereft of an opportunity for salvation. But the doctrine that all unbaptized children who die are damned in hell clearly implies that they do not receive sufficient grace or an opportunity for salvation. If Jesus died for all, then he died for unbaptized infants also. But if unbaptized children have no opportunity to benefit from the redemption in Christ, then the sin of Adam is more powerful and abounding than the grace of Christ.[10]

The ambiguity of Roman Catholic views on the destiny of unbaptized infants who die stems significantly from the Church's failure clearly to affirm or deny that salvation is uni-

9. George J. Dyer, "The Unbaptized Infant in Eternity," *Chicago Studies* 2 (1963): 146.
10. For development of this argument, see Adrian Hastings, "The Salvation of Unbaptized Infants," *Downside Review* 77 (1958): 172-78.

versally accessible. If it is universally accessible, then it would seem that the teaching of limbo is in grave jeopardy and a serious rethinking of the problem is called for. Until such time as it takes a stand on this issue, however, the traditional answer of limbo for unbaptized infants will remain the dominant view in the Roman Church. Nevertheless, many join Yves Congar in agreeing with the tradition of limbo but questioning whether unbaptized infants go to hell. Congar is certain only that baptized children who die go to heaven.[11]

## Through Election

John Calvin rejected the notion that only those who are baptized are saved in favor of the idea that only those who are elected according to God's sovereign decree are saved. This principle entails that infants can be saved whether baptized or not. In his *Institutes of the Christian Religion,* Calvin asserts that salvation is ordinarily obtained through the hearing of the word, but he also states that God is not limited to such means. He contends that all human beings — infants included — are sinful and deserving of eternal damnation. Those infants who are saved are not saved because they are innocent but because of the work of Christ (4.16.17). Any infants who are saved when they die had previously been regenerated by the Holy Spirit. Calvin explicitly rejected the idea that all unbaptized are consigned to eternal death (*Institutes,* 4.16.26, 31). Rather, he argued, there are both elect and nonelect infants. Some elect infants die, while others grow to adulthood. Are there nonelect infants who die and thus experience damnation? Calvin does not affirm this explicitly, but he does seem to imply that there are, since he asserts that he is only arguing against those who claim that all unbaptized are damned. He wants to open the

11. Yves Congar, *The Wide World My Parish,* trans. Donald Attwater (Baltimore: Helicon, 1961), p. 154.

door to the possibility of infant salvation without committing himself to the idea that all infants who die are saved (*Institutes*, 4.16.17). It seems best to interpret Calvin as believing that God elects some but not all children who die for salvation.[12]

The immediate followers of Calvin generally took the view that both elect and reprobate infants die. The Canons of Dort state that "godly parents ought not to doubt the election and salvation of their children whom it pleases God to call out of this life in their infancy" (art. 17). But while the theologians at the Synod of Dort affirmed the salvation of all children of the godly, they did not affirm a similar universal salvation for the children of the ungodly: "that there is an election and reprobation of infants, no less than of adults, we can not deny in the face of God, who loves and hates unborn children."[13] The Westminster Confession of 1646 says that "elect infants, dying in infancy, are regenerated and saved by Christ" (10.3). This, of course, leaves unanswered the question of whether all infants who die are elect or only some. By the nineteenth century a consensus had emerged among Reformed theologians that all infants who die are elect.[14]

Many Christians find the assertion that only some of the infants who die are elect problematic because it entails a denial of universally accessible salvation. It must be granted that this

12. Loraine Boettner contends that Calvin did not affirm infant damnation. He argues that Calvin believed nonelect infants never die, that they always grow to adulthood (see *The Reformed Doctrine of Predestination*, 8th ed. [Grand Rapids: William B. Eerdmans, 1954], p. 147). I find this less persuasive than Harry Buis's view that only children of Christian parents are elect. He states that "there is something unrealistic about universal infant salvation" (*The Doctrine of Eternal Punishment* [Philadelphia: Presbyterian and Reformed, 1957], p. 140).

13. Cited in *The New Schaff-Herzog Encyclopedia of Religious Knowledge*, ed. Samuel Jackson (New York: Funk & Wagnalls, 1909), 5: 491.

14. For a discussion of the Particular Baptists who adopted a Calvinistic stance on the issue of infant damnation, see Walker, "The Relation of Infants to Church, Baptism and the Gospel in Seventeenth Century Baptist Theology," pp. 256-60.

296 NO OTHER NAME

does not constitute a fatal flaw within the context of Calvinism, however, because Calvin did not believe that God makes salvation available to all people.

## The Destiny of Infants Who Die Is a Mystery

A great many Christians believe that we simply cannot know whether all infants who die are saved, that it is a matter to be left in the hands of God. Lutherans, in particular, have been identified with this view. Luther was not prepared to teach infant damnation, but neither was he prepared to teach the salvation of all infants who die. In his *Table Talk* (an informal forum which ought not to be considered either definitive or authoritative) he says, "we don't damn infants who die before they are baptized: the parents wish and intend to have them baptized. Consequently I don't judge such an infant but commend him to God. . . . The papists have alarmed us with wicked thoughts about children who die."[15] Luther endorsed the concept of the "baptism of desire," suggesting that the desire of Christian parents is sufficient to ensure the salvation of a child. He was silent, however, about situations in which the baptism of desire does not apply, as when a child of non-Christian parents dies.

Melanchthon took a more restrictive view than his co-worker Luther: "we should and must baptize little children. For certainly the promise of eternal life belongs to children, and this promise does not belong to anyone outside the Church, where there is no salvation. Thus we must bring children into the body of the Church and must make them members of the Church through baptism. . . . Those over whom the name of

15. *Luther's Works*, ed. Helmut Lehmann (Minneapolis: Fortress Press, 1967), 54: 56-58. Luther goes on to say that such fears should be encouraged, lest people thoughtlessly allow children to die unbaptized.

Christ is not invoked and who are marked by no sacrament are certainly not in God's Church."[16]

The Augsburg Confession of 1530 affirms the necessity of baptism for grace (art. 9). Although Lutherans affirm baptismal regeneration, most contemporary Lutherans interpret the Confession as saying that baptism is the ordinary means but not an absolute means of salvation. They affirm that baptism is necessary for salvation, but if baptism is not possible, they hold that the desire of the parents suffices to ensure the salvation of children who die unbaptized. Children who die unbaptized outside the church without Christian parents, they leave in the hands of God.

Many (most?) contemporary Lutherans privately hope for the salvation of all infants who die, whether baptized or not and whether of pagan or Christian parents. But this raises a major question. If all (or even most) infants who die are saved, then baptism must not be necessary for salvation in any ordinary sense, much less an absolute sense, since most infants die unbaptized. Hope for the salvation of all children who die appears to place in jeopardy the Lutheran understanding of the means of grace. Moreover, the question of universally accessible salvation arises once again. The assertion that the destiny of infants who die is simply a mystery suggests a relatively lower view of God's universal salvific will. Asserting that only baptized children are saved raises the question of whether salvation is in fact accessible to those who die unbaptized.

### Evangelization in or after Death

It has been the view of a minority in the church that young children who die are allowed to mature in the afterlife and then are evangelized. This belief goes back at least as far as the fourth

---

16. Melanchthon, *On Christian Doctrine,* trans. Clyde Manschreck (New York: Oxford University Press, 1965), p. 212.

century and Gregory of Nyssa.[17] The argument for this view is based on four premises: (1) people are condemned to hell for their own willful sin, (2) Jesus died for all people, including young children who die, (3) all people receive sufficient grace for salvation, and (4) the act of faith is necessary for salvation. The assertion that young children who die receive an opportunity to accept Christ after death is one of the few conclusions that does justice to all four premises.

A twist on this position has been affirmed mainly by Roman Catholics; they assert that in the moment of death, young children are granted full maturity and presented with the claims of Christ, thereby receiving an opportunity for salvation.[18] A few Protestants have also propagated this view. J. Oliver Buswell Jr. presents this idea as a "postulate" when he writes, "the Holy Spirit of God prior to the moment of death, does so enlarge the intelligence of one who dies in infancy (and I should make the same postulate to cover those who die in imbecility without having reached a state of accountability), that they are capable of accepting Jesus Christ."[19]

Whatever the drawbacks of these positions, it must be granted that they do a good job of affirming God's desire for all to be saved by making salvation universally accessible and that they do so without falling prey to universalism.

## All Young Children Who Die Are Saved

In the seventeenth century, it was the accepted view that there were a great many more damned than saved.[20] This had a

---

17. See Dyer, "The Unbaptized Infant in Eternity," p. 147.

18. See Ladislaus Boros, *The Mystery of Death*, trans. Gregory Bainbridge (New York: Herder & Herder, 1965), pp. 109-11.

19. Buswell, *A Systematic Theology of the Christian Religion*, vol. 2 (Grand Rapids: Zondervan, 1963), p. 162.

20. See D. P. Walker, *The Decline of Hell: Seventeenth Century Discussion of Eternal Torment* (Chicago: University of Chicago Press, 1964), pp. 35-37.

certain natural appeal for those who counted themselves among the elect, but it also served to raise increasingly difficult questions about why a good God would save so few. The German philosopher Leibniz pointedly found the Augustinian view of infant damnation problematic for his theodicy. The most popular solution to the problem was the assertion that all infants who die are saved. In the period since the seventeenth century, this view has proved to be so popular with so many communions — liberals and conservatives, Arminians and Calvinists, mystics and sacramentalists alike — that it is virtually unquestioned anymore. There remains some disagreement only regarding the justification for this conviction. I will briefly outline the Arminian and Reformed arguments.

## The Arminian Argument

Arminius himself believed, as a "matter of opinion," that all infants who die, whether of Christian parentage or not, are saved.[21] All such people are guilty of original sin, he felt, but the atonement of Christ overcomes that sin, and since infants are not guilty of actual sin, God is just in saving them. In other words, infants are saved not because they are innocent but because of the merits of Christ.[22] The death of Christ cancels out original sin. In effect, Christ's atonement serves the same purpose as baptism in Roman Catholic thought, but it creates fewer theological problems because it ensures the salvation of *all* infants who die, not just some.

A great many Protestants have made use of the distinction between original and actual sin in the discussion of salvation of

21. See *The Writings of James Arminius*, vol. 1, trans. James Nichols and W. R. Bagnall (Grand Rapids: Baker Book House, 1956), pp. 317-21.

22. Quakers Robert Barclay and George Keith were inclined toward suggesting that children are "innocent" until they reach the age of accountability and that they would be saved if they died in a state of innocence. For a discussion of Quaker ideas in this regard, see Frost, "As the Twig Is Bent."

infants. Seventeenth-century General Baptists, for instance, held
that the covenant God made with Adam (Gen. 3:15) was fulfilled
in Jesus Christ.[23] They maintained that this covenant applies to
all people because Jesus died for the sin of Adam. Infants who die
are saved by Christ in spite of Adam's sin, they argued, and are
thus part of Christ's "invisible church." John Wesley, who eventually came to hold the opinion that all infants who die are saved,
followed a similar path. He argued that prevenient grace absolves
all of Adam's sin by the atonement of Jesus and hence that infants
who die are automatically saved.[24]

But Arminians encounter a major problem with this line
of reasoning on infant salvation because it conflicts with their
control belief that an act of faith is necessary for salvation. If
infants who die do not exercise faith in God, how can they be
saved? In fact, how can it be claimed that *any* are saved? Appeals
to God's sovereignty might resolve this problem, but they too
would conflict with Arminian control beliefs regarding human
free will. The Princeton theologian B. B. Warfield chided the
Wesleyans on this point and concluded that the only consistent
means of escape for them would be to postulate a maturation
after death and an opportunity for salvation in the next life.

### The Reformed Argument

Zwingli went much further than Calvin was willing to go on
this issue and blazed the trail that most Reformed communions
follow to this day. He argued that God can elect whomever he
wills and that all children of Christian parents who die are elect.
He thought it probable that God's electing grace extends to
absolutely all infants who die. He suggested that death in in-

23. See M. J. Walker, "The Relation of Infants to Church, Baptism
and Gospel in Seventeenth Century Baptist Theology," pp. 242-50.
24. See *A Contemporary Wesleyan Theology*, ed. Charles Carter (Grand
Rapids: Zondervan, 1983), p. 268.

fancy might in fact be a sign of election.[25] Reformed confessions have gradually abandoned Calvin's belief that elect infants who die are saved but that nonelect infants who die are condemned to hell in favor of Zwingli's position. In 1886 Egbert Smyth observed that in New England even the "most rigorous adherents to the Augustinian and Reformed type of doctrine encourage the belief that all infants are 'elect,' and will be saved."[26]

Smyth attributed this significant change in opinion to a better understanding of the atonement and the character of God. I would suggest that changing attitudes toward children in Western civilization also played a decisive role in bringing about the shift. People gradually came to judge as inhuman any individual who could, like Augustine, sentence little children to hell. "Therefore," wrote Smyth, "the same church, with the same Bible as its rule of faith, now as commonly encourages the hope that all infants will be saved, as two centuries ago it discountenanced such an expectation." B. B. Warfield observed this same shift among his fellow Reformed brethren and endorsed it. In fact, he wrote a survey of the topic and defended the view that all infants who die are elected by God and are therefore saved.[27] In 1903 American Presbyterians produced a "Declaratory Statement" on article 10.3 of the Westminster

25. For a summary of Zwingli's position, see Butler, "Infant Salvation," p. 348. See also George Williams, "Erasmus and the Reformers on Non-Christian Religions and *Salus Extra Ecclesiam*," in *Action and Conviction in Early Modern Europe,* ed. Theodore Rabb and Jerrold Seigel (Princeton: Princeton University Press, 1969), p. 358.

26. Smyth, "Probation after Death," *Homiletic Review* 11 (April 1886): 286.

27. Warfield, *Studies in Theology* (New York: Oxford University Press, 1932), pp. 411-44. Other evangelicals who accept this view include Charles Hodge, A. A. Hodge, William G. T. Shedd, A. H. Strong, and Loraine Boettner. Studies by evangelicals on infant salvation who take a Calvinistic line include the following: R. A. Webb, *The Theology of Infant Salvation* (Harrisonburg, Va.: Sprinkle, 1981); Robert Lightner, *Heaven for Those Who Can't Believe* (Schaumberg, Ill.: Regular Baptist Press, 1977); and John Linton, *Concerning Infants in Heaven* (Grand Rapids: William B. Eerdmans, 1949).

Confession affirming that elect infants who die are saved. The official commentary says that this article "is not to be regarded as teaching that any who die in infancy are lost. We believe that all dying in infancy are included in the election of grace, and are regenerated and saved by Christ."[28]

There are those in the Reformed tradition who put a little twist on this line of reasoning. Neal Punt, for instance, argues that all people are saved except those who willfully and ultimately reject God. Since infants who die do not willfully and ultimately reject God, they are saved.[29] Punt does not argue that infants are innocent but that they are saved by the redemption in Christ. He does not believe that an act of faith is necessary in order to obtain the benefits of Christ's work. All are beneficiaries except those who reject it. This line of argument is not widely accepted by Reformed thinkers, however.

Reformed writers on this subject often claim that the Reformed doctrine of God's election is the only view that can logically affirm the salvation of all infants who die. This assertion has a certain validity: there is some degree of logical inconsistency in all of the other views we have surveyed. The Reformed position claims greater security on the grounds that it posits divine election as the sole means of salvation. If all who are saved are saved solely because of God's sovereign election, then God can sovereignly elect all infants who die.

But there is a problem with this argument. Why does God elect *all* infants who die but only *some* adults? After all, all people die and all people have original sin. Many Reformed would respond that this overlooks the fact that adults stand condemned by the actual sins they have committed in addition to original sin. But that is not really germane, since the doctrine

28. *The Constitution of the Presbyterian Church (U.S.A.): Book of Confessions* (New York: Office of the General Assembly, 1983), 6.193.

29. See Punt, *What's Good about the Good News?* (Chicago: Northland, 1988), chap. 11, and *Unconditional Good News* (Grand Rapids: William B. Eerdmans, 1980), chap. 11.

of election specifies that we are saved or damned solely on the basis of God's electing will, not on the basis of any human behavior. So we must conclude that God makes an arbitrary decision in electing all infants who die but only some adults who die. No convincing arguments have emerged from the Reformed community to account for why God would deal differently with the two age groups.

David K. Clark has criticized Warfield on this point specifically: "someone taking Warfield's gracious view . . . cannot hold that God acts reasonably in saving all infants who die and only some adults."[30] The traditional doctrine of election does not provide any grounds for suggesting that God would save all infants who die but only some adults. In fact, as Clark says, "if some adults are not saved and God's will is reasonable, then the logic of Warfield's Reformed position requires that some infants who die will not be saved."[31] If God is reasonable in his election and does not give preference to certain age groups over others, then it follows either that God elects and saves all people (universalism) or that he elects and saves only some infants and some adults.

Responding to the assertion that God does damn some infants who die, Robert Lightner says, "I do not believe that for a moment. It impugns the very character of God to believe such a thing."[32] But he does not go on to explain why this is the case. Augustine and Calvin did not believe it impugned God's character. I suspect the real reason is that current attitudes toward children in Western civilization make the prospect of infant damnation unbearable. I think there is considerable warrant for Clark to ask, "Is the salvation of all infants who die held for sentimental reasons?"[33]

30. Clark, "Warfield, Infant Salvation, and the Logic of Calvinism," *Journal of the Evangelical Theological Society* 27 (Dec. 1984): 462.
31. Clark, "Warfield, Infant Salvation, and the Logic of Calvinism," pp. 462-63. Clark himself takes this position.
32. Lightner, *Heaven for Those Who Can't Believe* p. 5.
33. Clark, "Warfield, Infant Salvation, and the Logic of Calvinism," p. 462.

## Conclusion

Today the Western church has reversed itself from saying that most young children who die are damned to asserting that all are saved. When called upon to console grieving parents, we wish very much to say with confidence that their child is now safe in the presence of God. In our pastoral concern, we desire to give a forthright answer to their question, but unfortunately we must own up to the fact that none of the positions we have surveyed is without its problems and also that the Scripture is not particularly clear on this issue. Once again, the view we take is likely to be determined primarily by our theological control beliefs.

Those who affirm baptismal regeneration, as Roman Catholics do, will find it difficult to rule out infant damnation. On the other hand, we have noted that other control beliefs within the Roman Catholic tradition conflict with this conclusion — namely, the beliefs that all people receive sufficient grace for salvation and that none are condemned to hell except for their own fault. These considerations lead some Catholics to the hypothesis of evangelization at the moment of death — and yet it should be noted that this does not guarantee the salvation of all young children who die either.

The conviction of many Reformed that all infants who die are elected seems to imply that God is unreasonable and perhaps guilty of partiality. The more logically consistent Reformed teaching that God elects some young children to salvation and others to damnation is to many minds a horrible doctrine that contradicts the universal salvific will of God.

The relegation of the entire issue to the category of impenetrable mystery — the assertion that we simply cannot speculate about the destiny of infants who die — also raises problems regarding God's universal salvific will. Although the Arminian solution affirms God's desire to save all people, it falls into inconsistency when it asserts that an act of faith is necessary for the salvation of adults but not of infants. A logical way out of this predicament would be to assume that infants who die are given an opportunity to mature after death and then to exercise faith in Christ. But it must be granted that, once again, such a process would not guarantee the salvation of all young children who die.

It seems clear that no position we have surveyed is free from serious difficulties. Despite the fact that the church has wrestled for nearly two millennia with the thorny issue of the salvation and damnation of the incompetent and infants who die, no consensus has emerged. Serious theological reflection is yet needed on this topic.

# Index of Subjects and Names

307

# Index of Scripture References

311